Ten Gates into the Garden

Spiritual Teachings for the
Awakening Consciousness

by

David Harry Davis and Katrin Louise Naumann

New Light Tarot Illustrations

by

Katrin Louise Naumann

~A School of the New Light Publication~

Dear Anne ~ Remember, you are Self, ever and always dwelling in the garden... Abundant Blessings ~ Katrin

First American Edition 2018

ISBN: 978-1-7325950-0-2

Published by
The School of the New Light
1583 North Road
Tully, NY 13159 USA

Copyright ©2018 The School of the New Light
Text Copyright © 2018
David Harry Davis and Katrin Louise Naumann
New Light Tarot Illustrations copyright© 2018 Katrin Louise Naumann
Cover Design by Brenna Merritt

All rights reserved under the International and Pan-American Copyright Conventions. No part of this publication may be reproduced, stored in a retrieval system, or transmitted in any form or by any means, electronic, mechanical, photocopying, recording, or otherwise, without prior written permission of the copyright owner. Published in The United States by The School of the New Light.

For more information contact:
The School of the New Light
1583 North Road, Tully NY 13159

Printed in the USA by DiggyPOD
www.diggypod.com

Table of Contents

DEDICATION	i
ACKNOWLEDGEMENTS	ii
PREFACE	iii
CHAPTER 0 : INTRODUCTION	**1**
TRANSPERSONAL TEACHINGS	**1**
OTHER DIMENSIONS	**2**
WE CREATE OUR OWN REALITY	**4**
TOOLS & MAPS	**6**
CONCENTRATION	7
THE SOUL	7
SCIENTIFIC PRAYER	7
HOLISTIC ASTROLOGY	7
MEDITATION	8
FOUNDATION WORK	9
KUNDALINI & THE CHAKRAS	10
THE DIVINITY OF DESTRUCTION	10
RELIGION	11
THE SELF	11
SPIRITUAL EXERCISES & MEDITATIONS	11
CHAPTER 1: CONCENTRATION	**12**
THE CAMERA	**12**
DIRECTION	12
FOCUS	12
FRAME	13
SHUTTER SPEED	13
FILM	13
TAROT CAMERA	13
THE AREA 51 TECHNIQUE	**14**
HIGHER DEVELOPMENT	**15**
CHANGE	15
THE KEY	**15**
BALANCE	16
CONCENTRATION	17
THE PICTURES	**17**

MISINTERPRETATION	17
THOUGHTS ARE SEEDS	**18**
ZEN STORY	19
WHAT IS HAPPENING?	20
CONCENTRATION EXERCISE	20

CHAPTER 2: THE SOUL   22

WHAT IS THE SOUL?	**22**
INITIATION	**23**
VIBRATIONAL SHIFT	**24**
REVIEW EXERCISE	27
RECOGNIZING SOUL PATTERNS	**28**
THE OVERSOUL	**29**
SOUL CONTACT	**30**
SOUL-MATES	**30**
THE TIES THAT BIND	**31**
MEMORY	**32**
THE THREE LAWS OF MEMORY	**33**
LAW #1:	33
LAW #2:	33
LAW #3:	34
THE AKASHA	**34**

CHAPTER 3: SCIENTIFIC PRAYER   37

THE ANSWER TO OUR PRAYERS	**37**
EASY AS 1, 2, 3	**37**
THE LAW OF THE TRIANGLE	**38**
PRAYER	**39**
FAITH	**40**
BEFORE WE PLANT	**40**
STEP ONE	41
STEP TWO	41
STEP THREE	42
AFTER THE LAST STEP	**43**
ACTIONS ARE PRAYERS	**44**
GOD'S WILL	44
VISUALIZATION	**44**
WORKING WITH THE SUBCONSCIOUS	**45**
THE LAW OF REFLECTED REVERSAL	**45**
DOUBT	45
NEGATIVE KNOWING	46
PERMISSION	46
WORTHINESS	46
FEAR OF FAILURE	46
FEAR OF SUCCESS	46
RESPONSIBILITY	47
PROGRESSED PRAYERS	**47**

AUDIBLE PRAYER	**48**
TO WHOM DO WE PRAY?	**48**
THE FLOWERPOT	**49**
DESPERATE PRAYER	**50**
PRAYER EXPERIMENT	**50**
PRAYER WHEELS	**51**

CHAPTER 4: HOLISTIC ASTROLOGY: THE CIRCLE DIVIDED	**52**
CONCEPTS & MISCONCEPTIONS	**52**
WHAT IS ASTROLOGY?	**53**
THE BIGGER PICTURE	**54**
THE SMALLER PICTURE	**54**
ONE	54
TWO	55
THREE	55
FOUR	55
FIVE	55
SIX	56
SEVEN	56
THE SEVEN SACRED PLANETS	57
EIGHT	57
BUDDHA'S EIGHT FOLD PATH	58
NINE	58
TEN	58
ELEVEN	59
TWELVE	59
ASTROLOGICAL SYMBOLS, PLANETS & CYCLES	**60**
THE SACRED SEVEN	60
THE PLEIADES	61
THE SEVEN SACRED PLANETS	61
PLANETARY SYMBOLISM	**63**
CIRCLE	63
THE LINE	64
THE CROSS	65
THE CRESCENT	65
PUTTING THEM ALL TOGETHER	**66**
THE SUN	66
THE MOON	67
MERCURY	68
VENUS	69
MARS	70
JUPITER	71
SATURN	72
URANUS	73
NEPTUNE	74
PLUTO	75
SOLAR CYCLES	**76**
LUNAR CYCLES	**76**
MERCURY CYCLES	**77**

VENUS CYCLES	**77**
MARS CYCLES	**78**
JUPITER CYCLES	**78**
SATURN CYCLES	**79**
URANUS CYCLES	**80**
NEPTUNE CYCLES	**81**
PLUTO CYCLES	**82**
PLUTO IN THE SIGNS	82
RETURNS	**83**
PLANETARY CYCLES	**83**
THE SOLAR SYSTEM WITHIN	**84**
AURIC MEDITATION	86
THE FOUR ASTROLOGICAL ELEMENTS	**87**
FIRE SIGNS	87
EARTH SIGNS	88
AIR SIGNS	88
WATER SIGNS	89
THE THREE ASTROLOGICAL MODES	**89**
CARDINAL SIGNS	90
FIXED SIGNS	90
MUTABLE SIGNS	91
THE YEARLY ASTROLOGICAL CYCLE	**91**
ARIES	91
TAURUS	93
GEMINI	95
CANCER	96
THE EGG OF LIGHT EXERCISE	98
LEO	99
VIRGO	100
LIBRA	102
SCORPIO	103
SAGITTARIUS	106
CAPRICORN	108
AQUARIUS	109
PISCES	112
TERRESTRIAL & CELESTIAL BODIES	**114**
ASTROLOGICAL MODIFIERS	**115**
ARIES MODIFICATIONS	115
TAURUS MODIFICATIONS	116
GEMINI MODIFICATIONS	117
CANCER MODIFICATIONS	118
TRANSMUTATION OF ENERGY	119
LEO MODIFICATIONS	119
VIRGO MODIFICATIONS	121
ASTROLOGICAL MODIFIERS CONTINUED	123
ASTROLOGICAL HOUSES	**123**
FIRST HOUSE	125
SECOND HOUSE	125
THIRD HOUSE	125
FOURTH HOUSE	126
FIFTH HOUSE	126

SIXTH HOUSE	126
SEVENTH HOUSE	126
EIGHTH HOUSE	126
NINTH HOUSE	127
TENTH HOUSE	127
ELEVENTH HOUSE	127
TWELFTH HOUSE	127
HOUSES: SELECT KEY WORDS	128
ASTROLOGICAL ASPECTS	**128**
CONJUNCTIONS	129
OPPOSITIONS	129
TRINES	129
SQUARES	130
SEMI-SQUARES	130
SEXTILES	131
SEMI-SEXTILES	131
PUTTING IT ALL TOGETHER	**131**
THE COSMIC THEATRE	131
TIME & SPACE	131
TIME FOR RELATIONSHIPS	131
THE BIRTH CHART	132

CHAPTER 5: MEDITATION — 134

MEDITATION IS NOT WHAT YOU THINK	**134**
SILENCE	**135**
SILENCE - 1965	135
SILENCE - EASTER	137
LISTENING	**139**
LISTENING EXERCISE	140
BREATH	**140**
CONSCIOUS BREATHING	141
KABBALAH	**141**
OM MANTRA	142
INSTRUMENTS OF MEDITATION	**142**
CANDLES	144
TRIPLE FLAME CANDLE MEDITATION	145
CONTEMPLATION OF THE ELEMENTS	145
PURIFICATION OF THE ELEMENTS: CONTEMPLATION	146
THE EARTH ELEMENT	146
THE WATER ELEMENT	147
THE FIRE ELEMENT	147
THE AIR ELEMENT	148
GUIDED MEDITATION	**148**
THE VISION ROOM	149

CHAPTER 6: FOUNDATION WORK — 150

REALITY IS PERSPECTIVE	**150**

CHANGE YOUR FOCUS, CHANGE YOUR LIFE	**151**
FIRST PRINCIPLES	**153**
SENSE OR NON-SENSE?	**154**
BE HERE NOW	**155**
THE COSMIC RADIO	**157**
NUMEROLOGY	**157**
NUMBER ATTRIBUTIONS	157
DESTINY NUMBER	158
BIRTH FORCE NUMBER	158
CHALDEAN NUMEROLOGICAL SYSTEM	159
GEMATRIA NUMEROLOGICAL SYSTEM	159
THE MEANINGS OF NUMBERS	160
TIME TRAVEL & PREDICTION	**161**
WE HAVE ALL SEEN THE FUTURE	161
LIGHT & DARK	**162**
CYCLES OF TIME	**163**
THREE REALMS OF WORK	**164**
PARTNERED ENERGY WORK EXERCISE	165

CHAPTER 7: KUNDALINI & THE CHAKRAS — 166

CYCLES WITHIN CYCLES	**166**
THERE IS NOTHING THAT IS NOT GOD	**167**
SHAKTI	**167**
JUDEO-CHRISTIAN THEMES	**168**
THE GARDEN OF EDEN	168
JACOB'S LADDER	169
EXODUS	169
CHRISTIAN MYSTERIES	**170**
CREATING A MYTH	170
THE CHAKRAS	**171**
ROOT CHAKRA	171
SACRAL CHAKRA	173
SOLAR PLEXUS CHAKRA	175
FROM MATTER TO SPIRIT	176
HEART CHAKRA	177
THROAT CHAKRA	179
THE CIRCLE OF LIFE	180
THE DOOR TO HEAVEN	181
FIGURE EIGHT PRACTICE	182
THIRD EYE CHAKRA	182
QUANTUM PHYSICS MEETS THE MIND	183
THIRD EYE INITIATION	185
DAVID'S TRAVELOGUE	185
CROWN CHAKRA	186
YOU CAN LEAVE YOUR HAT ON	187
KNOW FOOLING	188
KUNDALINI & THE CHRIST	**190**
THE CADUCEUS	**191**

BUDDHA, KUNDALINI & DRAGONS, OH MY	**192**
SOLAR MEDITATION	194

CHAPTER 8: THE DIVINITY OF DESTRUCTION — 196

THE BEGINNING OF THE END?	**196**
MULTIPLE REALITIES	**196**
ANCIENT TERRORISM	**197**
MODERN TERRORISTS	**198**
ARMAGEDDON	**199**
THE OTHER SIDE OF 9/11	**199**
PRIORITIES & THE BOTTOM LINE	**200**
CUTTING THE TIES THAT BIND	**204**
THE FINAL WALL	**206**
THE EGG OF LIGHT EXERCISE	208

CHAPTER 9: RELIGION — 209

PERSONAL RELIGION	**209**
SUPERSTITION AIN'T THE WAY	**210**
FAITH	**211**
EARLY DAYS	**211**
ASTROLOGY & RELIGION	**212**
CHRISTIANITY & BUDDHISM	**215**
ANGELS, HEAVEN & HELL	**216**
THE NEW AGE	**218**
MYSTIC ORIGINS & PRACTICAL SPIRITUALITY	**218**

CHAPTER 10: THE SELF — 220

THE NATURE OF THE SELF	**220**
KNOWLEDGE	**221**
SELF, SELF, SELF	**225**
MEDITATION: BECOMING A CONDUIT OF THE DIVINE	227

SOURCES — 229

GRATITUDES — 230

ABOUT THE AUTHORS — 231

DAVID HARRY DAVIS	**231**
KATRIN LOUISE NAUMANN	**232**

Dedication

This book is dedicated to all those who consciously seek the inward journey, for the purpose and pleasure of awakening their consciousness, reestablishing soul awareness, and reuniting with Self.

Acknowledgements

The teachings found in this book began to emerge in the early 1980s, as I designed a series of lessons on the Tarot and other Hermetic sciences. Many of my students had not received any preparation, and had difficulty understanding the more esoteric concepts in the material. So, the conception of this volume began, to create a true foundation, in order that others could receive the higher teachings.

Once the manuscript began to take form, with extensive help from Katrin Naumann, we recognized that this material could stand on its own. Thus: *Ten Gates into the Garden: Spiritual Teachings for the Awakening Consciousness*. It was not an easy task. We had many intense discussions as to its transcription.

For seven years, I was a monk, a brother in The Holy Order of Mans, a modern Mystery School. Doors were opened for me, and veils were rent, which brought me to a place where I could receive the "teachings." I am more of a scribe than an author, knowing nothing, receiving without distortion.

Ten Gates into the Garden: Spiritual Teachings for the Awakening Consciousness, is a collaborative work, bringing the essential wisdom of the Piscean Age into this one. This book was written to bring the esoteric into the exoteric, the mystical into the practical, in order to change our perception of reality. Yet, I had trouble making the teachings accessible to a wider audience. This has been the great work of K.N., who has edited and translated the more abstract ideas into understandable text. This provided her opportunity to expand on the ideas with fresh material from her own experiences.

I thank the many teachers and guides I have met along the way, in this life and others. I thank the divine Self, and the nameless One that includes us all.

Finally, I thank you, the reader, for completing this task. By reading, you balance the writing. If there is no one to read, there is no reason to write.

Thank you. Namaste. - David

Preface

Humanity has been seeking to know "Who am I?" and "Why am I here?" for eons. That inquiry has led us down infinite pathways of discovery and offered up equally diverse answers.

Whereas ancient seekers either instinctively knew to venture into the realm of the inner life, to discover what they sought, or were guided by those who had gone before them, the demands and distractions of our modern society have, generally, conditioned us to seek the answers to such perennial questions, and to pursue our deeply held desire for a sense of meaning and purpose, through external means.

While this volume is, by its very nature, an "external means," we endeavor in it to provide the reader with keys that will open a variety of gates, each of which serves as a portal to the inner life of Spirit, the "Garden of Eden." The teachings and spiritual practices found in these chapters comprise a primer, containing useful tools, offered as stepping stones that, when laid with care, will direct us along the spiritual path toward our center.

This book, and the companion audio: *Ten Gates into the Garden: Spiritual Exercises and Meditations*, are of practical use for the novice, who has just begun the inner journey, as well as for those who have been on the path for some time but may have wandered off course, or come up against obstacles that seem to bar the way toward further attainment.

This work sheds light on fundamental principles of various world wisdom traditions. As we look closely at each, we begin to recognize that, at the most basic level, each is saying the same thing, though the words and metaphors used may be different. Even the seeming gulf between science and spirituality we begin to see is, in many cases, only one of semantics. Note that the use of repetition throughout is to more firmly anchor the concepts into the subconscious mind. Rather than perpetuate the outmoded binary, the use of the pronoun *they* will be used, where appropriate, in lieu of she/he, in alignment with unity consciousness.

Ten Gates into the Garden offers the reader insights into where we have come from, as seekers of truth, where we may be at the present moment, as we travel along the path, and where we are headed, in the unceasing quest to find our way back to the Garden, which, we discover, we have never really left.

The answers we seek are always found within. Our intent is for these teachings to shed light on the inner landscape, that we may weed out what is of no use, and nurture that which supports and sustains us, in the process of fully awakening our consciousness, reuniting with our soul, and remembering we are Self, ever and always dwelling in the Garden.

CHAPTER 0

Introduction

TRANSPERSONAL TEACHINGS

We spend our whole lives living in the world, but the world is not what we think it is. We once thought the Earth was flat. All of our everyday experiences confirmed it. This was evidenced through our eyes and feet. It looked and felt like the Earth was flat. Simply walking here and there, we never would have perceived the curve of the Earth. Besides, everyone we knew shared the same belief.

We were not aware of the concept of gravity. It was thought, if the Earth were round, everything on the bottom would fall off. That was the "conventional wisdom" of the day. At that time, our parents knew it was flat. Schools taught us the same thing. Even the Church declared the Earth was not only flat but rested in the very center of creation.

If someone had tried to explain to us then that the Earth was round, as is our current perspective, they would have appeared to be insane, or "in league with the devil."

In order to accept the truth of the Earth's roundness that we understand presently, we would have had to change the way we perceived the planet. We would have needed to shift our basic concept of reality. This is not an easy thing to do.

The *Flat-Earth* was very real to many people. This view of reality is called "personal-reality." It is a personal, ego-centered perspective. From this place, we experience day and night, summer and winter, sunshine and rain. In the dim past, we believed the world we saw around us was the entire world. If we grew up in a forest, we might imagine the entire world is forest. If we were born far away from the coast, it would be difficult even to imagine such a thing as the ocean exists. It would have been hard to comprehend that most of the Earth's surface is covered with water.

We begin to expand our consciousness, by looking at what is around us from a higher and broader perspective. When we climb a mountain, our view opens up. We see a bigger picture.

When we travel by plane and look out the window, we view the world from an even more expanded perspective. David was amazed the first time he flew across the United States. He grew up near New York City, and believed the whole world was overcrowded. Flying over the country, he realized most of the land was sparsely populated.

In this age, we have set our sights much higher, into space. Now we have the ability to view the Earth from the Moon. With this altered perspective, we have developed an Earth-consciousness. We have expanded our personal reality to a planetary awareness. We find, from our broader perspective of the Earth, day and night happen simultaneously. Summer and winter occur concurrently. As a result, our previous ideas of time and space no longer apply.

The only way to see what the Earth looks like is to view it from space. This is where we gain the trans-personal perspective. Though, from this place of expanded awareness, we still see the Earth half covered in darkness, and half in sunlight.

Let's shift our consciousness again and view this from the solar perspective, as though we are the Sun. All the shadows on the Earth fall away, when we are the Source of Light. (Try to illumine a shadow holding a flashlight.) We also observe the center of the universe is not the Earth but the Sun. Nothing has changed other than our perspective, our awareness.

The teachings that follow are designed to take us beyond the three-dimensional *"Round-Earth"* view of reality to a fourth-dimensional awareness, and beyond.

OTHER DIMENSIONS

What we pose here may seem as crazy as our current views appeared to our ancient selves, who were certain the Earth was flat. From our typical everyday perspective, everything appears solid and real. We are not normally aware of other dimensions or inter-dimensional realities, because our five senses do not detect them. The senses only tell us about the physical world.

Nevertheless, most of the energy spectrum is beyond the scope of our ability to access it unaided. Radio waves, x-rays, blue-tooth connections, infra-red TV remotes, gamma rays, and so on, are real, but cannot be seen or heard without a secondary device such as radio or TV. Our eyes and ears cannot see or hear a single thought from those around us. In subsequent chapters, we will focus on how to open and use our higher faculties, such as spiritual sight and hearing, that do detect the unseen worlds.

There are plenty of books, films and TV shows about the "other dimensions." So many ideas are presented to us, some are based in truth, but most are pure fantasy. It's easy to group them all together, under the heading of "science fiction," and dismiss them. For many people they are all simply ideas; to others, they are very real.

As we move further into this New Age, we are becoming aware of many vibrational changes. One shift is called "the quickening," a word that has bounced around Christian circles for a long time. Simply put, it's a speeding up our Earth's vibrations. Everything is becoming quicker. Evolutionary charts show early life going on for millions of years. As more complex creatures evolve, the duration between shifts becomes shorter. When the human finally comes along in the time-line, we seem to occupy a mere sliver of the "total time" the Earth has been in existence.

It really is going faster. David's grandmother was born when the Wright brothers made their first flight, and lived to see a man walk on the Moon. Now that is fast!

Considering the information technology industry today, our computers are outdated about the time we open the box. Speed is increasing. Our language is being condensed, easily seen by abbreviations used in texting and speech (OMG, LOL, BFF). We now receive instantaneous communications from all over the globe, on our smart phones. If the Earth quakes in China, we can know it immediately through the internet, satellite, radio, and TV.

The current extreme weather conditions we are experiencing, at the time of this writing, are impacted by global warming/climate change, and continue to accelerate faster and faster. Our own vibration is also revving up, in alignment with our planet's energetic field.

The astrological sign of the New Age is Aquarius, which governs electricity. Its symbol is the wave sign, a glyph representing vibration. It brings a wave of new technologies, new consciousness, and new forms of energy.

In this age, we are able to see and work with these higher energies: light, color, sound, the chakras, our personal magnetic field, and so on. We find our spiritual work is much easier in the Aquarian Age. As matter becomes less dense, it is easier to transform it. In the past, it took intense physical labor to get anything done on this planet. We are shifting to a state where a simple thought will effect change.

Science is already interfacing human thought with computers. As we develop spiritually, we will no longer need any external apparatus to make things happen. Outer inventions are all reflections of inner abilities. All things begin within the mind, all ideas begin within ourselves.

When we have mastered the art of prayer, matter can be moved with our word. In future ages, the mind will easily move things about. Just because most don't yet have this ability doesn't mean we have to wait to experience it. There are always a number of advanced workers, who are not tied to "mass-evolution." Jesus was one such being. He said, "Follow me." He had progressed beyond the limited human condition and showed us a path toward spiritual evolution. There are no limits, except the ones we place on ourselves.

WE CREATE OUR OWN REALITY

We initiate our studies with this profound statement: *We create our own reality, 100%, with no exceptions.* This may be difficult to accept, because when we accept the idea, we must release all blame we have been directing toward others. When we accept this new consciousness, we can't blame anyone for anything anymore. There are no victims. We are never victims. This requires complete forgiveness, a tenet of the teachings of both Jesus and Buddha, as well as other Illumined Beings.

As we sow, so shall we reap. We cannot reap anything that another has sown! Everything we experience is a result of our own thoughts, feelings, and actions. Our experience is rarely what we perceive it to be. External events are mirrors, reflections of our own consciousness. We can only change the outer by changing the inner.

We will study the *Law of Cause and Effect* and the *Law of Prayer*. We will learn how to use these laws, rather than trying to avoid their reality. Instead of spending time and energy figuring out how to avoid the effects of our actions, let's learn how to create beneficial responses through right action. Avoidance and denial are not productive uses of our energy. David used to pray for his karma. He wanted to balance what he already had created, before piling up new stuff on top of it. If we have any debts to pay, let's do it now.

Once balanced, we can begin to do what we want to do, rather than doing what we have to do. This is like having the opportunity to take electives rather than required courses in school. Typically, they are much more enjoyable, because we have consciously chosen them. When we come into a state of balance, we find the door to inner worlds opens wide.

Astrologically, Libra, the scales, is the sign of balance and karma. If we move around the zodiac in a counter-clockwise manner, the sign that precedes Libra is Virgo. Virgo is a sign representing the dual energies of health and selfless service. To achieve a state of balance, our path must lead us through the energies of Virgo. Ultimately, we cannot be in true balance if we are ill or self-serving.

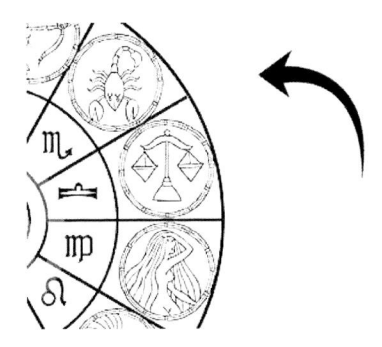

One path toward balance is through sickness, or burning off old karmic residue through "the sweat of our brow." The course of this path may appear as "bad things happening to good people." Behind the appearance is simply a rebalancing act. In this way, we work off the karma we have been carrying for many lifetimes.

The other option is to take the path of selfless service, putting our energy and attention on helping others. It's a less painful way to bring our soul into balance. We have put energy out and it must eventually return. Physics shows us that every action has an equal and opposite reaction. We can use the energy we emit to help others, or be purified through challenging, or "negative" experiences. We can only deal with our karma, the effects of previous actions, in these two basic ways. We may choose a path of service, or we may choose to experience disease. This doesn't mean that if we're sick, we are a bad person. It may simply mean we "think" we are bad. This judgement must be released.

Disease isn't experienced to make us suffer, it manifests so we can learn a particular spiritual lesson. God never punishes us. We do that well enough ourselves. We can see "lesson" as "less on." As we balance, there is less karma on our plate. We can also see our karmic lessons as "*blessins*," as they always serve the evolution of our soul.

Remember, we are responsible — able to respond. At first, it may appear being "responsible" is just another guilt burden we must carry, but it's actually key to our liberation. If someone "out-there" is causing our problems, then we can do nothing until they stop. We place the need for action on their shoulders. "Stop doing this to *me*!" On the other hand, when we realize we have been causing our problems all along, we are in position to address them and make change, if we choose.

We are the only one able to act to alter our experience. We always choose how we react, when someone is triggering us. We may even begin to re-wire the patterning. It always takes two to sustain conflicts. When we decide to stop the "karmic dance" with another, the dance ends. If we put down the tennis racket, the game is over. Our opponent can't play without us.

If we travel around the zodiac clockwise, we find Libra comes after Scorpio. When we consciously walk the spiritual path, we move contrary to the ways of the world. The world proceeds to Libra through Virgo. Let's take the spiritual path, and travel the zodiac in reverse, in a clockwise direction. How can cycles be moving in opposite directions?

We will take the path of Scorpio, the path of Initiation, the path of the *Kundalini*, which we will explore in Chapter 7. This is a more intense path, a spiritual pressure cooker, that leads us through complete transformation. It may appear to be a much shorter/faster path toward balance, which it is; though much steeper and more strenuous. Consider Jesus' crucifixion, for example. That experience afforded a very fast evolutionary jump for Jesus, but what could be more arduous? The more condensed and accelerated the path, the more potent it is. Humanity, it would seem, is happy to take all the time in the world to achieve balance. Are we?

These chapters follow the path of Initiation, the fast track. As we move into the initiations of Scorpio, we take a path through conscious death, death of the false ego-mind. This very often deters those who are not really serious or ready to make such a commitment.

TOOLS & MAPS

Just who are we, anyway? Are we our job or our possessions? Are we our thoughts and ideas? Are we our feelings, our body, our name, or how we look? Who are we? The ancient mystery schools in Greece were guided by the statement, "Man, Know Thyself." All the answers are found therein.

In this life, we are all given tools to help us know the Self, the highest aspect of our being. The objective of these lessons is to become aware of the tools we already have and remember how to use them. We have our word, our knowing, our imagination, our will, our mind, and so on. Even our ego can be a productive tool, once mastered. All outer tools are external representations of the same tools we have within.

There are a number of road maps and resources for roadside assistance, when consciously traveling the path. In this volume, we will be focusing on the maps of Holistic Astrology, Kundalini, and the Way of the Christ. These lessons serve as steppingstones on our spiritual path, and are the foundation for further, deeper studies in the Tarot, *Kabbalah*, and the Cube of Space, which we will address more fully in subsequent volumes.

We will also explore the map-less path to the unknown. We shall know the Truth and be set free.

Concentration

How do we advance this journey? The first thing we will learn is the art of concentration. As it was with the creation of the universe, concentration is always step one. We must develop the ability to focus our attention; otherwise, we will only perceive a reality that is out of focus or scattered. If we are unable to focus our attention, we cannot continue on with much benefit.

When reading these chapters, try to maintain the thread of consciousness contained between the words. During this study, pause to ponder what is written. There are many truths contained within each sentence. If the new information begins to blur, stop. Allow the mind to process what is read.

It is clear that if we eat without pausing periodically to digest, we will get very sick. Even if we are consuming the healthiest food available, too much will bring us to a state of imbalance. We not only need time to assimilate what we have taken in within these pages, but eventually we must eliminate what no longer serves us.

Concentration is the "magic wand" in all magical actions. In using concentration to focus the energy of our intent, we clarify the image of our desired result. All things come forth from a point of concentrated energy. Science describes the creation of our universe, the "Big Bang," as a rapid expansion of matter and energy streaming out from a single concentrated point.

The Soul

In the second chapter, we will focus on the nature of the soul, which is the amalgamation of the essence of our experiences from all our lifetimes. The subconscious mind is an expression of the soul. Through meditation, we can enter our subconscious mind and find pathways to the soul.

Scientific Prayer

Chapter three will reveal the inner workings of prayer. Through prayer we communicate with the Divine! Prayer gives us a technique to make things happen. Contrary to popular belief, every prayer is always answered. We will focus on scientific prayer, so we can understand how prayer really works. We will also examine how we contribute to the appearance that our prayers are going unanswered, and what to do about it.

Holistic Astrology

In the fourth chapter, we will explore the science of astrology and its symbolic language. We will gain a greater understanding of what astrology really is. Moving beyond the personal signs, we will see their universal application. The word astrology is derived from the Greek *astro*, which means "star," and *logos,* which means "word" or "reason." Astrology teaches the message of the stars. A true astrological birth chart is a map of the soul patterns we choose to work with in this life.

Looking out at the night sky, we perceive no end to the myriad collection of stars. Astrology, as well, has no limit in its scope. The universal patterns that it employs are at the foundation of all creation.

Meditation

Chapter five covers meditation, or rather uncovers meditation. We will learn how to quiet the mind, so we may hear the Inner Word, the Inner Teacher. Meditation is really the key to this work, the doorway to the inner worlds. It is the bridge we walk, as we withdraw our conscious focus from the five senses.

Once we have some mastery over our ability to focus our thoughts, we can begin to learn how to meditate. In meditation, we relax our will, the power used to concentrate, and place ourselves into a passive, receptive state. Some may experience difficulty trying to meditate, because, in fact, we cannot meditate! Meditation is a passive state, while doing anything is active in nature.

As with sleep, we must surrender our conscious mind and allow our subconscious to take charge. We cannot will ourselves to sleep. We can only allow ourselves to drift off into slumber. Even when we stay up for extended periods of time, our efforts are directed in trying to stay awake. Once we relax, sleep comes. We can never force meditation. All our efforts only delay the experience.

When we learn how to quiet our mind, we will be able to hear the teacher within, the Inner Word. We learn to discern the difference between guidance from our Higher Self and the false self (ego).

We each have the Higher Self within. Simply stated, our work is to uncover this great treasure, listen to it, and respond to its instruction (inner-structure), putting our Divinity into action. This is what is meant by the kingdom of heaven. We must now remember that it is within us. What is asked for in the Lord's Prayer? "Thy kingdom come…on earth as it is in heaven." How do we do that?

In order to bring God's kingdom from heaven to earth, we must reveal it. It is buried deep within our being. Jesus spoke a parable concerning this. The kingdom of heaven is like a man, who, finding a great treasure, sells all that he has to obtain it. This treasure is the Self, the Christ within. It has many names: the Pearl of Great Price; the Diamond; the Philosopher's Stone; the Cornerstone Rejected by the Builders; the Rock of Ages; Atman; Sun of Man; Buddha Consciousness, among others.

To "sell all that we have" is to give up everything else. We must sell all of our attachments to the material world. As long as we allow ourselves to be distracted with the outer, we can never find the inner. We cannot serve two masters.

We begin by removing the covers, unveiling the Divine within. These veils are our false ego, ideas, judgements, desires, opinions, fear, and the like. We are the ones who are covering up this inner kingdom. No one is hiding it from us. The more we uncover, the more we become aware of the reality within us, and can receive our soul, and, ultimately, the Inner Being, or Self, the I AM Presence.

Once we accept this inner reality is real, we may listen to it and heed its instructions. In so doing, our outer world is re-structured, to be in harmony with our inner one. "As above, so below." This is how the kingdom comes to Earth.

We may attract a group of like-minded people, who have created an environment based on inner reality. This group acts as the third jewel in Buddhism. The first jewel is the teacher, the Buddha. The second jewel is the teachings. The third jewel is the community of those working with the teachings, the *sangha*. These "companions on the way" help disarm our false reality through personal support and guidance.

If we can find one, a true teacher is the prime jewel. We listen to the outer teacher, that we may find the true teacher within, the Self. We may initially begin by finding a spiritually based group of some kind. We study their teachings and may be fortunate enough to be in the presence of a Master Teacher, who can reveal the Supreme Teacher within us. They say, "When the student is ready, the teacher appears."

Foundation Work

Chapter six deals with foundation work. When we construct a building, we begin by laying a foundation. It would then stand to reason that this should be the first lesson. However, in approaching these teachings, we already come with our own foundation firmly in place, a false foundation. If we were functioning with a true foundation, there would be no need for any lessons. We would continually receive instruction directly from Source.

This work is an enormous leap and therefore done in stages. We will go through these stages, dissolving one foundation and creating another that is ever closer to Source. If we take the long view, we see each lifetime as an opportunity to evolve, toward a purer state of being, as we become one with the Higher Self. We can take our time. We are given eternity to find our way back home. The purpose of this course of study is to provide a "short-cut" to this end. It is "short" because we will "cut" away all limitation.

As this lesson follows meditation, we can assume that a great deal of our false perception, our old foundation, has been removed by that point. Then we begin to build a new foundation, putting our "new wine" into "new wineskins," a reference to the parable Jesus spoke, which is mentioned in all four Gospels. Old concepts will not accept new thought.

> *"And no one puts new wine into old wineskins; or else the new wine will bust the wineskins and be spilled, and the wineskins will be ruined."*
>
> *Luke 5:37 KJV*

Kundalini & the Chakras

Chapter seven provides introduction to the *Kundalini* and the *Chakra System,* aspects of the energy body. Chakra means "wheel," or "whirling disk of energy." When the awakening of the Kundalini energy takes place, reality is no longer just a mental idea, but a force that involves our entire being. This is when everything changes. We must approach this work safely, and only once we are ready. The movement of the Kundalini parallels the eternal path of Initiation. As this is high, inner work, we will not open that door prematurely. By the time we open that gate, we will be in a higher state of consciousness, and will be able to better understand what is presented.

The Divinity of Destruction

We live within divine creation, and yet it often appears to be falling apart. Yes, it is divinely falling apart. In chapter eight, we explore how destruction and creation are a polarity of the same energy. When we create a painting, we must destroy the wholeness, the completeness, of a blank canvas.

All the heavy elements on Earth are the result of an exploding star. The form is what is destroyed. All form holds divine Light, creating the illusion of an independent object. When we ultimately experience the Oneness of God, all our previous ideas and concepts of God are destroyed.

Science tells us that nothing can be created or destroyed, it can only change form. If everything is God, does God destroy God? No, creation and destruction are just concepts. God will always be whole. We also cannot be destroyed, but we certainly change form (reincarnation).

Relax. The destruction we see around us is only an appearance. All of creation is evolving toward a greater expression of itself, the One. Focus rather on the creative power within. As we are beings created in the "image" and "likeness" of God, this means we are also creators. What are we creating?

Religion

In chapter nine, we look closely at the nature and purpose of religion. What is its source? Why do we have it? What is its purpose? Our aim is to understand religion, as a tool for spiritual growth. Does religion move us forward or hold us back? Why are there so many? Why do they seem to be so different? How are they similar?

Our relationship with religion spans more than one lifetime. It is a pattern of the soul that contains many dimensions, including the concepts of heaven and hell, angels and spiritual guides.

We will also examine the essence of the major religions of the Earth. As we progress in this study, know that each being on this planet has their own individual path toward the expression of Divinity. As God dwells within each of us, no other path can lead us to the Divine but our own. We will give insight on personal guardian angels, as well.

All religions are tailored to meet the needs of the people who adopt them. Not all religion is formalized. Many today are cultivating their own "personal religion." Finally, we will focus on the concept of trans-personal religion.

The Self

Finally, in chapter ten, we explore the false self, Self, Higher Self, and Supreme Self. Eventually, we will be able to know who we really are. The Higher Self is the Christ, or Buddha Self, within. The Supreme Self is the God Self, the Source of our being.

These are, collectively, the "Foundation Teachings." Once this material is understood and assimilated, we are ready to build our Inner Temple, to understand our divine nature, and, ultimately, to comprehend the nature of the creation in which we exist. The gate is open. The path has been cleared. We are each invited to enter.

Spiritual Exercises & Meditations

An additional tool you have at your disposal, to support the awakening of your consciousness, is the audio companion: *Ten Gates into the Garden: Spiritual Exercises and Meditations.* You have the choice of purchasing a CD or the downloadable version. The spiritual exercises and meditations found in the book augment the teachings and help you to anchor them in your consciousness. The use of the audio version frees up the conscious mind, so you can delve more deeply into the experience at the subconscious level. We recommend this, so you may optimize your experience.

CHAPTER 1

Concentration

THE CAMERA

We begin our study of concentration, using the camera as an analogy, with the assumption most have some awareness of a pre-digital 35 mm film camera.

Direction

In photography, we use a few simple tools to help us capture the images we want. As with all this work, it begins with intent. Our intention might be very specific. We may wish to take a photo of an event, person, or scene, for example. Our first step toward that end is to point the camera in the right direction. If we wish to take a picture of a sunset, we must first point the camera at the Sun.

This may seem obvious, yet so many are looking for God, positioned with their backs to God. We don't do this purposefully; we simply think, imagine, or believe God is "out there" somewhere.

The first requirement to take a snapshot is to aim the camera at what we intend to photograph. When we are in a state of confusion or indecision, or just feeling lost or stuck, we often seek direction, but may not know where to look. To find the Divine, we must direct our attention within.

Focus

Next, we bring the image into focus and frame the shot. By focusing, we establish a center of attention. We key in on a single focal point and bring clarity and sharpness to our vision. There is an immediacy and vividness now to our subject.

When we go to the movies, they are shown in focus. In the days before the digital age, periodically that was not the case. If the film were out of focus, people yelled to the projectionist to "focus, focus!" Once focused again, our attention naturally returns to the screen. Unless the film is in focus, it does not hold our full attention.

Frame

Framing allows us to remove any unnecessary or distracting elements from our composition. We make sure the telephone poles and wires are cropped from the shot. When we frame, photographically, we look at the edges of the image in the view-finder, and create a frame for our focused subject, using surrounding objects; a tree trunk along one side, or a hedge along the bottom may serve this purpose. When we place the subject within a framework of familiar objects, free of extraneous distraction, the mind more easily perceives the photo's focal point.

It is surely more difficult to concentrate, when we are immersed in an overly stimulating environment. Consider focusing on any object in the room where you sit, now imagine trying to do the same at an amusement park. Some feel this is actually the best way to learn the art of concentration, for when we can focus in the midst of chaos, we are able to focus under any circumstance.

Shutter Speed

When taking a photo, we also need to choose the shutter speed that controls how long the film is exposed to light. When the shutter moves at high speed, we freeze an image in time. When we opt for a slow shutter speed, we capture moments that may indicate motion and directionality. When we see the blur of a runner in a photo, we understand in what direction they are moving.

Film

Pre-digital, camera film came in rolls. This recording medium is placed in the left chamber, then threaded across the shutter curtain, and attached to the take-up spool on the right side. With each shot taken, the film is advanced, as though we are writing on a scroll.

Tarot Camera

The Magician is card number one of the Tarot. This card represents focus and concentration, as does the number one itself. In the camera, The Magician represents the lens. We will address these concepts more thoroughly, in a forthcoming volume on Tarot.

The second Key in the Tarot is the High Priestess, symbolic of the subconscious and memory. She is the film in the camera. She is pictured sitting between the two pillars, analogous to the spools that hold the film.

The pillar on the left is black, symbolizing the unexposed film, while the light pillar on the right indicates its exposure to light. The film is the veil stretched between them. The metal associated with The High Priestess is silver, incidentally used in the initial making of film (silver-nitrate). She represents the subconscious mind, a place where all images are reversed.

When we snap a picture, the shutter opens and light moves through the lens, striking the film. If we have focused properly, the image is sharp. The image received, due to the nature of the film, appears as a negative that reverses light for dark and dark for light.

Through the developing process, the reversed image is righted and fixed as a positive print. It's significant that, other than the instant the lens is open, the developing process takes place in total darkness. The workings of the subconscious also take place in darkness, that is, they are unseen.

There is a "space and time" within us, between our exposure to an image and its chemical "fixing" in our brain. Consider witnessing a disturbing image on TV. Any time we view images on TV or elsewhere we wish not to become part of our soul makeup, we can eliminate them before they become fixed in our consciousness, using the following technique.

THE AREA 51 TECHNIQUE

If we were caught sneaking around taking pictures of "top-secret" Area 51, at Edwards Air Force Base in Nevada, the camera would be confiscated. The authorities would remove the film and expose it to light, which would ruin any pictures we had taken.

We can apply the same technique to our "inner camera." To rid ourselves of unwanted mental images, all we need do is expose our subconscious mind to the Light. If we wait until these images become fixed in our consciousness, they are more difficult to remove.

When we find ourselves in any disturbing situation we can flood ourselves with Light. The key is to flood our subconscious with Love, before the image sets. The Divine, Love, is Light. When we truly love the God/Self within our self and others, we can only see the positive. No negative images come from God. Love's active, outwardly pouring, or centrifugal, energy pushes negativity away.

HIGHER DEVELOPMENT

The photographic cycle continues as we develop the negative. Now, the photographic paper is exposed to light, as it is projected through the film negative. Finally, the image is reversed again, resulting in the photographic print.

Before the final print is complete, we can be very creative in the darkroom, when working with the negative. We can crop the image, enlarge it, and make areas of the photo lighter or darker, emphasizing particular details. In each of these processes, we work with the original image, utilizing the creative-subconscious, our imagination, to alter or emphasize aspects of the composition.

The camera represents the mind. The lens and shutter are controlled by our consciousness. The film is our passive subconscious. We are continually taking pictures, whenever our eyes are open.

Change

We can change our lives, by changing the images at which we look. On what do we choose to focus, and with what degree of clarity? How much Light do we allow to penetrate our subconscious? What do we want to remove, or crop out of view?

We so often make quick judgments of a situation, having no clear sense of the direction it is moving, or the elements of its composition, what actually led to this particular unfolding of events.

Let's imagine we want to lose a few pounds, but continually keep looking at food. Our eyes focus on the many wonderful meals we see prepared on TV, or in magazines that offer pages of mouth-watering recipes. Each time we focus on food, we snap another picture for our subconscious to develop. We don't realize we are actually working against ourselves.

THE KEY

The film is simply recording the object of our attention. The film cannot hear "good" or "bad," "yes" or "no," "I want this," or "I don't want that." It only ever registers the subject of our focus. If we want to lose weight and keep looking at food, even though we may say or think,

"I don't want to eat all this," the only thing the subconscious acknowledges is the food. As a result, it is impossible to develop anything else. Food rather than weight loss is in our "viewfinder," so that's what we manifest.

This is the great secret behind Jesus' teaching, to "Resist not evil." *(Matthew 5:39 KJV)* When we resist "evil," we are sending "evil" pictures into our subconscious mind. This gives more and more life to these images, making them stronger and stronger. The subconscious doesn't understand the word "resist," it only captures and "prints" the mind pictures we are taking.

Even if our intent is to "slay the devil," the subconscious reads it differently. It understands that in order to slay the devil, the devil must exist. We continually, unwittingly create what we wish to avoid. Why does our subconscious operate this way?

Balance

The subconscious is simply serving to create balance. It stands to reason, if we are focusing on something, we must have some unfinished business with it. We must need to have another experience with this energy, in order to bring about the necessary balance. If the energy were balanced, it would not even enter our mind.

Many of the issues that troubled us as children, we have resolved by adulthood. As a child, we may have been afraid of the dark. As an adult, this fear no longer plagues us. When we walk into a dark room now, it doesn't even occur to us to be afraid. The energy has been balanced. We generally place more emphasis on the challenges we face, rather than those we have already solved.

We need to take conscious control of our thoughts, or we will always be operating on automatic pilot. Though automatic works, it is not optimal. When we are ruled by our unconscious drives, our spiritual development progresses much more slowly. Work at seeing the positive in everything; give it life; help it grow. This is how affirmations work.

When we look in the right direction, focus our attention, frame out the distractions and press the shutter release, we plant a seed. We plant a seed in the subconscious. Our conscious mind is the sower and our subconscious mind is the fertile earth. Adam, of the Old Testament, symbolizes the conscious mind. Adam is the gardener.

We have found a gateway into the garden, into the subconscious mind, represented by Eve. If we only plant positive seeds, the fruit they bear can only be positive.

Concentration

Concentration, as defined by www.yourdictionary.com, means "to direct or draw toward a common center; focus; to make a solution or mixture less dilute; to direct one's thoughts or attention." We may find the first definition interesting, when we consider that if we are drawn to our "common" center, we are all at the same place.

Our consciousness is the solution or mixture we wish to make less dilute. All the insignificant sensory stimuli we encounter every day is what dilutes our minds. When we turn on the computer, TV, open a magazine, or engage with our phones, we dilute.

We do not imply any of this is "good" or "bad," rather we highlight that if we attempt to do some "work" with any potency, dilution will not further our goal.

Diamonds are concentrated coal, which is black and opaque, while light flows through translucent diamonds. Concentration can lead to transformation. We can concentrate the mind. We can concentrate the will. Lasers are concentrated light.

In the Tarot, card number one, The Magician, represents concentration, and indicates concentration is primary to any spiritual work. Science confirms, before the "Big Bang," the entire universe was "concentrated" at a single point. Then, bang!

THE PICTURES

Ok, now our wonderful pictures are processed, printed, and displayed. Many of us place these images in photo albums. We also have photo albums within, though we rarely look at them closely. We revisit them as recollections of childhood and earlier life, or special events that seem to have made deep impressions in our memory.

All the photos we have taken of ourselves are not pictures of our self but of our experiences. It is actually impossible to take a picture of our "self." Even if we take a "selfie" on our phone, the image is reversed, like our reflection in a mirror. When we picture ourselves in our mind, it's just a mental image, not our true self. We are not the pictures.

Misinterpretation

Often when we have an experience, we misinterpret it's meaning. That misinterpretation then becomes a foundation for more error.

It is quite common for children to blame themselves, if their parents break up. This misunderstanding arises, because the children were not given all the facts. Their minds were registering the input but recording false information. The meaning they have drawn from the experience is what is false.

The child is making a movie titled "This is What Marriage Is." As an adult, we subconsciously refer back to it for instruction. We utilize this model, as our example of how a husband or wife should act.

We don't need to change the movie. We just need to change the title to "This is What Marriage Is Not." Then we can reframe and reinterpret the experience.

Did our parents break up because we did something "wrong" or were "bad?" Perhaps they were discontented with each other, suppressing their own unresolved issues, or overburdened with the stresses of life, were unable to communicate their needs. Their separation and divorce never had anything to do with us.

In meditation, we can go back and review our life, and look at the events in a different light. We can re-remember. This process allows us to change our past, or what we thought was our past. When we do this, we alter the present, our present experience of reality.

Everything we experience is merely an image imprinted in the mind. What we see, and how we see it, becomes our present reality. As we progress in this work, we will be using our spiritual sight more than our physical eyes.

St. Paul said:

> *"For now we see through a glass, darkly; but then face to face: now I know in part; but then shall I know even as also I am known."*
>
> *1 Corinthians 13:12, KJV*

True knowing is when we come face to face with Self.

THOUGHTS ARE SEEDS

We plant every thought into our subconscious. The fruit then grows and later manifests as our experience before us. The world we experience in this moment is the result of our own past beliefs, based on our interpretations of previous events.

Let's say, for example, we get mugged in the park. Our subconscious connects the assault with the park. The park then becomes a much more dangerous place than it was previous to our experience. The park has not changed, we have.

If we think we got mugged because we went into the park, the park becomes fearsome. This is, however, only one way to look at it. In fact, it's really about us, and has nothing to do with the park. Perhaps, had we avoided the park, we still would have gotten mugged.

We often believe we are victims, and those around us continually conspire to keep us in this mind-frame. "It's not your fault, there should have been more police around." That's easy to accept, because it puts the responsibility elsewhere.

If I walk into a fire, I am responsible for getting burned. I can't blame it on the fire. "Oh, the fire was too hot. If it was only an eighty-degree fire, I would have been fine."

Do we put ourselves in danger on purpose? Who said it was danger? Who said we got mugged?

Zen Story

This wonderful Zen story offers us some perspective.

There was a Zen monk, who lived alone in a hut. One night he was awakened and found a thief rummaging through his things. "Good evening" he said to the intruder. "Are you hungry? Let me get some food and water."

The thief stopped cold. "I want your money, old man."
"Why of course" said the monk, "Take the money, but leave me enough to pay my taxes."

As the thief left, the monk chided him for not saying thank you. The thief begrudgingly obliged. Later, when the local police apprehended the man, the old monk was called in to testify.

The authorities said, "We have caught this thief, who stole from you."
"Oh, no." said the monk. "This man came here for a visit. I gave him the money as a gift, and he thanked me for it. He has not stolen anything from me."

Years later, when the man was released from jail, he returned to the monk and became his student. The monk interpreted the events differently, creating a different reality.

What is Happening?

What happens to us is whatever we cause to happen! We write the script. The Magician, representing the conscious mind, sows the seeds. In what way are we a magician? Our magic is that we can change our reality at any time, simply by changing our thinking. When we change our thinking, we alter the contents of the subconscious mind, which will adjust our attitudes and beliefs. This will transform how we react to situations around us, affect our speech and movements, and even impact the vibration of our electro-magnetic field.

The act of reframing opens the way for us to attract new streams of people into our lives. We may also find ourselves attracting new experiences that serve as reflections of our new state of consciousness. We call this the *Law of Attraction*. We will examine its workings, when we further study the subconscious in the next chapter, The Soul.

As we begin to look inward, we have the opportunity to wean our mind from the barrage of stimuli around us. We can choose to plant positive and life-affirming seeds in the fertile soil of the subconscious. As they grow and manifest in fruitful experience, we gradually regain control of our lives. Once regained, we may then hand that control over to the Divine within. Then we'll reap fruits far beyond our present awareness, and we will again return to Eden.

Explore the *Concentration Exercise* below, to hone your powers of concentration. We recommend you experience the meditation using the available audio recording, *Ten Gates into the Garden: Spiritual Exercises and Meditations*.

Concentration Exercise

(This exercise can be found on the digital recording Ten Gates into the Garden: Spiritual Exercises and Meditations, or consider recording the meditation, to play back for yourself, rather than reading it as you go.)

Sit comfortably at a table clear of clutter. Place an orange with seeds on the table in front you. The exercise will take between ten and fifteen minutes. Practice it daily, at a time when you will not be disturbed. Morning is recommended, as it is a good way to begin the day. The exercise will only benefit your concentration with consistent practice.

Initially, keep your consciousness on the orange. When other thoughts creep in, just acknowledge them and bring your awareness back to the orange. You'll have plenty of time for other thoughts after the exercise is complete. Don't push or force yourself. Relax the body and breathe. Just as physical exercises support our strength and endurance, so do spiritual ones.

*****

Consider the orange. Observe it. Keep your attention on the orange. Begin to look at the outer skin. Notice the color; is it consistent? Are there areas of color that appear lighter or darker? Notice how the light reflects off the fruit. Does it seem shinny or dull? Look at the shadows. Become aware of the orange's presence. Consider the texture of the skin. Is it uniform, or varied? Be aware of the end where the orange was attached to the tree…

Concentration Exercise, Cont'd

In your mind, imagine you are peeling the orange. Feel the white pulp under the skin. See its thickness, how it protects the fruit. Now notice the veiny membrane surrounding the segments, creating a web of fine tubes that bring nourishment and water to the fruit. In your mind's eye, slowly peel it off.

The segments within surround the center, where each accesses the Life Force, as it moves through the stem. We could imagine each section is like a house or sign in an astrological chart. Using this analogy, we can visualize the seeds as the planets revolving around the Sun. Some sections are empty, while others contain multiple seeds. Some seeds are nearer the center; some are farther out. Others are spaced higher or lower in relation to the center.

Choose one seed on which to focus. Look at the outside of the seed, its shape, color, and texture. Observe how the seed is formed. Peel back the seed's casing and see inside. Reduce it to its smallest part. Now, in your mind's eye, plant a seed in the earth. Place it a few inches underground and cover it up. The seed is in total darkness.

Sense the Sun's rays penetrating the earth to warm the seed. Water it and watch it begin to sprout. See it send roots down into the earth, while its shoot reaches up through the soil toward the Sun. Observe as it moves through its growth cycle, as day turns to night and back to day again. Each cycle brings more growth. Speed up the action. Watch the cycles of the plant, rising toward the Sun during the day and resting through the night. The days get longer as we move from spring into summer. Fall arrives and daylight diminishes. The Sun rises ever farther south each morning. See the seasons change as the orange seed grows into a tree....

Observe the trunk thicken, in order to support more branches. See the leaves emerge and slowly open, notice the tightly closed buds gradually bloom into flowers. Now bees arrive to dip into each flower, spreading pollen about. From the flowers we begin to see the emergence of new fruit. The fruit grows, as the oranges mature and ripen. We have come full circle.

Pick the orange and see the complete cycle within it. Imagine the tree that is in the orange. Trace the history of the orange and tree. This cycle of the orange has repeated for thousands of years. Now, in your mind's eye, eat the orange and savor the totality of the cycle present in every bite. Notice your current state of mind.

Were you able to stay present to the visualization or did you notice your mind wandered to thoughts, concerns or preoccupations? Know that with continued practice you will be able to stay focused on the cycle of the orange unfolding throughout the entire concentration exercise. This level of focus will begin to permeate other areas of your life. Practice brings proficiency.

Once the exercise is complete, eat the orange. See how close your vision was to the physical orange.

CHAPTER 2

The Soul

WHAT IS THE SOUL?

Once, a college student put his soul up for auction on eBay, listed it in near perfect condition, and started the bidding at five cents. Many of us lead our lives in constant fear of losing our souls. Others, denying their soul's existence, feel they are at liberty to engage in any sort of activity, with no fear of repercussion. These attitudes stem from a great misunderstanding of just what the soul is.

In reality, neither can we sell, save, nor lose the soul. The soul is not something we possess or have; rather, it reflects who we are. Simply, our eternal soul is an energy field, containing the impressions of all we have ever experienced since our creation.

What is meant by our "creation?" Before the initial Creation takes place, before time and space come into being, even before the "Big-Bang," only One Being exists, only One Being. This being is All That Is, eternal, having no beginning nor end. This nameless One, the eternal One, is God, infinite, divine Consciousness, the universal Mind. This One, or cosmic Cell divides itself into the multiplicity of creation, that it may know itself.

At the point of Creation, the parts, including us, take on the illusion of individuality. Although One, the creation *appears* to be many. We forget our divine union with All That Is and falsely believe we are separate individuals.

What is individuality? If we view it as a three-part statement of truth, we recognize the words in/divi/duality, and we may begin to get a clearer picture of the word's meaning. At center resides the Divine, "divi," our divinity, preceded by "in" and followed by "duality." The oneness of the divine Consciousness finds itself in duality, and so experiences itself as separate from the Whole. When we say, "I am an individual," we are stating, "I am the One, (Divi)ne, in a state of polarization or duality." The yin yang symbol is a beautiful representation of this phenomenon. These two *seeming* opposites are contained within the same whole. They are not separate; they are symbiotic, the one necessary and essential to the other's existence, and each contains its opposite.

Duality is expressed all around us in day and night, father and mother, masculine and feminine, etc. We step even deeper into this sticky substance, if we fall into judgement mode. Then we perceive "good and evil," "right and wrong," "this and that." In actuality, the contrast we experience as duality is merely an expression of an energetic continuum or spectrum.

What is duality? The root word is "dual," meaning two. If we start with the One, and divide it into two, we have initiated the source of all the belief in separation that follows. The first "One" appears to be apart from the other "one," which creates the illusion of "two." This false perception initiates the desire to return to Oneness, through union.

In the physical world, this desire manifests as the sex-drive, which compels us to merge or unite with another. What we are really seeking is divine union, an idea that for many is simply an idea. Physical sex, on the other hand, seems to be more "real," more tangible. For the initiated, however, sexual union is just a lower vibrational manifestation of a higher vibrational reality.

INITIATION

To initiate is to begin. The initiated are those who are beginning to live within a different state of knowing. As our consciousness raises, it moves through many octaves of vibration. Each time we transcend a lower vibration, we are initiating. We are beginning again, and such is the path of Initiation. Once we are initiated, we see everything from a totally new perspective.

Initiation is still practiced in many tribal cultures, as a rite of passage for a child to become an adult. After passing through a trial or test, they take on a new identity within the group, perhaps they may serve a new function. Now that their consciousness has changed, the initiate has access to new tools. This is their reality, rather than some fabricated system of growth.

When pledges are initiated into a college fraternity or sorority, they will likely view themselves as part of this new group. They may even have a new set of responsibilities, and perhaps be seen in a new light by others. The raising of consciousness or vibration is seldom the result of this form of initiation. In some cases, when hazing is instituted, it may even lead to a lowering of vibration or consciousness. The 1978 movie, *Animal House*, is a quintessential representation of lower vibrational consciousness in action. At this writing, such practices, to one degree or another, continue to happen on college campuses all over the US.

There are certainly many socially minded organizations that focus on doing good works. A number of "Greek" brother and sisterhoods are based on true initiatory groups, but any sense of spiritual transformation has been lost. Even though there may well be an upliftment of ideals and goals, the raising of consciousness is not their intent. The Masons, on the other hand, are an organization with at least thirty-three separate initiations members may pass through toward spiritual advancement.

Tests that result in true changes in vibration do not come from outside of oneself. These may appear to manifest externally, even though the real causes originate within. As we begin to perceive things differently, old patterns rear their "ugly" heads. These play out as the true tests or initiations. They ask of us, "Are you really going forward with this at any cost? Are you willing to let go of the old ways?"

How they manifest in our experience differs for each of us. We all have our own lessons. We can't look at anyone else's paper. It's impossible to cheat. Some patterns are so deeply set that it may take some heavy work to become aware of them. They have become so ingrained in our lives, we accept them as our true nature. Often our immediate reaction to any change is to resist, to dig in our heels again and defend our defenseless positions.

The solution, then, is humility. It's easier to remove a false pattern, when we can acknowledge it is not a true part of our being. The false ego holds tightly, motivated by fear. It is afraid to relinquish control, afraid the new change will weaken its hold over our thoughts and behaviors, and it will "cease to exist."

VIBRATIONAL SHIFT

We are vibrational beings, emitting a pattern signal, based on our core beliefs and concepts of ourselves. We can begin to change our chronic vibrational baseline, by changing a habit-pattern. As an example, let's say that we are interested in giving up caffeine. Very soon we will notice a few things, the first of which is *coffee*. Our old pattern has been repeated so often it has created a magnetic charge in our subconscious. So, before long, we will attract coffee, in some form, to us. Someone will offer us a cup, a thought will arise to make or buy one, or we may see it in an advertisement. It may also become evident this is the "worst" possible day to attempt to give up coffee. Our experience is amplified for "effect." We create, although unconsciously, multiple opportunities to release the pattern of our coffee habit.

Let's look more closely at how the process of breaking an old pattern works. The first time coffee, or the idea of it, is presented to us, we may say, "No thanks." One rejection causes no real change in our vibration, as we typically don't drink a cup every time one is offered to us or we see an image of coffee. Our inner pattern faces no real challenge yet.

The "test" then returns, and we are offered coffee again, later in the day, perhaps, when we are feeling a bit sluggish. Now the aroma of the brew brings up memories and desires, but again we decline. We've just refused two in a row. The subconscious notes the change. We've missed a cup here and there in our life, but likely never twice in a row. It senses a shift, though the subconscious is not yet certain it will hold. Are we truly giving it up or not? Then a third cup is proffered. This is known as "the charm," the pattern maker, as it initiates the new pattern. The triangle pattern creates a gateway, a portal into new experience.

If coffee is offered yet again, the subconscious need not take notice. It's now following a new "law" we've laid down. This example can give us a clue why certain things are repeated three times. Recognize, however, certain patterns, such as addictions, may require us to reaffirm the new pattern continually for some time, until it is well ingrained enough to keep us from backsliding into old ways of thinking and being. We can also recognize temptation stems not from some "devil" trying to trip us up, but as a way for the subconscious to find out what we really want. We are advised to keep this in mind, whenever we attempt to make a change in life.

An established pattern is like a dance we can do without any thought. We move our feet, unconsciously, to a particular rhythm, enacting a modern ritual. Each pattern, like each dance, evokes a different feeling, awareness or vibration. When we decide to learn a new dance, we use different steps; we learn new moves, we take on a new consciousness.

If we're out of rhythm with our "dance" partner, or one is dancing the tango and the other a waltz, toes will get stepped on. When we begin to change our vibration, we may no longer be in harmony with people and experiences aligned with the old vibration. This new discord may be painful. If each partner is dancing a different step, they may soon seek new partners. This is why people drop out of our lives, or we choose to release them. Old habits no longer appeal and we move on, because there is no longer a vibrational affinity.

We have patterns of speech and thought. We have patterns of belief and knowing. We have soul patterns, which are the deepest and most difficult to change. Yet when we do, the results are completely life altering.

How do we establish soul patterns? Each day's experiences are absorbed into our consciousness. The energy of those experiences is transferred to the blood, which gradually circulates the resulting vibration to all the cells, bringing them "up to speed" regarding the events. Finally, when we go to sleep, that vibration is assimilated in the four lower bodies (physical, mental, emotional and memory) of each cell. When someone has experienced a trauma of any kind, sleep will, ultimately, lessen the intensity of the initial shock, by spreading it out over trillions of cells. The physical body retains the experience at a cellular level, and the occurrence also becomes established in the subconscious. As a result, a traumatic experience can be triggered quite easily, resulting in such conditions as PTSD.

Even when we drop the body, transitioning through what we refer to as "death," consciousness remains, as the essence of all of the experience of this lifetime, which is then integrated into the soul's memory bank. They say, "You can't take it with you," referring to material possessions, but we do absorb the distillation of all of our experience into our personal Akashic Record, the soul.

How do we get rid of lower vibrational thoughts and feelings? If we can "get a handle on them," we can "pick them up," or, more accurately, raise them up. We are literally "giving them up," letting go of them and allowing them to raise in vibration. We can imagine the lower vibrational energies circulating around the base of the spine, the pelvic or solar plexus regions (where we typically feel the effects of denser energies in the physical body) disentangling from those centers and moving up the spine and out the top of the head, through the crown chakra energy center, which has its locus a few inches above the head. God is more than happy to take away this burden. It only serves as a barrier between God and us, anyway.

We may pray that our resistance is removed. It works! Also, we can visualize a fire and throw the destructive thoughts and feelings into it. Using the phrase "into the fire" is impactful. After all the junk has been put "into the fire," the mantra takes on new meaning. Now we go "in" to the fire. We pray at the altar of the divine Flame within, the Triple Flame of the Heart, representing the Power, Wisdom and Love of the individualized God Presence that is each of us. When the outer no longer holds us, we can go within and approach the Divine. The final meaning becomes clear; as we actually turn "into the fire," we become the Light. This is a true stage of enlightenment (in-light-en-ment).

Practicing the *Review Exercise* below, every night enables us to weed-out the destructive and charge up the constructive/creative/life affirming energies. Then, when we go to sleep, our cells are bathed in "good vibrations." At the end of this lifetime, as we go through "transition," we look over our life from death on back to our birth. This process is truly our life "flashing before our eyes," and then our life-experience transfers from our blood to our soul, so it may be accessed in subsequent lifetimes, for the sake of our continued soul evolution. We recommend you experience the meditation using the available audio recording, *Ten Gates into the Garden: Spiritual Exercises and Meditations*.

> **Review Exercise**
>
> This spiritual exercise lets us in on a very useful secret. We are given a window of opportunity for transformation that opens just before sleep.
>
> As you lie in bed at night, begin to focus on your rhythm of breath. Allow it to gradually deepen and slow down. As you relax more fully, look back over your day. Start from where you are in the present moment. Take in the ambient sounds in your environment. Feel the support the mattress and pillows provide you. Sense the textures of the fabrics of your night-clothes and bedding against your skin.
>
> Slow the breath down even more. Now begin to move progressively backward through time. Remember getting into bed, brushing your teeth, getting into your pajamas, taking off your day clothes, etc., continue back through the day in these segments, until you imagine yourself waking from sleep this morning.
>
> As you become aware of things you did or said that are in alignment with your divine Self, give life to them, affirm them in the mind. Open the heart to them. If you recall actions, feelings or thoughts that are out of alignment with your highest Self, transform them. Imagine, without judgement, how you might have behaved, or what you might have said that would have allowed you to remain in alignment with the highest aspect of your being. Allow the vibration of this present alignment to permeate the mental, emotional, memory and physical bodies, to transmute the energetic residue of the earlier incident in your day. Notice how you feel. What has shifted for you energetically?
>
> Resolve to make a different choice, based on this new vibration of equanimity, when you draw this kind of experience to you again. Were you angry with someone? Visualize the barrier around the heart dissolving, so the Love Light within you may flow more freely. Surround the being or event in this high vibrational energy. Alter the way you use the Life Force energy. Direct it away from the negative and destructive toward positive and generative expressions.

Remember the secret? We don't actually have to carry everything over. We may reenter the editing room. As the film of our day rolls by, we can cut out the parts we want to remove and amplify the parts we want to keep.

Practicing the exercise every night on the smaller, daily scale benefits us in two ways at the time of our transition. First, there will be a lot fewer "scenes" that aren't working that need revision in the next life, because we will already have transmuted the denser energies. Additionally, we will have created a pattern of editing, so when we find our self at this place again, we will know just what to do. In fact, we will do it automatically. What an opportunity! We will no longer be operating under the rule, "What you see is what you get."

RECOGNIZING SOUL PATTERNS

For a pattern to exist, it must be repeated multiple times. We may have had a disastrous relationship, broken up, only to attract a new partner, who is virtually a clone of the old one, perhaps again and again. When this happens, we are running up against a soul pattern. Our partner is only ever reflecting back to us our own mis-alignment, so we must discover and uproot our own soul pattern underlying the dysfunction, or we will continue to attract others who mirror it back to us.

Perhaps one of our parents expressed the same pattern. Does that make it a family pattern? It is both a soul pattern and a familial one. In order to transcend our patterning, we choose, as a soul, to incarnate through a parent or into a family expressing the same pattern. Again, they only serve to reflect back to us our own mis-alignment. Our old patterns are familiar and therefore comfortable, however dysfunctional they may be. Our work in this lifetime is to transmute that old energy so we may transcend the outmoded soul pattern.

One way we may discover these patterns is through the astrological birth or natal chart. The soul patterns, present at birth, are activated through our current life experience. Each had its origin in another lifetime, and the soul has carried the patterns forward into this life, for the purpose of liberating our consciousness from its own self-created limitations.

These patterns may be very hard for us to see, because they seem so much a part of our makeup. It is like trying to see our own eye without using a mirror. In the same way, we have difficulty seeing the pattern from a position within the pattern. An astrological chart, however, serves as a mirror, as a reflection of our soul's current energetic vibration, and can be seen more objectively by an astrologer, who is able to analyze the chart, and discern the patterns.

The second way to discern is to look directly at the soul and see the patterns. How can one "see" the soul, if it's only a pattern of energy? We are able to see the physical body, and that's only a pattern of energy, too. We see what we look at. If we are only interested in seeing the flesh, how will we be able to see the aura? How many people, who read "adult" magazines, would buy them, if they only showed the model's aura? Perhaps, a few would. We see what we look for; we get what we see, and this can be a very vicious cycle, depending on our point of view.

How can we walk through the world without looking at it? We do so with great difficulty. If we only look at the aura, how can we possibly see the soul? We must shift our focus away from the world and even the aura, toward the soul-plane, where the soul resides. So, let's progress.

In order to see the spiritual world, we must use more than our physical eyes. Our spiritual sight must be activated. All of our senses have a spiritual counterpart. More accurately, it is our spiritual senses that have a physical counterpart. We begin to explore this awareness in meditation, placing our focus on the mind's eye. This process will begin to offer us alternative visionary experiences, helping us to be more open to other types of sight.

When we focus our awareness on the mind's eye, we are still relying on mental sight. We have not yet tapped into our spiritual sight, that, when developed, may be used when the eyes are open as well as closed, because we are not using the physical eyes at all. Soul-vision is not commonly applied on Earth. We must first be able to discern our own soul, before we can see someone else's. If we are truly viewing the soul, we have access to all the other incarnations.

It is said the eyes are the "windows to the soul," and that is correct, but only partially. You may look deeply into a person's eyes and catch a glimpse of the soul, but you may have no awareness of the soul-patterns. Looking into the soul this way is like seeing someone across the street, yet without knowledge of what they are doing or where they are going. It is important to realize the soul is genderless. It is neither male nor female, nor is it solely "human." At our soul's inception it is Light and nothing more.

THE OVERSOUL

Does an animal have a soul? Well, yes and no. The soul records experiences. Many living things share collective experience. Look at cows in a pasture. There isn't much variety in the experience department. For the most part, all the cows have the same experience. Sure, there are some differences. Maybe the farmer takes a few cows to the State Fair. Do we think the cows know they are at the State Fair? It's the same thing only a different day. They eat, poop, get milked, and sleep. A few get to go for a ride.

So, this uniformity of experience is shared in a common soul, what's described as an "over-soul." This over-soul may stay with this group of cows for many generations. It may even be connected to various groups of cows, although they would necessarily be the same type of cow, like all Herefords or Holsteins.

We often see flocks of birds or schools of fish moving fluidly in unison. A "murmuration" of starlings expresses in pulsating undulations, expansions, contractions and twists. They appear to be one body, orchestrated by one mind.

We can apply this same analogy to ourselves. Our body is a combination of countless cells. Each cell does not have an individual soul. They all share our soul. Our soul is their over-soul.

All our cells, therefore, share in the same experiences. Typically, they all respond to the same guidance, because they have the same DNA blueprint.

It is important to note that some domesticated animals and pets, like cats and dogs, through their long, close association with humans are rapidly shifting away from rulership by the over-soul, and in many cases, expressing as individualized souls.

SOUL CONTACT

The most direct link to our own soul is through the subconscious mind. This is why many are able to recall past lives, while in hypnotic trance, or through meditation and dreams. As we develop our meditation practice, we can safely begin to consciously enter the subconscious.

Let's look at a three-dimensional example of a multi-dimensional reality. Consider, again, the cells in the body. Each cell has a nucleus, which contains the genetic code for our particular form. The DNA within all the cells is the same. As the cells develop, they take on specialized functions, depending on their location in the energy field of the body. Let's call this their environment.

Similarly, within each of us, at the very center of our being, resides a nucleus we will refer to as the Self, the individualized aspect of the Divine. Within the Self, as in the nucleus of the cell, is an instruction set. Just as all the cells in our body have the same set of instructions, so do all the people on the Earth. We are all cells in the body of God. This is what makes us all "created equal," and what unifies us, our point of Oneness. As the cells of God's body, we each take on different aspects of the Self. We serve different functions that support the Whole. We might see ourselves as Cosmic "stem cells," with the ability to become anything.

What makes each of us different, however, are our individual experiences. We know a blood cell has a different experience than a liver cell. It looks different and functions differently. No two beings have the same experience, as we are always viewing our lives through our own set of filters. The imprint, or memory essence of these unique energetic occurrences, is stored in the repository of the soul, and will color any future experiences we have.

SOUL-MATES

We are generally very aware of our genetic or adoptive family, and the families we may have married into, or acquired by choice in other ways. In addition to these, we also have soul-families. These family structures are made up of those souls with whom we have interacted lifetime after lifetime. Our soul holds the memory of each incarnation and the impressions left by those we have known. As we meet up with them in different incarnations, we may still be working through old energies, while also creating new patterns.

Even if we are with someone in only one life, a pattern of energy is created by the relationship. The souls we have incarnated with many times are those with whom we have the most potent relationships. They may be our teachers, friends, colleagues, relatives or mates. The patterns of these relationships are transferred to our soul through the memory, through our subconscious mind. We continually retain the essence of every experience, which works like hypertext; if we "click" on it (focus on it) it expands and leads to more information, and the potential for greater growth. Nothing is lost.

We may meet someone who has an immediate impact on us, whether "positive" or "negative," or we may feel uncannily attracted to someone we just met. The strong reaction indicates it is not our first encounter with this soul. "Love at first sight" is rarely at *first* sight. Our soul has an affinity with the other's soul, because we have been with them in one or more incarnations. It all seems so familiar. There is in place an energy connection that was created before this embodiment.

When we meet up with the same soul in a third lifetime, a triangulation is created. The trine brings the relationship into another dimension. At three, a link is established, (three is the pattern maker) and they become part of our soul-family. The process of energy triangulation lays the foundation for the development of a star-pattern.

As these two souls interrelate, lifetime after lifetime, more points of a geometric star are established. We can only see these geometric patterns by observation over thousands of years. As the star grows, a bond is created that is termed soul-mate. We have created many stars with many people over many incarnations. We are all working on star-points, even now. This lifetime we may put many more points on our stars. We experience what we create.

THE TIES THAT BIND

Our consciousness tends to project us into the future. We are asked to think about the future all the time. We are asked what we want to be when we grow up, if we intend to marry or have children. We are encouraged to make out a will and plan for retirement. We project and plan. The indigenous peoples of Earth try to be conscious of how what they do now will affect the next seven generations. Taking this view expands one's awareness.

What we cannot forgive ties us to the past, and brings the past up again and again. This "hyper-focus," or "obsessive concentration" limits our awareness. As we play out hurts over and over in the mind, we lose sight of what's happening now. There is a great deal of energy liberated for new creation when we are able to release the past.

The Greeks call the soul the "*psyche*," the root of the term psychedelic. Using such substances is a less than safe path to greater awareness, as exploration with drugs can plunge us into areas of soul exploration for which we are not prepared. Certainly, we can never really be prepared for something new, but we can learn how to more easily navigate through new territory.

During the 1960s many found out why the drug LSD was also called "acid." With the high doses used, during the early days of experimentation, the drug could dissolve away soul patterns, cleanse the karma. Many people had incredible soul experiences. Without realizing it, they were witnessing the transmutation of their old patterning. The "shaman's path," which often utilizes psychotropic drugs, is not to be underestimated, nor entered into lightly. Using "mind altering drugs" is no substitute for doing the actual work required for spiritual evolution and karmic balancing.

Today, when we think of someone having "soul," we are referring to the depth of "feeling" or "emotion" they possess. As these attributes stem from the subconscious, when we are "soulful," we are, at the very least, tapping into the realm of the soul.

MEMORY

Memory is the basic function of the subconsciousness mind. If our memories are based on what we observe, it's easy to see how poor observational skills can create false memories. We are not able to accurately judge what we are seeing, if our vision only sees the outer, or superficial event. When we come from a purely self-conscious, or egoist position, our sight is already distorted. When we only consider how something relates to us, we severely limit the field of possibility.

Attempt to remember when John F. Kennedy, Martin Luther King, Jr., or John Lennon was assassinated, or perhaps the events of 9/11, the Columbine or Parkland school shootings, or another significant world or personal event that was unexpected. We may recall being home from school with a cold, for instance. We might recollect the weather on that day. Perhaps we were watching TV when the NEWS suddenly interrupted the programming. We likely remember who was present with us. When we recall an event from the past, we are doing so from the vantage point of our unique experience, how it affected *us*. It is easy to see how any given memory has little to do with the event itself and everything to do with our personal experience of it.

There is an anecdote in which two people suddenly come charging into a psychology class, and "shoot" each other with bananas, before dashing out. Although each student observed the same event, they all had entirely different recollections of the incident. Though some looked away, sensing it was "staged" for demonstration purposes for the class, many were caught up in their own personal reaction to the events. Nonetheless, they each had widely differing experiences.

Why are stage magicians easily able to fool us? Our faulty powers of observation lead us to a different conclusion than what is actually taking place. We *saw* the magician locked up in the trunk, therefore he must be in the trunk. Surprise! He's not in the trunk; he never was. Our subconscious mind believes what we thought we saw. It is easy to recognize the benefits of cultivating our powers of concentration.

Look at what has been created in God's name, based on the false conclusions that result from a severely limited understanding of sacred texts like the Bible and the Koran, for instance. We may begin to see how much of our suffering is caused by our false concepts and beliefs.

THE THREE LAWS OF MEMORY

Three Laws demonstrate the memory faculty's ability to make associations. A multitude of ideas are introduced to the subconscious mind continually. The ability to sort and arrange these ideas is at the very foundation of memory.

Law #1:
We associate things that are similar. It's easy to remember vegetables, or colors, or the names of the States. We group the individual units together in our mind. We get the same result when we use a search engine on our computer, typing in a "keyword."

Law #2:
We remember things that are close together in space or time. Our memory of Kennedy's assassination or 9/11 falls into this category. We make associations, remembering things that took place at the same time. We recall a special vacation to an exotic locale. This memory group contains the hotel room, the people we encountered, the food, the weather, our activities, and so on. We easily put together various experiences and meetings into a single framework. For example, try to remember something like a first kiss and where it happened. See how many details you can remember.

Law #3:

We remember things of great contrast, or opposite quality. When we play word association games, we often respond to "hot" with "cold" or "sweet" with "sour." It's as easy to remember as day and night.

The two pillars, on the Tarot's High Priestess card, illustrate the three laws. The two pillars are similar in shape, are close together, and opposite in color. The High Priestess is symbolic of the subconscious and the soul. Much may be gained that is beyond the limitations of words, by meditating on the card. We will explore the 22 Major Arcana more deeply in our next book on Tarot.

THE AKASHA

In metaphysical circles, we often hear the term, *Akashic Record*, which refers to Nature's memory, a record of all that has ever happened, the totality of which is God's soul. We each have the potential to access and read these records. If we wish to see God's soul, however, we must first access our own.

When David travelled to Bali years ago, for a workshop on the *Seven Rays*, he had occasion to visit "The Hall of Records." The following is from his Bali travelogue:

Our workshop continues and I find myself in deep space during a meditation we are doing. Beyond the Earth and Moon, beyond the Sun, our local star, and into space. I come across a pod of "space whales." There were a number of pods and I was drawn to one. I had read that whales were the "record keepers" of this planet, and so my subconscious used this symbol to represent my impending experience.

I go within the whale. I am just there, inside. Before me is a room, though lower than where I stood. I can barely see in through a number of windows, as they are at (my) ground level. The room is dark and I can make out a number of bookshelves. At once I know this is the "Hall of Records." I also know I have no business being here. I look over to my left and see an Asian man, dressed in ornate red clothing. He stands before a red door. He is silent, but the door begins to open. A blinding solar light, from behind the entrance, floods into the space where I am. I dissolve into the light. I come out of meditation.

I tell Helen my experience and she tells me to return, to receive information for the group. Later that evening I return.

That night we meditate by the fire. We sit around the flames and go within. I put myself in the fire, so that what is not Self is consumed in the flames. I see fire elementals (conscious beings that live in the fire dimension, they are not physical) and send them love. It looks as though they are wearing a blue "skin" that covers them completely, melting all features into a singular form. It feels cool but not cold. Very pleasant. I go deeper into meditation.

I go to the "Hall of Records." I am immediately overcome with the immensity of it. I ask to be shown into the Hall. It is a very large room. I cannot see the far or side walls. Before me are infinite shelves of books. I think it is too much for my mind to comprehend, too much to fit in my head. For the sake of the group, however, I strive forward.

My mind tries to get in the way, pulling up concepts of where I am, and any ideas I have ever heard about the "Hall of Records." Every thought that bubbles up is tossed into the fire before which I meditate. My mantra becomes "into the fire," repeated over and over. Any thoughts - into the fire. Ego puts in an appearance - into the fire. All distraction - into the fire.

I look across the Hall. I am not in my comfort zone at all. Actually, I feel very uncomfortable being here and would much rather leave, but I am not here for myself. I ask what they want us to know.

A large book is put before me and opened to the first page. The letters appear to be flame-letters but are not Hebrew or anything I have ever seen. They are gold and the pages are parchment. The book looks very old. (Ancient wisdom?) I look at a word I cannot read, and my attention is directed to just one letter in the word. Upon closer examination the letter seems to be alive and in constant motion. The shape does not change but there is an internal flowing movement so it always looks different.

Again, I want to leave, but "they" say there is information for the group. I say, "they," but only one presence is there. I do not see who "they" are.

I am told the letter is our entire universe in its complete cycle of life. The shimmering of the letter is the living creation. It contains past, present, and future, though this "time" is not linear. Rather, it appears that all time is happening at once. The letter is flat but also multi-dimensional. It is active. It does not represent the universe but is the universe. It contains everything and feeds on itself, constantly renewing, or re-birthing itself.

I want to leave again, but they say there is more information. The letter is actually a sound vibration. Our entire universe in this one sound. (OM?) It is the "Word." All matter, all thought, all feeling, all perception is just sound vibration. From this perspective I see the unifying energy field. The rocks, oceans, people, cans of soup, angels, and worms cannot be separated out. There are no separate things. All of creation is a manifestation of the single note. I see all separation as a "miss-perception."

It really is all one. To realize this, and to realize the magnitude of letters in these never-ending shelves upon shelves of books, is too great to comprehend. I am stunned. We are to know that because everything is sound, sound touches everything. By working with sound we're working with the universe itself. We cannot hear it because we are it.

CHAPTER 3

Scientific Prayer

THE ANSWER TO OUR PRAYERS

The word prayer has different meanings for different souls. To some, prayer is the repetition of verse in a house of worship, or a heartfelt request in private. We may consider prayer a religious practice or view it in a spiritual context. Let's see how it works scientifically.

Prayer actually enables the Universe to become aware of our specific needs. It is said that Nature abhors a vacuum. Our needs create a vacuum to be filled. In the act of prayer, we are asking that the vacuum be filled. When we don't ask, the needs are not fulfilled, and we experience discomfort.

Some individuals repeat prayers over and over until they become the prayer. If we become the prayer at the start, we would save a great deal of time. To become the prayer, we shift the energy from words to actions.

In Chapter 1: Concentration, we looked at the conscious mind, and practiced The Concentration Exercise, which focuses our thoughts. Chapter 2, on The Soul, dealt with the subconscious mind. In the Review Exercise, we discovered a way to clear our subconscious of unproductive energies.

In this chapter, we will learn how these two faculties work together, so we can use prayer as a tool to shape our reality. We will come to realize our every prayer is answered every time.

EASY AS 1, 2, 3

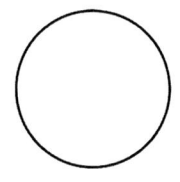

The Introduction was titled Chapter O, this number is represented by a circle, the undifferentiated Whole. When we learned to focus and concentrate in Chapter I, we created the dot within the circle, which is the geometric shape representing the number one. A dot is static, however, a number without action or movement. Next is the number two. How do we jump from one to two?

When we focus and center our being in the center of the circle, we create two realms. There is the circle-realm and also the dot-realm. The relationship between the inner dot and the outer circle becomes the field of experience, the three-dimensional world. This is the realm of *prakrti*, which, in Hinduism, represents, among other things, the "stuff" that makes up what we perceive as reality. It is all illusion, or *maya*, which, in Sanskrit, refers to our distorted thinking about the three-dimensional world we experience. It may now become clearer why Chapter 2 is about the soul. The soul records our adventures (experiences) in the field of the three-dimensional plane.

Geometrically, the number two is sometimes depicted as a line, for it has two ends. Here it is drawn between the center of the circle and the outer rim. As the line is created, so is polarity. Through our actions, in the field of experience, we amass soul patterns, which spiral around the center, creating the scroll script of our soul's evolution. The High Priestess holds this scroll in her lap.

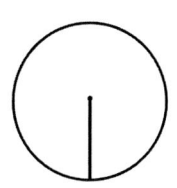

Three-dimensionally, visualize the dot as the very center of a sphere. We can draw a line, or radius, from the center point to any place on the outer surface, no matter how large the sphere.

The image to the right illustrates how the one and the many are connected. We might consider the point in the center to be omniscient, simultaneously knowing everything about every part of the sphere. It has a direct connection to all aspects of the whole from within. In the same way, God is connected to all of us, from within.

THE LAW OF THE TRIANGLE

The *Law of the Triangle* governs prayer. The geometric shape for the number three is the triangle, an ancient symbol of action. With a triangle, we can envision energy moving around a circuit. The triangle also represents the One, manifesting as three.

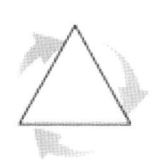

The Christian Holy Trinity: Father, Son, and Holy Spirit is an expression of this directional energy flow. In Hinduism, the Godhead is also depicted as a trinity, seen as *Brahma*, the Creator; *Vishnu*, the Preserver; and *Shiva*, the Destroyer.

We are guided by some religions to picture God as a triune being that veils God behind the mysteries. This enables some religious leaders to hold onto the real power, while the masses are encouraged to believe that they can't understand the nature of the Divine, and therefore must submit to the beliefs of the group, and can only reach God through one who is a member of the hierarchy. The priests know, while the masses only believe.

The teachings in this volume will begin to remove the veils, opening the way toward knowing, for all who seek it.

PRAYER

Many people understand prayer to be a plea made to God for the granting of some wish. We may pray to pass a test or win a football game. We might pray for patience, healing for ourselves or others, or we might pray for world peace. To whom are we praying? God? Jesus? Mother Mary? Buddha? Quan Yin? A Saint? An Angel?

All the great spiritual teachers tell us not to pray to them but to the Creator, God. God, as the Source-Creator, is our necessary point of contact, if we wish to create, or more accurately, co-create anything.

How do we manifest our intentions? We must first begin with an idea of what we wish to create. For a clear result, we must start with a clear idea.

We then call on our powers of focus and concentration. First, we think about the idea, then visualize an image of what we will create in our mind's eye. Now we plant the concentrated seed idea, the thought-form, into the fertile soil of the subconscious mind. Finally, we must let go.

If we are planting a garden from seed, first we prepare the soil. We weed the garden, removing them at the root, so they won't grow back. We plant seeds in the subconscious in the same way, and we must, likewise, weed the subconscious mind.

If we allow weeds to overrun our vegetable garden, the vegetables will have to compete with the weeds for sunlight, water, and nutrients from the earth. In the same way, our prayers will necessarily compete with so many other of our conscious and unconscious wishes, and become entangled or choked off.

It is essential that we completely uproot negative and destructive thoughts (conscious and unconscious). If we just remove what we see above the surface, the pattern will return. We aren't looking to remove the effect of our actions, but the cause. In gardening, we turn over the earth, before planting. Similarly, we may have to overturn some unconscious beliefs we hold.

Imagine trying to plant tomato seeds while still holding on to them. At some point, we have to let them go. We also need to cover them with soil, so they will germinate. How well will the tomatoes grow, if we keep digging them up every hour to see how they are doing? In the same way, we must let go of whatever we pray for, in order for it to come to fruition. We cannot put an idea into the subconscious mind and continue to hold on to it. We can't recall it to mind every few minutes, or we will disrupt the natural cycle of the creative process. We must really let go.

FAITH

Now faith enters the picture, as it is what enables us to let go of the seed. We have faith the tomato seed we planted will produce fruit, in due time. When we continually practice this technique, and see it work again and again, our faith transforms into knowing. We no longer believe; we know. Then we can even let go of the knowing and it becomes automatic.

When we walk across the room, we know we will not fall through the floor. Our knowing is so complete, we don't have to do so consciously anymore. Our subconscious mind takes over the knowing.

BEFORE WE PLANT

As we develop an idea in our mind, we apply our powers of imagination. We imagine how our idea might grow, its various potentialities. We can visualize an action and then imagine the outcome, the possible effects. In this way, we can eliminate poor ideas ("bad" seeds), before we put them into practice (plant them). We have discovered a place of experimentation and investigation. It is our creative subconscious mind, the seat of the imagination.

The subconscious mind is made of a substance the Hindus call prakrti. It is the root-substance of creation, upon which all objective planes of being rest. It is the principal material energy, the Holy Spirit, of which all matter is constituted. Also referred to as the Cosmic Water, it is the source of matter, even as all energy has its origin in the divine Flame, or *Purusha*.

Step One

First, we create the seed of our initial idea, a thought, and envision the form it takes. As we focus, the thought-form coalesces. As we speak our prayer, like a super-saturated solution, eventually the thought-form precipitates out, descending, or lowering in vibration, to become a blueprint for the ultimate concretization, or material manifestation to follow. This thought-form reflects the original pair, the Father (Energy) - Mother (Matter) God.

We symbolize the Source Energy, underlying the thought, as a blue sphere. Blue has the highest relative vibration among the primary colors. The circle represents the spiritual realm, and again refers us back to the seed.

Step Two

Next, we must activate our thought-form, with our word, for it to manifest in the material world - the germination of the seed. Words carry power. Anyone who has ever been yelled at can attest to this. Our intent determines how this power is used.

A large yellow triangle symbolizes the Word, or the *Law of Prayer*. As most of us associate prayer with words, the triangle symbolizes prayer itself. Recall the *Law of the Triangle,* which is like a circuit board, running energy in a particular pattern.

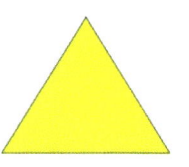

We begin by visualizing the blue sphere of Source Energy at the top of the large triangle, manifesting as an idea. We place the small, yellow triangle, symbolizing the thought-form at the right corner of the large triangle, representing the *Law of Prayer*.

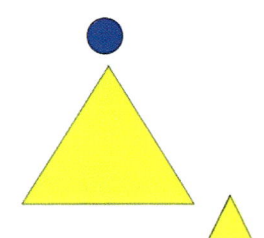

Words harness and limit sound energy, for the purpose of specification. If we scream "ahhh" when we are in trouble, we emit sound without the form of words. When we limit the sound to the word "help" or "fire" we are being more specific, concentrating the energy, and communicating the nature of our situation. When we verbalize prayer, we are energizing our "though-form" with our Life-Force Energy.

When we take an idea (seed) and plant it in the subconscious (water) and add the energy of the word (sunlight), it will bear fruit. We are now at the point of voicing our prayer. To whom, then, shall we voice it? Where shall we direct the flow?

If we accept that God is within us, then this is where we must direct the prayer. If we acknowledge we are individualized expressions of God, then we already are within. Do we pray to our self, or do we pray to our Self?

If in reality there is no such thing as space, how can we offer our prayer in any particular direction at all? We may have been taught to lift our hearts in prayer, or perhaps to bow our heads. Is there anything, or anywhere we can speak and not be overheard by God? Does God not know our thoughts already? If God is everywhere, why do we direct our prayers at all?

All of these instructions are not for God's sake. They are for us. If we ask how to pray, will we not be told? Over the ages we have asked and have received countless techniques. Do we really need all these instructions? Only if we think we do.

We find so many ways to pray, because we have over complicated our lives. If we merely simplified to what is essential, all we need do is ask. Knowing God is everywhere, we wouldn't need to put ourselves into any particular position or use any increased volume. We wouldn't need to close our eyes or go into meditation. It is very simple. We ask, and we receive.

It's not about being worthy, or deserving, or even about being good. Jesus never said, "Ask and ye shall receive, if you are good." That was attributed to Santa Claus.

Verbalization has an additional effect that we tend to overlook. It lets our biology (flesh body) know what's going on. When we speak out loud, the sound vibration is received by our ears, and translated by the brain. The outer (body) gets to know what the inner (mind) is up to. Knowing what is coming, the outer already begins to change.

Step Three

After we have asked, the final stage of prayer is letting go. We have created a thought-form, activated it with sound vibration, and must now let it do its thing. Just as the seed could never sprout if we kept holding on to it, our thought-form can never materialize, if we continue to hold it in our minds.

The magic continues. This third step is the third point on the *Triangle of Prayer*. At the lower left point resides the red square. This is the point of the Holy Spirit. We may simply use the word Spirit. By saying that it is "Holy," we mean that it is whole or complete. It is the totality of Spirit.

In the illustration, we see "idea" at the top of the triangle. "thought-form" and "silence" are at the base. As the idea descends in vibration, the thought becomes the thought-form, and the form, then, moves into silence. The triangle represents energy in motion, and the square signifies the stillness of matter.

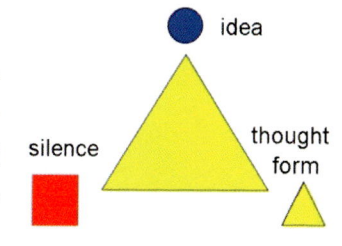

It has been said that matter is polarized Spirit, or prakrti. The magnetic fields that are created cause a temporary division of Spirit, into an endless number of smaller energy fields that appear to us as the physical plane.

As matter is demagnetized, or depolarized, all forms dissolve, and Spirit returns back to a state of Unity. When we speak of matter as polarized Spirit, the polarity manifests, in the physical plane, as protons and electrons. Protons and electrons do not exist as independent entities in unified Spirit.

Consider Spirit, using the analogy of water. As we polarize (freeze) the water, its vibration is lowered, until it becomes solid ice. We can build any number of structures and forms with the ice. However, when the vibration raises up, the ice melts and the forms dissolve. The water becomes vapor, no longer seen, touched, smelled, heard, or tasted. The water is no longer in a state of separation. As Spirit is lowered in vibration it appears solid and separate. When the vibration is raised, it lets go of form and regains its Oneness.

AFTER THE LAST STEP

When we finally let go of our prayer, knowing it will be answered, we return to the blue circle at the top of the *Triangle of Prayer*, and we thank God (or Self) for answering our prayer.

Two purposes are served here. First, by thanking God, we solidify that we know it worked. We also complete the circuit of energy as we return to our starting point. The circuit becomes sealed. This means the beginning and the end of our wire are soldered together. Soldering works much better than electrical tape, which we can view as a symbol for the ideas we keep wrapping around and around the connection point, like when we keep telling ourselves over and over we've prayed correctly.

We have just cast our energy pattern into the ocean of Spirit. As stated previously, there is a natural law that states, "Nature abhors a vacuum." The empty pattern of our prayer is now filled with Spirit. It can do nothing else but descend into manifestation. Our prayers work every time, if we offer them correctly.

As we continually pray, we create a positive cycle, where answered prayers increase our belief and, ultimately, our knowing, which dissolves away all doubt.

We can pray in the name of the Father, the Son, and the Holy Spirit, Brahma, Vishnu and Shiva, or the Triple Goddess. We can pray in the name of the blue circle, yellow triangle, and the red square. God doesn't care.

Eventually prayer becomes automatic. We will arrive at a point where everything we think, happens. It can be very dangerous, if we get to this point, before we learn mind control. Fortunately, there are a number of safety measures built in, which make it impossible to get to this point, until we have the proper degree of mind control. A kind of un-catch twenty-two. They are as follows.

ACTIONS ARE PRAYERS

It is said that in this present age our actions are our prayers. Whatever we do is a prayer. Doing the dishes is a prayer. Giving someone a hug is a prayer.

Are there "good" prayers and "bad" prayers? Do "good" and "bad" even exist? If we are concerned our prayers are going to up-end creation, all we need say is "Thy will be done" or "in right action."

God's Will

When we are on the other side, between incarnations, we understand all we do is already God's Will. Is it God's Will that we cheat or steal? Is it God's Will that we hurt each other? How can this be God's Will? Let's not look at it in such a limited way. Instead, imagine that it is God's Will for us to have free-choice and learn from our mistakes. Broader perspective is crucial.

VISUALIZATION

Of all the beings that walk the Earth, the human is the only one who can visualize. We're not saying animals don't have visions. Anyone who has ever watched a dog sleep and seen its legs moving, might feel pretty confident the dog is visualizing something in a dream. The difference is a dog cannot decide to visualize a certain thing intentionally, we can. We are able to use our imagination, to visualize something we have never seen before. Imagine what it would be like to win ten million dollars. It's easy to imagine how that would impact our life. When we use the imagination in this way, we create a thought-form.

Using visualizations, we can have real experiences. In an experiment done with high-school basketball players, half the team worked out and practiced, while the other half sat and visualized themselves working out and practicing. The results were equal. The physical body couldn't tell the difference, simply because there is no difference.

The more real we can make our visualization, the easier it will manifest. Try to involve all of the senses. Feel it, taste it, touch it. Make it real. This type of prayer is not usually seen as prayer, but just a way to bring something into manifestation. It is most definitely prayer.

We may think we can make something happen without having to ask God. We may believe we are separate from God. Even if we don't acknowledge it, even if we call the process something else, we are always co-creating with Source Energy.

WORKING WITH THE SUBCONSCIOUS

There is a relationship between our subconscious mind and the other kingdoms of Nature. The mineral, vegetable, and animal kingdoms are more greatly influenced by our subconscious than by our conscious minds. Our pet does not understand all the words we use when we speak to it, but our pet does know how we are feeling.

If we wish to change the weather, speaking directly to the wind or the clouds will not work. "Move over here, cloud." When we speak to a cloud in this way, we make the subconscious assumption the cloud is something separate from us. We experience the cloud as "over there." We must go into ourselves to that place where there is no separation between the cloud and us. Then, as we change ourselves, we can change the cloud. We can never affect the cloud, as long as we think it's "out there."

THE LAW OF REFLECTED REVERSAL

Sometimes it seems that the exact opposite of what we are praying for happens. Perhaps we imagine ourselves not smoking cigarettes any longer, or going to the gym more regularly. But, alas, we're still smoking, and we haven't worked out in weeks. Even Saint Paul writes of finding himself doing what he "wants not to do." Sometimes it seems that our prayers are never answered at all. Why do the things we want happen or not? What's really going on? Quite a lot is happening, in fact. Let's look more closely.

Doubt

"It's impossible!" This is a very common mind-set, and one at the root of why our prayers appear to go unanswered. We just don't believe it can work. We reason, if everyone could get whatever they wanted, the world would be a much different place. In what way would it be different? Look around. Everyone is getting exactly what they want. Some people want failure, some want frustration, some want excuses. Such desires are rarely conscious, however.

They operate under the surface in the realm of the unconscious, where they have that much more power to influence us.

Do we really believe in God? Do we believe there is anything beyond the physical plane? Is it possible to know one way or the other? Are we under the influence of the limited consensus reality of physical science? The bottom line is that it won't work, because we know it won't work. We create what we know.

Negative Knowing

"I know I can't do this." This can be remedied by knowing that we can. We take the mantra from *The Little Engine That Could*, "I think I can," and amplify it into "I know I can do this." The Higher Self knows we can do anything. Jesus and Buddha know we can do it, too. The power of our knowing is great.

Permission

Sometimes we believe we need permission to manifest our desires, to change our life. We are taught from a very young age, by our parents and elders, by religion, school, and government, others know better and are in control. They have instilled this belief to wield power over us. We have permission, it has always been granted. Now we must give it to ourselves.

Worthiness

Low self-esteem is another block to our answered prayers. "Who am I that God would answer my prayers? I am not worthy." This thought is a prayer, and we receive confirmation of our unworthiness, as a result. Our negative self-image serves as a barrier to manifesting our desires. Perhaps, we have been taught those who do God's Will are rewarded. We know we have not always done God's Will, so we know we are undeserving of this divine gift. We believe we are lowly sinners. These very thoughts are counter to our actual intentions.

Fear of Failure

"I am afraid I will fail, if I try. I won't fail, if I don't try." If we pray and it doesn't work, it becomes one more damning nail in our coffin of loss, one more weight we carry on our backs. We believe, if we try and fail, it's much worse than not trying at all. We seek safety in immobility. We must learn to see every experience as an opportunity for growth and expansion.

Fear of Success

Success will surely change our life. Is it something we truly want? Are we ready for more responsibility, visibility, accountability? Perhaps we are comfortable with the life we have now. How would we actually live, if we accepted that we are the cause of our experience? We would have to give up all of our excuses.

Responsibility

If we can make anything happen, if our every prayer is answered, then we take on tremendous responsibility. *Response-ability* is the ability to respond. If prayer works, then we are able to respond to everything. Can Super Woman lead a so-called normal life?

PROGRESSED PRAYERS

The very nature of our subconscious mind can trip us up. If we are focused on quitting smoking and visualize throwing cigarettes away, the subconscious only hears and focuses on "cigarettes." It deduces that in order to throw away cigarettes, we must have cigarettes. As such, the subconscious continues to manifest them in our experience, perpetuating the cycle of smoking. The subconscious is only ever trying to manifest the focus of our visualization.

Indirect suggestion and active imagination are the keys to the attainment of our goal. We must begin by progressing our consciousness in the direction of the outcome we wish to achieve. Instead of visualizing ourselves throwing away the cigarettes, we progress our vision into the future to a time long after we have quit. We might imagine ourselves getting our teeth cleaned at the dentist, where the hygienist comments on how much easier our cleaning is this time, and how much whiter are our teeth. Perhaps, we envision ourselves running a 5K race or walking our dog with vigor and vitality each morning.

After we quit, we'll have freed up a good deal of money we had previously used to purchase the cigarettes. We might see ourselves buying something special with it. Perhaps we take a family vacation, or purchase a gift for someone else. We might imagine ourselves on the beach, or the person's reaction when they open the gift.

We're actually fooling our subconscious here. If we are able to envision this positive reaction in the dentist's office, our subconscious assumes we must have already quit smoking, because it cannot discern the difference between the future and right now. The subconscious is always focused and creating in the now. We want to conjure a vivid vision right now of the beneficial effects our prayer will achieve, and our subconscious will attract to us all we need to manifest that vision.

In the work of healing, we go beyond seeing our subject as healed (to be healed we must assume dis-ease). Imagine them out walking or playing. See them doing something that must require they are totally well. David broke his ankle some years ago. He might have envisioned a party taking place, because he had just bowled a 300 game. For the party to happen, the subconscious mind must assume his ankle is healed.

A more effective healing technique is to envision the client as a perfect, divine being, throughout the session. This requires great focus of intent, but it is a much more powerful tool, and can manifest instantaneous healing. Jesus demonstrated this in his works.

AUDIBLE PRAYER

Our word, which is spoken sound vibration, has power. When we consciously use our knowing, we create a form within which we may carry that energy.

The less limitation we place on our knowing, the more powerful will be our word. As we simplify our thinking, our knowing becomes less limited. What could be simpler then speaking the word and having it manifest instantly? Again, Jesus had it mastered.

TO WHOM DO WE PRAY?

It is said, in Catholicism, saints have a special position in heaven. Praying to them, we have a better chance of our prayer being answered. They symbolically sit on God's shoulder and whisper in the Creator's ear. Angels are also said to be divine messengers.

How many pray to Jesus or Buddha? Better to focus our thoughts directly to Source, the Creator within us. This is what might be called the "cut out the middleman" religion. Many religions don't want us to know about this.

Some think God, as the Universe, as All That Is, and as All Powerful, is so big our petty lives mean nothing to such a Consciousness. Does God really care who wins the Super Bowl? Does it come down to which fans pray the hardest?

Let's look at it this way. We have a physical body. Imagine we are God and each of our cells is a conscious being. We are in all of our cells and they are all in us. From the cell's perspective, we don't exist. The cell can't see us. We are so large that we are invisible. The cell can't comprehend the whole picture; it's not aware of anything we are thinking or feeling, although our thoughts and feelings affect it entirely.

We stub a toe and the toe reacts. The nerves start sending us messages that we need to pay attention to this part of the body. It focuses our attention; then we can take action. We might sit down and rub the toe, or just shrug it off. The toe is praying to us!

God is connected to us, in the same way we are connected to our cells. Take time to ponder this parallel. See the stars as cells in a really enormous body.

Saints and others energetic masters, who have the connection, act as the nerves. They call God's attention to an energy event. They focus the universe. Their purity and simplicity create an intense electro-magnetic field. Impurity and complexity can only dilute the potency of the One. This is what makes the One Mind so powerful. We can get to this state of simplicity, by letting go of our false life. The letting go purifies us. Let go. We can focus Spirit. We can talk with God, within. Even better, we can listen.

We no longer need the saints. We must be our own saint and focus the universe in a positive and conscious way. The truth is we are already focusing the universe, although not always so consciously or positively.

Whatever our mind centers on becomes our prayer. Many think they cannot pray and get results, but they are praying all the time. Every action is a prayer. Everyone is already living the life for which they are constantly praying.

As mentioned, all actions are prayers. If we eat too much, we are praying to gain weight. If we state (words are actions too) that we cannot get along with so-and-so, that is our prayer. If we think (thoughts are also actions) we will never find that special someone, guess what? If we want to change our life, we have to change our thinking, our speech, and our actions.

THE FLOWERPOT

As we begin to awaken, we realize everything we have been experiencing has been our own creation. When we really understand this, we give up any blame or excuse for our current state. This is a primary teaching in this work. *We are totally responsible for everything we experience.*

Consider this example: We are strolling along the sidewalk, when a flower pot falls off a windowsill and drops onto our head. How can we be responsible for that? We are responsible for our reaction to the event. How did we respond? Did we yell and get really angry, or just keep going, happy no one was seriously hurt? Was our thought process that this is simply a karmic event, or did we run to a lawyer's office?

Let's back up. Was there any inner guidance that morning we ignored? Did the idea of taking a different path pop into our mind? Was it an idea quickly dismissed, because it didn't make any sense at the time? Had anyone else tried to change our path? "Could you pick up some bread, while you're out?"

Let's look at the flowerpot itself. Is that what it really is? Is it not just an energy field we have translated into the idea of a flowerpot? This notion of flowerpot was presented to us as a child and we accepted it. We created, in our mind, an association between the word and the idea.

We have accepted a consensus of meaning, to enable us to perpetuate the illusion we are communicating with each other. If we want to tell you about something, we must at least believe we share the same meanings for words as you do. What you see in your mind, when I say tree, may be a completely different picture than the one I imagine.

This particular composition of matter or polarized energy we call a flowerpot. But that's our creation, you see. As far as the flowerpot is concerned, it's just a piece of the Whole. Actually, the flowerpot has no self-consciousness of being a flowerpot. We have created the flowerpot in our minds.

The famous psychic, Peter Hurkos, discovered his abilities only after falling off a ladder onto his head. Who knows what the flowerpot will do?

As we perfect our techniques, and clear away the blocks we initially erected, prayer becomes instantaneous. All we need do is know that something needs doing. That's it. As we become aware of anything, the Universe becomes aware of it simultaneously. It's automatic.

DESPERATE PRAYER

We pray a certain way, when we are really desperate. I'm not talking about the deals we're trying to make with God. It happens after we've exhausted every effort to make something happen. It's when we finally have to go beyond ourselves and pray in earnest.

Have we ever faced death? That time the car went out of control…and we prayed so intensely. Our prayer was answered. We are still alive. These types of prayers seem to get immediate response. It's the focus, the concentration of intent. An emergency situation gives us no time to doubt.

PRAYER EXPERIMENT

There are a number of experiments that demonstrate the effectiveness of prayer. In one study, two groups of people prayed over plants to observe prayer's effect on growth. The first group made general prayers over the plants. The second group prayed more specifically, visualizing the plants growing, praying that each plant would be filled with life. They prayed for each plant individually, trying to say the best prayer for each plant. When the results came in, they found the first groups' plants did much better with only their general prayers.

The first group stayed open, letting what was needed come through. The second group thought they knew what was needed. The blessing was limited by their own "knowing." It's so easy to get in the way, especially when we think we are doing the most good. The best thing we can do is to just call God's attention to a situation. God knows what to do.

PRAYER WHEELS

Tibetan Buddhists use a tool called a prayer wheel. Inside the wheel is a scroll inscribed with a prayer. It's usually, *"Om Mani Padme Hum."* A simple translation would be, Om, which is the sound of creation, followed by, "The Jewel is in the Lotus," and ending with Hum, the sound of dissolution. As we practice with discipline and wisdom, we dissolve our impurities and develop Buddha mind.

It's the triangle again. We create the universe with the cardinal Om. We stabilize and fix creation, by having the Jewel exist within the Lotus. Finally, with Hum, the universe dissolves back into the One. As we spin the wheel, each revolution sends the prayer out to all of the universe.

So how does it do that? It doesn't. It's just a reflection of our mind. As we spin the wheel, our knowing is what's sending out the prayer. If we thought it was a dumb superstition, nothing would happen. Prayer is a tool. We only need our tools when we are doing something. When the work ends, we put the tools away. We can spend our days and nights in constant prayer, or we can simply live, and be a prayer.

CHAPTER 4

Holistic Astrology:
The Circle Divided

CONCEPTS & MISCONCEPTIONS

Most people associate astrology with daily horoscopes. This prediction, or guidance for the day, might be true, if there were only twelve people on Earth. As we know this is not the case, we can consider these horoscopes virtually worthless. The true value of astrology is infinitely greater than mere personal perspective.

Holistic Astrology is also known as Transpersonal Astrology, a study that goes well beyond horoscopes and personal lives. If we seek to know our self as a whole, divine being, when we think only in terms of birth sign, we consider a mere fraction of who we truly are. Actually, we are a manifestation of all the signs, just as our body is composed of all of our organs. In this chapter, rather than looking at ourselves through Personal Astrology, we will explore the greater macrocosm, the universe, as viewed through Transpersonal Astrology.

How does astrology work? How can the distant planets and stars possibly affect us? The Sun is nine million miles away, and our lives depend on it. The stars are much farther away still. Yet, they affect us at an energetic level. Astronomers learn about a star, by passing its light through a spectroscope, to discern its chemical makeup. All the variables have yet to be discovered, but we do know each star has a different energy signature. To see a far-off star, its light must pass through the optic nerve, then into the brain. In this way, an energetic connection is made between us and the star. By intensifying our focus, we can strengthen the connection. These distant lights do, certainly, impact us all.

It is true that the stars are not where they were 2,000 years ago when the star groupings lined up with the signs that gave them their names. Other than the mythological symbolism they represent, the constellations have no correlation with astrology.

As David was growing up in the late 1950's, some were of the belief that "God is dead," an idea first espoused by the philosopher Frederick Nietzsche. At sixteen, David went to Confirmation classes at the Temple. When the Rabbi asked them if God really exists, they all concluded there is no such thing as God, so they all were confirmed atheists. The Rabbi was attempting to teach them they should care for humanity and do good works, even if God does not exist, instilling in them a socially moral code.

Through that teaching, David's false idea of God died. At the time, the common Judeo-Christian image held in many Westerner's minds portrayed God as an old man with a long, white beard. This was the God who "died." This "God" was not really God at all. Today, we understand God more universally, with no particular form or other limitation, though many still cling to the "old age" vision. This will pass in time.

In the same way, our ideas of what astrology is must also die. Then we may begin to see what astrology really is. Since the late 1960s, David has had to let go of what he thought astrology was, many times. So, what is it?

WHAT IS ASTROLOGY?

The word astrology is a combination of *astro* and *logy*. Astro means "star" and logos is "story" or "words." Thus, astrology is the story of the stars, or message of the stars. In order to receive these messages, we have to be open and receptive. When we think we "know," then we project that onto others.

When David began his study of the signs of the zodiac, he projected, as many do. If he knew someone was a Scorpio, for example, he would begin to see them through the filter of what he knew about Scorpio.

He soon changed his ways. When he met a Scorpio, he would observe, thereby learning what Scorpio was. David would let the signs teach him what they were, rather than accepting what the books said. After years of doing this with many people, he began to understand the essence of each sign. David also learned very well how to read people.

Similar to the cycle of the year, astrology is one expression of the larger Cosmic Cycle. Astrology is the study of the whole, divided into twelve parts. The whole what? Its focus is the whole of creation, the entire cycle of manifestation, involution and evolution. It's the study of the Circle of Life.

THE BIGGER PICTURE

In ancient times, the Greeks held a yearly initiation and celebration. The goal was to offer an understanding of the seasons, and the cycle of planting and harvest. This was presented in a theatrical presentation of the myth of Demeter and Persephone, called the *Eleusinian Mysteries*, which we will examine further in a later chapter. The esoteric teaching of the story is that everything cycles again and again, including human incarnation.

One of the most well-known cycles is the journey of the Earth around the Sun, which we call a year. Those of us who have been on this planet for some time are aware that the cycle repeats over and over. On a smaller scale, we observe the monthly cycle of the Moon, and the 24-hour cycle of the day.

We can witness the shorter cycle of ocean waves, or the longer cycle of the tides. Within our own body, we have the short cycles of the heartbeat, the longer cycle of the breath, the even longer cycle of the digestive system, and the still infinitely longer cycle of reincarnation.

All cycles, whether large or small, slow or fast have a beginning, middle and end. The astrological year begins with Aries, on the first day of spring (Northern Hemisphere). The cycle initiates here, when day and night are of equal length. With the new thrust of Aries energy, the light slowly starts to outlast the darkness.

The first day of spring initiated in Aries is not contingent upon a particular constellation coinciding with a certain place in the heavens, but, rather, on when the light begins to increase. Even if all the constellations moved 180 degrees, spring would still begin at the vernal equinox. The signs represent different parts of the Universal Cycle. By subdividing the One Cycle into smaller segments we gain understanding of the greater whole.

THE SMALLER PICTURE

One

As we divide the One, each successive division creates smaller and smaller pieces. In the mystical Hebrew teachings, it is said that when Creation took place, the One was shattered into infinite pieces, as reflected in the theory of the "Big Bang." Our apparent work is to reassemble the Divine, though, truly, it has always remained as One.

Two

Dividing the circle into two parts creates polarity, commonly illustrated with the yin yang symbol. It shows the relationship of feminine and masculine energies. The night and the day, the principle of cause and effect, magnetism, the digital world of zeros and ones, and duality itself! The more segments we create, the more complex the result. This is the root of polarity.

We view the world through two eyes and listen with two ears. In the study of Hermetics, we learn of the Principle of Polarity, which states *everything* in the material plane is dual, consisting of two poles. Everything has an equal and opposite energy. Each astrological sign has its opposite, two expressions of the same energy.

Three

If we divide the circle into three, we manifest the Holy Trinity, a tenet in many religions. In astrology, we have three modes through which the energies express: cardinal-creating, fixed-establishing, and mutable-dissolving. We will soon look at these in greater depth.

In Hindu philosophy, there are the three fundamental tendencies of the universal nature (*prakrti*) called *gunas*: *sattva* (creation), *rajas* (preservation), and *tamas* (dissolution). Sattva also relates to consciousness or intelligence, rajas to energy or action, and tamas to substance or matter. The geometric symbol for this number is the triangle.

Four

Geometry expresses the division in four parts, as the square and the cross, and we easily observe the cycle in our experience of the four seasons. Spring becomes summer becomes fall becomes winter becomes spring again and again. Even around the equator there are four seasons, though they manifest in weather patterns quite differently than in distant latitudes.

In Western traditions, there are four basic elements: Fire, Water, Air and Earth. We also divide the circle of space around us into the four directions of the compass, also depicted in the Native American Medicine Wheel. DNA, a basic building block of life, is a combination of four basic substances: guanine (G), adenine (A), thymine (T), and cytosine (C)

Five

Traditional Chinese Medicine shows one expression of the division by five, as manifest in the Five Elements Theory or *Wu Xing*: Wood (spring), Fire (summer), Earth (late summer), Metal (fall) and Water (winter).

We experience the world through our five senses, and we have five fingers and toes on each hand and foot. The human body, standing with arms and legs outstretched, mirrors the five-pointed star.

Although, today, many associate the pentacle with paganism, the early Christians used the five-pointed star to represent the five wounds Jesus received in his wrists, feet and side, during the crucifixion. When Constantine came to power in the 4th century CE, he changed the symbol to a cross. The star is now relegated to the tops of Christmas trees.

Six

The One, represented through six divisions, is expressed in the Star of David, one triangle pointing up and one pointing down. It is a prominent symbol in the Hebrew religion, as well as a key in the study of the Kabbalah. This symbol also has an affinity with the Hermetic teaching, "As above, so below."

It is a more complex expression of the yin yang polarity. In astrology, two triangles connect the elements. An upward facing triangle connects the earth signs: Taurus, Virgo, and Capricorn. A downward facing triangle connects the water signs: Cancer, Scorpio, and Pisces. Our bodies are made up of Earth and Water. When mixed together we have mud, the material God used to "make" our bodies in the Bible's creation story.

Seven

In this number, the whole of time is separated into weeks that contain seven days. Every week we go through the cycle again and again. The manifestation of the week has its root in the creation story in the Bible.

When the ancients gazed up at the heavens, they saw seven lights, known as the Seven Sacred Planets: Sun, Moon, Mercury, Venus, Mars, Jupiter, and Saturn. They believed these heavenly bodies governed all activity in the world. Today, we know the Sun and Moon are not planets. Still, we recognize them all as seven potent energies above us.

These energies are also represented in the seven chakras, energy vortices spinning within us that serve as an interface between our physical body and the subtle bodies. The root chakra is associated with Saturn, the sacral center relates to Mars, the solar plexus is aligned with Jupiter, the heart center is associated with the Sun, the throat chakra connects with Venus, the third eye has affinity with the Moon, and the crown chakra resonates with Mercury. In this way, we are all our own solar system.

> **The Seven Sacred Planets**
>
> **Sun:** Our individuality; how we see ourselves.
> **Moon:** Our soul, subconscious mind, and basic need in this lifetime.
> **Mercury:** Our conscious mind; ego consciousness.
> **Venus:** Our feminine energy; creative nature.
> **Mars:** Our masculine energy that initiates action and moves our muscles.
> **Jupiter:** Our karmic blessings and expansion.
> **Saturn:** Our karmic debt; the lessons we need to learn in this lifetime.

In the same way the seven sacred planets are associated with the chakras, white light divides into the seven colors of the rainbow (ROYGBIV), and sound is divided into the seven whole notes of the Western musical scale as C, D, E, F, G, A, and B, each aligning with the chakras from root to crown, respectively.

Astrologically, the center of our solar system is the Sun, which governs the sign Leo. In terms of the body, Leo rules the Heart. When the Heart becomes the center of our life, we are able to harmonize with creation.

Eight

The infinity sign, or lamnescate, is an eight on its side. The four-part system of the seasons is easily divided once again, creating an eight-part cycle. This is the foundation for the eight holy days or *Sabbats* that Wiccans celebrate in honor of the cycle of birth, life, death and rebirth, witnessed again and again in the yearly seasons. They are *Samhain, Yule, Imbolc, Ostara, Beltane, Litha, Lammas,* and *Mabon.*

As the circle is further divided, we observe how energy expresses in various ways. Through the celebration of the Sabbats, one aligns with the Greater Cycle, as played out in the relationship or polarity between the Earth and the Sun.

In the *I Ching*, a divination system long used in China, the Circle of Life is split into eight trigrams. A trigram is made up of three lines, either whole __ or broken _ _ . The whole lines represent yang, while the broken lines symbolize yin. If we divide each of the eight sections of the circle into eight more divisions, the result is 64.

The *I Ching*, which divides the great wheel into 64 hexagrams made of six lines each, offers a clue to the Masonic concept of "squaring the circle." The Great Wheel of the Circle, which represents Spirit, is brought into matter, manifested in the square. So, the *I Ching* takes spiritual wisdom and gives it practical application.

In Buddhism, the Wheel of Life has eight spokes. This Buddhist symbol is a steering wheel we can use to navigate through life. Gautama Buddha taught that liberation from the wheel of birth and death is achieved by following the Noble Eightfold Path.

> **Buddha's Eightfold Path**
>
> 1. Right Understanding
> 2. Right Thought
> 3. Right Speech
> 4. Right Action
> 5. Right Livelihood
> 6. Right Effort
> 7. Right Mindfulness
> 8. Right Concentration

Nine

Depending on how we view Pluto, there are nine planets in our Solar System: Mercury, Venus, Earth, Mars, Jupiter, Saturn, Uranus, Neptune, and Pluto.

This division of the One is also represented in the nine months of human gestation, as well as in the Catholic novenas that are prayed in preparation for feast days or a specific intention. The Greeks and Romans attributed artistic inspiration to nine Muses.

Another system dividing the circle into nine parts is the Enneagram, typically used in personality analysis. A framework that can be applied in various ways, it was first created in ancient Egypt.

Ten

The Kabbalah uses a symbol named the Tree of Life, to encompass all of creation, from the Infinite Light above to the densest manifestation of physicality. The Tree is made up of ten spheres. The study of this system will be addressed in subsequent volumes, as it is a higher-level teaching.

Eleven

Eleven becomes manifest in the Sun Spot cycle. For eleven years the number of spots increases, and then they decrease for eleven years. This is a core rhythm of our solar system and is influenced by the Sun's magnetic activity. It's magnetic poles also reverse every eleven years.

Twelve

In school, we were taught the decimal system, one through ten. We also learned a base-twelve system, specifically to tell time with an analog clock. The old, non-digital clock face has twelve numbers on it, which also align with the twelve months of the year.

The human body is composed of twelve major systems: Cardiovascular, Digestive, Endocrine, Integumentary, Lymphatic, Muscular, Nervous, Reproductive (Female and Male), Respiratory, Skeletal, and Urinary.

If we use our musical scale of seven whole notes and add the five sharps and flats, we manifest sound in twelve notes of the chromatic scale. There is much in this mystical number yet to be revealed. In Chapter 6: Foundation Work, we will look at numbers in more detail.

Why did Jesus have twelve Apostles? Why were there twelve tribes of Israel? Why are eggs sold in dozens?

Our system of astrology consists of twelve signs and twelve houses. A blank astrological chart has a circle in the center, surrounded by a twelve-spoked wheel, which is surround by a larger circle.

In Geocentric Astrology, we place the Earth in the center of the circle. Since most people still believe that the Earth is their solid ground, we will be using this type of chart. Heliocentric Astrology places the Sun in the center. When the Sun truly becomes the center of our being, we may use that type of chart.

According to Einstein, there are no actual positions, only relative ones, so we can only say that this is the relative position of the Earth. With the Earth in the center, then the outer circle describes the heavenly progressions across the sky. The top of the circle refers to that area in space directly above our head. The bottom indicates the area of space below our feet, below the planet itself.

The left side represents east and the right half is west. The horizontal line dividing the top half of the circle from the bottom signifies the horizon. Horizon is plainly the root of the word horizontal. The Sun, as well as everything else, rises in the East, on the left. At high noon the Sun is at the zenith. It sets on the right side and sits directly below the Earth at midnight, at the nadir.

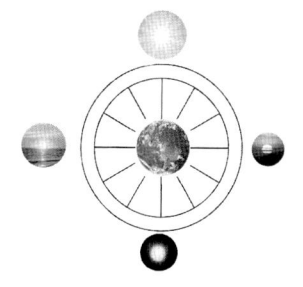

As we correlate the daily cycle with the yearly one, sunrise equates with spring, and summer aligns with noon. Fall begins, as the Sun dips below the horizon at sunset, and the dark of winter corresponds with midnight.

In the esoteric study of astrology, we acknowledge that the day begins with sunrise and the year is renewed in spring. This is the exact opposite of the Hebrew calendar, which begins each day at sunset, and the year with autumn. By contrast, the Roman calendar begins in winter on the first day of January.

Why do we begin our cycle in the spring? As the esoteric spiritual work involves increasing the Light on the planet, we align the beginning of the cycle with the increasing light of spring. The spring season commences when the Sun is observed at the vernal equinox point. The word equinox means "equal night," that is, the day and the night are of equal length. From the perspective of the Northern Hemisphere (which will be our vantage point, unless otherwise noted) this equality wanes, as the days increase in length.

ASTROLOGICAL SYMBOLS, PLANETS & CYCLES

The Sacred Seven

There are seven basic energies in our creation. They are represented in a number of ways in various traditions and systems. We shall begin our exploration with how they manifest in ourselves. We all have seven openings in our head: Two eyes to allow in light; two ears to receive sound vibration; two nostrils to detect scent; one mouth, with many functions beyond taste. The flesh on our skull is the vehicle for the final sense, touch; however, the receptors for touch, the nerves, lay beneath the surface of the skin, so this sense is not included in the seven.

Our eyes enable us to see in 3-D, and our ears, either side of our head create a stereo effect. If our smell was as well developed as other animals, or as it was for the earliest humans, our nostrils would even allow us to detect the direction from which an odor was coming.

Within our spiritual or etheric body, we have what is known as the Chakra System. It consists of seven basic energy centers that run more or less parallel to the spine. They are situated at the base of the spine, sacral center, solar plexus, heart, throat, third eye, and just above the top of the head. We will devote an entire chapter to this system farther along in the book.

As mentioned previously, the Western music scale is composed of seven whole notes. The musical scale is broken into twelve notes, when sharps and flats are added. Seven and twelve are mystically connected with the triangle and square. 3 (triangle) + 4 (square) = 7 and 3 (triangle) x 4 (square) = 12. These equations are part of the mysteries of the Great Pyramid, a square base with triangular sides, contained within its sacred geometry.

In the arc of a rainbow, the Sun's light is broken into seven colors through a prism, which is a triangle that refracts the one light into seven colors, symbolic of creation. The One God, manifesting as a trinity, creates the Seven Spirits or Rays that bring about creation.

The Bible uses the number seven extensively. For example, the creation story in Genesis describes how the universe was created in seven days. When we read the Bible esoterically, we understand the description of the creation of physical manifestation is not to be taken literally. Rather it is symbolic of the creation of an etheric blueprint, through which physicality was eventually created. This original model is known as the "Seven Spirits Before the Throne of God," the Elohim, the Master Builders. They are the Sacred Seven in its primal manifestation, and the source of all other expressions of the Sacred Seven.

The Pleiades

Also known as Seven Sisters, the stellar constellation Pleiades is referred to in many indigenous and ancient cultures. It is one of the nearest star-clusters to Earth. Although our telescopes can see that there are more than seven stars in this constellation, the naked eye only picks out seven lights. Many believe the Pleiadians are our ancestors, the seed race, or origin of our human species here on Earth.

The Seven Sacred Planets

The ancients saw seven lights in the sky, which they called the Seven Sacred Planets. The word planet means "wandering star." More accurately, they are not all planets, as we define them today, since they included the Sun and Moon.

The pattern of seven, through these planets, is expressed in the days of the week. The Sun inspired Sunday, and the Moon gave us Monday. Tuesday derives from *Tiu*, the English/Germanic god of war and the sky. His Norse counterpart is the war god, *Tyr*, related to the Roman god, Mars. Wednesday's source is *Woden*, the chief Anglo-Saxon/Teutonic god, aligned with the Norse god *Odin*, associated with Mercury. The Roman god Jupiter, creator of thunder and lightning, finds his complement in the Norse god of thunder, *Thor*, whose name gives us Thursday. The Teutonic goddess, *Freya*, related to the Roman Venus, is the root of Friday. Finally, Saturday stems from the Roman god, Saturnus.

In astrological terms, the seven sacred planets represent the following: self-awareness (Sun); conscious-mind (Mercury)/subconscious-mind (Moon); masculine (Mars)/feminine (Venus); blessings (Jupiter)/debt (Saturn); needs (Moon)/drives (Mars). We are more than our self-awareness, a set of polarities, our consciousness and history. Yes, we are self-aware. We know we exist, because we experience existence. Our aspiration is to become Self-Aware.

What are we, existing as we do? This is one of life's great mysteries. The answer is almost too simple. We are Self. We are God. Our difficulty arises, because we do not know we are God. We have forgotten the true nature of our being.

We may have heard people speak of the indwelling God. What a wonderful idea! At this point, though, for many, it's no more than a concept on the page. We need to realize we are God, before it will truly mean anything to us. Therefore, our goal is God-realization.

We are self-aware. We think and can reflect on the past, our history. We are able to recall ways in which we have manifested our energy both productively and destructively. We understand the polarity of masculine and feminine. On the way to God-realization, we will begin to manifest both equally.

Through the use of our consciousness, aided by our subconscious mind (history of past action), we can begin to recognize both the productive and destructive effects of past actions, and learn to balance them, by using the electro-magnetic aspects of the masculine-feminine polarity.

The Seven Sacred Planets not only correspond to the physical planets dancing around the Sun, but they are universal symbols in and of themselves. For example, they represent the seven sacred metals of alchemy. The Sun is gold, while the Moon is silver. The Moon reflects the light of the Sun, and silver is a reflective metal. The Sun is our Self, and we use mirrors (originally made of silver) to see the reflection of our face (also the Sun). Mercury is quicksilver, an appropriate element for the fastest planet. Venus aligns with copper, Jupiter is tin, Mars is iron, and Saturn corresponds to lead. These metal attributions are also clues to the esoteric meanings of the metals spoken of in the Bible.

The Seven Scared Planets are also represented in our Chakra System, so we can also associate the metals with our own energies. We will make this plain in our chapter on Kundalini and the Chakras. The alchemical recipes, outlining the mixture of various ingredients, were actually veiled formulas for combining energies to achieve specific effects. For example, if a formula required that gold be added to a mixture, with the knowledge that gold is the Sun's metal and aligned with the heart chakra, one would amplify Love energy.

PLANETARY SYMBOLISM

Whether or not we are conscious of it, we continually use a system of universal symbolism, based on archetypal patterns. These archetypes are the basic patterns of creation. Their meanings are intuitive, and are, most readily, revealed through meditation. As universal symbols, they speak to us through a universal language.

We have found that information gathered in other lives can manifest in this one more easily, if it was first learned in the same language one is fluent in presently. Though we may have gained some awareness of a concept in France in another life, we don't currently speak French, so it is more difficult for us to access that information or knowledge. We speak here of mental information, not "karmic lessons," which are understood universally. Specifically, David has been an astrologer for many lifetimes. In each, he has used the same symbols, the same language. As a result, he can easily access information about astrology received in other lives. He has, however, had to learn, during this life, about Uranus, Neptune, and Pluto, because they were unknown entities, during those past lives before the advent of the telescope.

Circle

Our understanding of planetary symbolism begins with the circle, which has no beginning or end. A circle has no time. If we look at an analogue clock and remove the hands, time no longer exists. Time is the division of the circle. We divide the circle the Earth makes, as it revolves around the Sun, into twelve months of time. Time only exists in its relation to space.

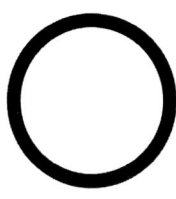

When the Earth is in a particular place in space, in relation to the Sun, it's January. It is 3:20 pm when the clock hands are in a particular place on the dial. We have also designated different times for the same moment, in different places. 3:20 pm in New York is 8:20 pm in

England. So, time is relative. This explains why an exact time and place of birth are needed to calculate an astrological chart.

In our mathematics, the circle is the symbol for nothing, no-thing. The circle exists beyond time and space, and so symbolizes unending space and time. It represents Spirit unbound.

The circle is manifest in the ancient Egyptian and Greek O*uroboros*, a snake biting its tail. It is the universe feeding upon itself. What else can God eat, other than God? Energy cannot be created or destroyed, it can only change form. This is the *Law of the Conservation of Energy*. Matter consumes energy, and energy consumes matter.

The circle is like a cosmic egg, containing the potential for all expression. When we think of an egg, the ovoid chicken-type may come to mind, but when we look at a human egg, or ovum, it is round. The circle is really part of a spiral, moving infinitely in both directions, like the inner tube of a tire.

If we place fire out in space, away from any gravitational fields, it assumes the shape of a sphere. Our Sun is a perfect example. When astronauts look at water in a gravity-free state, it also takes a spherical shape. The Earth typifies this same phenomenon. The sphere is the natural state of matter. Simply, the circle is a symbol of Spirit and the spiritual world.

The Line

There are many line qualities. They come in all lengths and widths. They may be straight or curved, solid or broken, and they also have infinite directionality. We will focus here solely on vertical and horizontal lines, representing the electric and the magnetic, respectively. The vertical line is energy/Spirit, while the horizontal denotes matter.

Our spines are usually oriented on the vertical axis, while four-footed animals, like dogs, cats, horses and pigs, orient theirs on the horizontal axis. They run parallel with the Earth's magnetic field.

In meditation, we are guided to align the spine in a straight, upright position, perpendicular (at a 90-degree angle) to the earth, so we are aligned with the Spiritual plane. When our spine is in a horizontal position, we usually fall asleep. The horizontal spinal orientation is also common during sex. The strong polarity of the sexual experience is intensified by the magnetic fields of Earth. In Tantric sexual practice, many positions are seated or standing, with the spine oriented on the vertical axis, as a means to induce a spiritually transcendent sexual experience.

The Cross

When we integrate a vertical and horizontal line, they form the cross, a symbol aligned with Christianity for thousands of years. The symbol, however, has been around for far longer. It represents the four elements: Fire, Earth, Air and Water and denotes the four directions on the compass. It is symbolic of the human, specifically the physical body, which is our "rod" and our "staff." (*Psalm 23 KJV*)

The vertical arm of the cross represents the spine along which the Kundalini, the creative Life Force Energy, runs. When the horizontal cross bar is positioned in the center, we have the equal-armed cross, which signifies the balance of opposing forces.

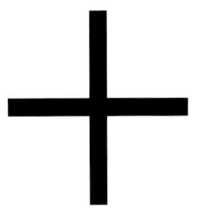

The Christian cross forms the conjunction higher up at the heart center. The Rosicrucians, a mystical order that arose in the 17th century, place a rose at the juncture of the heart center, creating the Rose-Cross, one source of the group's name, which illustrates eternal life, and also signifies the opening of the heart chakra.

The cross is often identified with Jesus and death, as a result of prolonged Christian influence. Esoterically, the cross represents, as mentioned previously, the four elements and the physical body, which is composed of the four elements. Jesus' crucifixion symbolizes the soul, which occupies a flesh body, attached (nailed) to the material form. From birth, we are already crucified on the cross of the physical body.

As Jesus, the Christ, was sacrificed ("to make sacred or holy/whole") on the cross, he was freed from the gravitational limitation of his earth-body. The truth of his crucifixion is just the opposite of what we have been taught. This is why the way of the cross is a path toward liberation. Jesus was actually un-crucified!

When the equal-armed cross is placed within the circle, it indicates spiritualized matter, where all four elements are unified by the circle. This is also the astrological symbol for planet Earth.

The Crescent

The crescent is another staple in our symbolic collective, one seen by all in the changing phases of the moon, and is, thus, a symbol for the Moon. This shape is also reminiscent of a bowl, which holds the waters of Spirit. Additionally, it resembles an antenna dish, and implies the ability to receive. The Moon represents the soul, which holds all the memories from our collective lifetimes.

PUTTING THEM ALL TOGETHER

We are able to create all the planetary symbolism, by combining these few simple shapes in various permutations.

The Sun

We begin with the circle. Then we place a dot in the center to show the creation point, the Self. This is the astrological symbol for the Sun. It is the atom, the cell. It is representative of our solar system, with the Sun at the center. In a birth chart, the Sun relates to our individuality, and how we see our self. It symbolizes our basic drive for significance, the will to be. When we are asked what sign we are, we typically offer the sign the Sun occupied at the time of our birth. At the time of our birth, every planet is in one sign or another. We are, quite simply, very complex beings.

The Sun is at home in the sign Leo, which is its ruler. When in the opposite sign Aquarius, it is said to be in detriment. The Sun is exalted in Aries, and has its fall in Libra, the opposite sign. What does this mean?

The Sun moves through Leo, its home, in the middle of summer, the season when we experience the longest day of the year (Northern Hemisphere), and which is, typically, the hottest time of year. Six months later, in Aquarius, we are in the middle of winter, just having experienced the darkest (shortest) day at the winter solstice. In this sign, the Sun is in detriment, which means the effects of its energy are diminished.

Spring, on the other hand, is a time for nature's reawakening, and so the Sun gives it a little push of energy. Aries, which heralds the commencement of spring, is the exaltation of the Sun. Six months later we enter autumn, where the Sun is in its fall in Libra. When the life-force dwindles, leaves drop to earth. This exploration gives us a better idea of what happens to the energy of a planet when it moves through particular signs.

The Sun is the *Lord* of our solar system. It is the Source of life, light, heat and food, and the axis of our system, holding it all together with its magnetic field. As the cornerstone of the creation around us, strength is a solar quality.

In the Tarot, the Sun manifests as The Sun card. It represents the heart, as well as the heart chakra. Its symbolic color is orange, or gold, in relation to the mineral kingdom. The musical tone associated with the Sun is D-natural. In the Tarot, each of the seven planetary lights corresponds to a pair of opposites. On one side we find fruitfulness and on the other sterility. The Sun will bring forth food from the earth in a well-kept garden. When out of balance, too much Sun will dry out the land and make a desert.

The Moon

When we divide the circle, the crescent is born. The Moon symbol is created by the division of the Sun's symbol. In the Garden of Eden story in the Bible, Adam (atom) represents the Sun, the divine Masculine principle. As Adam was created in God's image and likeness, Adam was both male and female. To create Eve, the Moon, or Divine Feminine principle, God had to divide Adam into two, male and female. The story says Eve was created from Adam's rib, which is crescent shaped. More detail and greater clarification on this creation story is offered in the next volume on the Tarot in Lesson 6: The Lovers.

In an astrological chart, the Moon represents the soul, the subconscious mind, memory, emotion, and our mother. The Moon indicates needs. We have incarnated to bring our soul into balance. If our soul had no need to be here, we wouldn't be here.

The Moon's light reflects the Sun's light. Moonlight is reversed sunlight, a difference which is easily felt. When we look at ourselves in a mirror, our image is always reversed.

The Moon, symbolic of the emotions, has sway over the tides, with its magnetic pull dramatically affecting the water on this planet. Considering our physical body is mostly water, we are surely affected by the Moon. Women's menstrual cycles are linked to the lunar phases. The Moon affects the body, not us. Since most people identify with their body, they may feel they are at the mercy of their emotions. The solution is to identify instead with Self.

The Moon rules the sign Cancer, its home. Since the Moon, symbolic of the divine Feminine, also rules the home, it has traditionally been the assumed place of women. It is obvious today that all the old patterns are changing. Still, it is interesting to learn where societal norms originate. The opposite sign, Capricorn, is the detriment of the Moon. Capricorn rules profession, and, up until relatively recently, the societal belief was "a woman's place is in the home," not "at work." We are moving toward a more balanced expression of these energies. We are also now witnessing a broader change in gender identification, as it moves beyond the binary to the multi-expressive.

As the ages change, the energies change, resulting in a change in consciousness. We may feel we need to fight for change, but if we are patient enough (it may take lifetimes), everything will eventually evolve in the direction of balance. Though change is initiated by people, as the ages progress, ideas change and new possibilities open up.

Over the course of a month, the Moon moves through all its phases, constantly altering in appearance. It is exalted in Taurus, fixed earth, which brings stability to the changeability of the Moon's energy. The opposing sign Scorpio is the Moon's fall. The Moon governs the female reproductive cycle and birth. As Scorpio is a sign of death, this is not the best place for birth to flourish.

The Tarot card for this planet is the High Priestess. The spiritual center for the Moon is the third eye. Its main affiliate organs are the stomach, and breasts. The Moon's vibration has affinity with G#. The symbolic color of the Moon is blue, and is often portrayed as silver, which is its metallic association.

The energy polarity for the Moon manifests as peace and strife. Is our home peaceful or full of strife? How we respond subconsciously to events creates subtle currents or emotions that manifest as feelings, which are registered in the physical body as sensation. Be mindful of emotional reaction. It can cause great volatility, disrupting the balance in our mental-emotional complex.

Mercury

For the planet Mercury, we use the Venus symbol, the circle on top of a cross, and place a crescent above the circle, the bowl opening to the heavens. If we view the cross as the body, and the circle as the head, then the crescent becomes a crown. As Mercury governs the crown chakra, just above the head, this is very apt. Mercury, messenger of the gods, uses the dish antenna on top of its head to receive messages.

Mercury represents Adam in the Garden of Eden. When we remove Adam's rib, the crescent symbol, Eve (Venus) emerges. This is the symbolic creation of the divine feminine. Eve also represents our subconscious mind. In order to create Eve, God put Adam (conscious mind) "to sleep" (subconscious).

Mercury rules both Gemini and Virgo. Some astrologers see Vulcan as the ruler of Virgo. The only problem is that this planet has not yet been discovered, though it is believed to orbit between Mercury and the Sun. In Roman mythology, Vulcan worked the forge, creating the weapons and armaments for the gods. The forge is the Sun.

Mercury's home is Gemini, and its detriment is Sagittarius. Mercury rules the nervous system and Gemini governs communication, and the nervous system is the means by which the body communicates with itself. Mercury is in its fall in Sagittarius, because Jupiter, the largest planet, offers the energy of excess, so the conscious mind becomes overloaded.

When in Virgo, Mercury is exalted, because Virgo governs analysis and mathematics, which allow the mind to function at the height of its power, to discover the makings of the universe. The intelligence of Mercury is applied in Virgo, while in Gemini Mercury just communicates the messages. Mercury has its fall in Pisces, because Pisces is the unconscious, and the conscious mind does not function well under water. This is why it is hard to think straight when we are drowning in our emotions, or inebriated with drugs or alcohol. Pisces is poetry, while Mercury is the mathematical mind.

In the Tarot, Mercury is The Magician card. Its color is yellow, the tone is E-natural, and the metal association is quicksilver, also called mercury. It carries the energy polarity of life and death, associated with the creative or destructive nature of the consciousness.

Venus

To create the symbol for Venus, we place the circle of Spirit above the cross of matter. Heaven above; Earth below. Beautiful! Venus is the planet of beauty and harmony, and its symbol is associated with women in general. Spirit is able to move freely above the foundation of matter, like clouds moving through the sky. The circle represents the endless cycle of life. Life manifests in the physical world through the four elements. The ancient Egyptians used the ankh, as a symbol of eternal life.

Venus is at home in Taurus and Libra. Taurus rules the upper back and shoulders, while Libra is the lower back and kidneys. The opposite signs to these: Scorpio (Taurus) and Aries (Libra) are Venus' detriment. Venus is exalted in Pisces and falls in Virgo. As the planet of love, it has more difficulty relating with Virgo the Virgin, and Scorpio can distort love into a merely sensual and self-fulfilling energy. Pisces brings selfless love, exalting Venus' vibration.

Venus rules the vegetable kingdom, so its color vibration is green. The musical tone is F#. Venus governs the throat chakra, the throat itself, and is associated with The Empress card in the Tarot. Venus is the planet of the creative subconscious mind, and our responses and interpretations of its messages will lead us into either wisdom or folly, the energetic polarity associated with this sign.

Mars

If we turn the Venus symbol upside down, it becomes the symbol for Mars. We now have Spirit (circle) below matter (cross). Spirit is conquered by matter. The ancient glyph initially consisted of a cross placed on top of the circle, which eventually evolved into its current iteration, one we associate with men. When we place matter above Spirit, the resulting conditions are evident in our experience on Earth today.

In general, this orientation, and its outcome, have, primarily, been the work of men. Clearly, we are witnessing a change, as more men are embracing the divine feminine within themselves. Mars rules Aries, the warrior. We can see the symbol as a shield and weapon, and also recognize the phallic masculine connection.

Mars has also been associated with the fires of hell. It is said, in hell, we all burn for eternity. (it only feels like an eternity, until our consciousness changes) What is hot? Compared to the mean temperature of space, 98.6 F is hot. We are burning in hell at this moment. Buddha said our desires have created a burning house around us. It's difficult to wake people from sleep, when they don't even realize they are on fire.

If we put the Mars symbol in the center of the zodiac, the arrow points to Scorpio, the sign it governed in the last age. Scorpio is now ruled by Pluto, the higher octave of Mars. Scorpio is the higher octave of Aries, as it is the eighth sign.

Mars is at home in Aries, in detriment in Libra, exalted in Capricorn, and has its fall in Cancer. In Aries, martial power is needed to begin any cycle. In Libra, as with the Sun, the energy is lessened. Capricorn puts the power of Mars to use. The sensitivity of Cancer then mutes that power.

In the Tarot, Mars is The Tower card, also called "The House of God." Its color is scarlet (Mars is the red planet), and it is attuned to the note B-natural. As the god of war, Mars' metal is iron, used to make swords, guns, and armor. The chakra association is the sacral center.

Looking at the vibrational polarity, we see it expressed in two pairs, grace and sin, or beauty and ugliness. How we choose to use our energy, as expressed through speech, results in the creation of either pair. Note how these two polarities are describing the same energy.

Jupiter

We use the cross and crescent to make the glyph for Jupiter, placing the crescent on the top left of the horizontal line. The soul symbol (crescent) is placed above the balance beam on the credit side, what we might call "good karma." It is positive energy we created through our actions in previous incarnations. It functions as healing and blessing. Everything below the crossbeam falls on the debt side.

In Roman mythology, Jupiter was the father of the gods, Jove. As the largest planet in this solar system, it brings expansion, and is known as the planet of wealth, the "Greater Fortune." Jupiter brings forth the positive effects of the past (our "good" karma) through blessing, healing, and abundance. In this way it acts as a guardian angel. Jupiter even acts as a planetary guardian for the Earth. Due to its mass, (the heaviest planet) it pulls into itself many asteroids that have gone off course.

Jupiter rules Sagittarius and is in its detriment in Gemini. Jupiter governs philosophy and the Higher Mind. Gemini focuses on a narrower view, ruling the lower mind. Jupiter is exalted in Cancer, bringing prosperity into the home, and it has its fall in Capricorn, a sign of contraction.

Jupiter is The Wheel of Fortune, in the Tarot. A# is its musical note, and it has an affinity with the color purple. The chakra association is the solar plexus. The metal for Jupiter is tin. As the Wheel of Fortune, it represents the polarity of wealth and poverty.

Saturn

Saturn's symbol takes the crescent and places it below the cross, on the right side. Here the soul is pinned down by the weight of the cross. It indicates great limitation and bondage. Saturn says, "Thou must fulfill." This means we must deal with all the accumulated junk from the past. It is the collection of all that we avoid, what is often termed our "bad" or "negative" karma.

As we work our way out of the limitations we created for ourselves, as we clean up all the crap that we've created, our soul will begin to rise up above the limitations of matter.

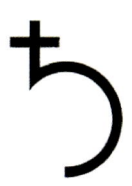

Saturn manifests as the teacher, who will not let us get away with anything. Saturn brings us face to face with all the problems we try to avoid. Saturn is very patient and will wait many lifetimes, bringing the lessons back again and again, until we learn what we need to. Each time the lesson resurfaces, it hits a little harder, until it gets our attention. Don't wait for a crisis to transmute the energies that bind.

Saturn is encircled by a ring that was seen even in ancient times. It was known as the "Ring-Pass-Not," and was thought to be at the outer boundary of our solar system, and is why the planetary energy manifests as limitation, but also as perfection. It is also why Saturn is aligned with the skin, the outer boundary of our physical body.

Saturn rules Capricorn. Jupiter expands, while Saturn contracts. As Capricorn governs system and structure, the limiting power of Saturn makes things more concrete. It keeps Capricorns' structures from falling apart. Its detriment is Cancer, as the sign of the womb needs to be very pliant and free to grow. It is exalted in Libra and falls in Aries. The unforgiving teacher, Saturn, works best in a balanced situation. All the lessons are to bring our soul into a state of balance. Saturn, when in Aries, manifests more severely, showing very little compassion. In order to be compassionate, one must consider the other, walk a mile in their shoes, as it were. This is the Libra attitude. In Aries the "me first" attitude prevails.

In the Tarot, Saturn is the final card, "Cosmos," alternately called "The World," or "The Dancer." Saturn vibrates to the tone A-natural, and its color signature is indigo. Saturn is associated with the root chakra, and the metal, which is the heaviest, is lead. Our final pair of opposites attributed to the seven sacred planets is dominion and slavery. Saturn offers us the opportunity for right interpretation and use of limitation. In one instance, limitation, or discipline, empowers us, and in the other it binds.

Uranus

This glyph is one of the more complicated astrological symbols. It looks reminiscent of a capital H, with a pendulum hanging from the middle. We begin with a cross, which stands atop a small circle, with two crescents attached to the arms of the cross. One of the crescents is "positively" charged, while the other is "negatively" charged. We cannot say which is which, because they constantly change as alternating current. Uranus rules electricity. Uranus plugs into the cross of matter, enlivening it with its electromagnetic nature. Uranus's energy is inherent in the creation of the cyber-world of this age.

Though the circle is below the cross, in this symbol, almost out of the way, Spirit becomes our assumed foundation. We have entered an age of science, and an age of constant change. We have entered the Age of Aquarius.

Uranus, Neptune and Pluto, the three outer planets of our system, work outside our material experiences, relating more with universal energies, and having influence over entire generations, due to their slow cycles around the Sun, as compared to Earth. The Tarot separates these three, appointing them to the positions of the "Elemental Mothers." Uranus is the Mother of Air, Neptune, the Mother of Water, and Pluto, the Mother of Fire. These planets no longer align with opposite pairs, for they go beyond the limitations of the physical plane.

Originally, Aquarius was ruled by Saturn. The science that arose out of this age enabled the discovery of Uranus. This new age, with all its advances, was hidden from the ancients, who only saw through the limitation of Saturn, which served as a veil of limited thought. Now, we recognize the real ruler of Aquarius as Uranus, which brings freedom and liberation from all bondage.

Aquarius is ruled by Uranus, and its rapidly alternating energies are at the core of the "electronic" revolution. The internet, also under Aquarius's rulership, takes us into a new dimension, where all people have the potential to move beyond their individual abilities, to create a synergy of consciousness.

Our individuality comes under Leo, the sign of the ego. Here, Uranus is in detriment, as it is difficult to become part of a group, when our ego is only concerned with its own needs and desires. Uranus is exalted in Scorpio, the sign associated with death. When one has not yet been born, it is impossible to die. This "non-material" energy has difficulty working in Taurus, the sign of fixed earth.

Uranus' color is pale yellow. Uranium is the periodic element associated with this planet, and its musical tone is A-natural. It represents the aura, an electro-magnetic emanation reflecting the state of the chakras. Uranus governs the electrical body and the meridians, and also rules the circulation of the blood. In the Tarot, Uranus is The Fool card, illustrating the soul before incarnation.

Neptune

Neptune, as ruler of Pisces, governed the age we are now leaving. Its symbol is simple, utilizing the cross and crescent. The cross is inverted, with the cross-beam at the bottom. When placed in this position, it resembles a sword. Shall we live by the sword, or by the cross? Do we not invert Christianity, whenever we fight?

The Age of Pisces was an age of suffering. Here, we see the soul pierced by a sword, as was spoken of Mary, in the New Testament. It was said a sword would pierce her heart, that she may hear the hearts of many. The death of a child, something Mary endured, is said to be the greatest piercing of the heart.

During the crusades, this symbol was played out in the conflict between the cross, or sword of Christianity, and the crescent moon of Islam. Again, there was much suffering. We are still dealing with the residual effects of the Piscean Age, as witnessed in continued conflict in many parts of the world. Suffering also can conjure the image of this symbol, as the "devil's" pitchfork. Additionally, it is called Neptune's Trident, a symbol claimed by the Roman god of the sea (Greek - Poseidon).

Neptune rules Pisces, and is in detriment in Virgo. There are no exaltations or falls for Neptune. Neptune is the higher octave of Venus. In the Tarot, this planet is the Suspended Man, also called the Hanged Man. It is associated with the periodic element, Neptunium. The color correlation with Neptune is blue, and its note is G#.

Pluto

Similar to Mercury, Pluto's glyph is composed of a cross, a circle, and a crescent. Here, however, the crescent rests between the cross and the circle. Mercury, which elevates the Moon above the circle, is a mental sign. Pluto puts Spirit above the mental plane.

Pluto holds some opposing energies locked within it. In the Tarot, this planet is aligned with the Judgement card. Often referred to as "frozen fire," Pluto is considered the Mother of Fire. Perhaps, it is frozen, because Pluto is so far from the Sun. Yet, on the Tarot card that illustrates it, there is no fire represented, only icebergs. Frozen water! The glyph itself can be seen as a chalice holding the circle of Spirit, made of both Fire and Water.

This glyph represents the transformation we have gone through to be able to enter this next age. The suffering of the last age awakened compassion in the soul, which lifted up the soul. We balanced the aggression of the sword with the self-sacrifice of the cross. We are now in a place to receive Spirit.

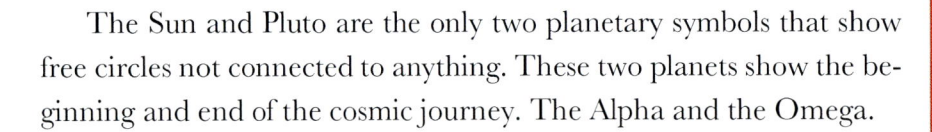

The Sun and Pluto are the only two planetary symbols that show free circles not connected to anything. These two planets show the beginning and end of the cosmic journey. The Alpha and the Omega.

Pluto is the higher octave of Mars, as the sign it rules, Scorpio, is the higher octave of Aries. Pluto and Mars share the same musical note, B-natural, only for Pluto it resonates at a higher octave. Scorpio is the eighth sign after Aries, and eight is the number of the octave. Before Pluto's discovery, Scorpio was ruled by Mars. Pluto is exalted in the sign Aries. There, it can manifest its hidden power in the material world. This puts the opposite sign Libra as the realm of its fall.

In the myth of Persephone and Demeter, both represent the energy of Venus, the ruler of Libra. Persephone is kidnapped by Aries, ruled by Mars and Pluto. She is taken underground to Hades, symbolic of Scorpio. As fallen energy, Pluto is weak in Libra.

Here we have introduced the planets. The first level lessons in this volume create a foundation of understanding for the more advanced material. As we progress into the second volume of study on the system of Tarot, a book of pictures that reveals the journey of the soul through involution and evolution, we will focus on the Major Arcanum, each of which represents an astrological sign or planet. We will dedicate an entire chapter to one card, as we explore these energies in greater detail.

SOLAR CYCLES

The Sun is at the center of all planetary cycles in this solar system, so it serves as the foundation of all our astrological calculations. Because everything is relative, we must have another point with which to compare it. For our study, we use the Earth. Now that we have a relationship, we can examine the apparent cycle, the Earth as it revolves around the Sun. This gives us a benchmark number of "one year."

We then use this number in relation to all the other planets. For example, Jupiter takes twelve Earth years to make its circuit around the Sun. If we were not relating Jupiter to Earth, its cycle would simply be one Jupiter year.

Our solar cycle includes two solstices and two equinoxes, which differentiate our four seasons. The Sun has an internal magnetic/Sunspot cycle of twenty-two Earth years. The Sun's cycles are so significant to our identity that each of us carries that reminder in our date of birth. We also pin most of our holidays on this yearly Sun cycle. Some holidays, however, are aligned with the movements of the Moon.

LUNAR CYCLES

The Moon gives us two frequencies to work with, the twenty-eight-day monthly cycle and the thirteen-month yearly cycle. The Moon affects the Earth's tides, and as our physical bodies are mostly water, it affects us, as well. No doubt, there is a strong connection between the Moon and a woman's menstrual cycle. Astrologically, the Moon is associated with the womb. The more our consciousness is attached to the flesh body, the more open we are to the influence of the Moon's magnetic field.

How else, then, might the Moon affect us? Such descriptions as "full moon madness" or "lunatic" may come to mind. Why is the Moon associated with madness? The Moon, astrologically, governs our emotions, our needs, and our subconscious mind. On a much deeper level it is a link to the soul.

If we lack emotional stability, we can easily be knocked off balance. If we were on a boat, we would need to use our "sea" legs to balance the ups and downs of the waves. We must also gain an emotional footing, so that we are not pushed here and there by our feelings or the collective mood of a group.

There is a collective consciousness, as well as a collective subconscious, we share with those around us. It's easier to recognize when we look at the bigger picture. We can see it in the various "moods" into which many may fall, and these may change as rapidly as the weather. Consider the stock market, for example. The Moon only spends two and a half days in each sign, as it revolves around the Earth.

The Moon's phases, constantly moving from new to full and back again, offer us another cycle. Before the use of electric light, the Moon was the biggest light-show around. Everyone was conscious of its phases, which created a connection between each individual. This was the beginning of the earthly collective consciousness.

MERCURY CYCLES

As we look at the patterns of planetary movement around the Sun, be aware that most people's awareness goes no further than the Sun and Moon. Anyone can point to the Sun or the Moon, when they are visible. Who could point to Mercury? Who, but the ancient astrologers, priests, and the learned knew of its presence? This rare knowledge gave much power to the "elite," allowing them to "see" into the future. They were conscious of a more complex reality, detecting patterns "over the heads" of the general population.

Mercury, the fastest planet, takes eighty-eight Earth days to zip around the Sun. In Greek mythology, he was messenger of the gods, with winged feet. Mercury rules the hands, used in communication. Coincidentally, a piano has eighty-eight keys. Mercury and Venus are closest to the Sun and travel around the zodiac together. From our perspective on Earth, they are never more than about 90 degrees from each other.

VENUS CYCLES

As we just learned, Mercury and Venus are always relatively close to each other. Venus' cycle is 225 Earth days. In Ancient Greece, their names were Hermes and Aphrodite. Together, they create the hermaphrodite, a being displaying both genders, a balanced expression of the Mercury and Venus energies. Many view Mars (Aries) and Venus (Aphrodite) as the expression of this polarity; however, this view is a distortion of the truth of the divine being we are.

Venus gives rise to the senses, a requirement for creative expression, and Mercury rules the conscious mind. These energies represent and manifest as the balanced expression of our outer and inner experience. This understanding shifts our dualistic consciousness out of the male-female binary. When the Venus energy moves to unite with Mars, its direction moves away from the Sun. When it works with Mercury, it moves toward the Sun.

Mercury and Venus are the two fastest planets orbiting the Sun. They show us that our thoughts and the world around us are in constant flux. The only way to get off the merry-go-round is to be the Sun, the Center. We must be the enlightened Master of our reality. We already are the Sun. When we are able to truly be ourself, our *Self*, then everything will stop spinning.

MARS CYCLES

While Venus orbits closer to the Sun than Earth, Mars's orbit is just beyond the Earth's, and takes two years to circle the Sun. This larger and slower cycle deals with energy and power. It fuels our activities.

There is an affinity between Mars and the Earth, because its transit is twice as long as the Earth's. Musically, we can tune a vibrating string to a particular note. With any stringed instrument, when that string is divided into two equal parts, then plucked, it plays the original note in a higher octave. If we double the length of the string, the same note vibrates an octave lower. Earth and Mars have the same relationship. This creates an affinity in vibration. Now, we are learning that future space missions intend to go to Mars.

When the planet Mars moves into the sign it occupied at our birth, our personal energy and vitality increase. As we evolve, we raise our vibration or "sound," and the energy and frequency we emit shift to a higher note. As the same note manifests at different octaves, when we move through spiritual transformation, we resonate at a higher octave, but are still the same soul and Self. We may not appear any different to others, but we are.

JUPITER CYCLES

Jupiter has a twelve-year cycle. Similarly, the Chinese zodiac operates on the same cycle, in which an animal is assigned to each of twelve years. In India, a very sacred gathering called the *Kumbh Mela* is repeated every twelve years.

In Judaism, childhood lasts twelve years, where upon the thirteenth birthday one has a *Bat* or *Bar Mitzvah*, and becomes a woman or a man, in the eyes of the congregation. Consider these customs are thousands of years old. In the distant past, when an average life-span was only thirty years, puberty meant adulthood, aligned with the ability to procreate.

Earth's one-to-twelve revolutionary relationship creates an "affinity" with Jupiter. We cycle the Sun every twelve months, while the big planet cycles every twelve years. This affords Jupiter the bigger picture, and so is related to the Higher Mind. In Roman mythology, Jupiter was the father of the gods.

SATURN CYCLES

Saturn takes twenty-eight to thirty years to journey around our Sun. For the ancients, thirty was an average lifespan. Saturn was, therefore, given rule over old age and time, and referred to as Father Time.

One Saturn cycle is made up of four seven-year periods. We move through these seven-year periods, like rungs on a ladder. Twelve rungs bring us to an age of eighty-four. 7 x 12 = 84. We will examine the relationship between seven and twelve in a later chapter. For the time being, note that we have seven days in a week and twelve months in a year.

Saturn governs the skeletal system, a structure and form upon which our physical body is built. These seven-year periods also create a framework upon which each life is built. As we grow, we reach certain pivotal points every seven years. Our various bodies (physical, emotional, astral, mental, etheric template, celestial, causal) mature at different rates, but not everyone awakens all seven bodies within a lifetime.

In our first seven years, we learn how to function in our physical body. When we are around seven years old, we begin school, a whole new experience. At this time the emotional and sexual nature are activated, and the etheric body is awakened, culminating in another rite of passage, puberty, which occurs around age fourteen. From age fourteen to twenty-one, the astral or lower mental body begins its development, igniting the intellect, along with our thinking and reasoning abilities.

At twenty-one our physical bodies have matured, and society declares us "adults." Now we are considered responsible for ourselves, and we may pass through another gateway, opening the portal to the mental body, this allows the ability for contemplation of abstract concepts, and, in rare cases, the potential to awaken the Kundalini. We will explore the Kundalini, in a subsequent chapter.

Saturn's first return (one complete revolution) comes between twenty-eight and thirty years of age, at which time the spiritual body may be awakened, if the Kundalini has been activated. This is "truly" when we enter adulthood; by this point, some may even be parents.

As Saturn works with form and structure, we become more set in our ways. It takes more energy to change a pattern now. Again, we come up against our sense of limitations and boundaries, the "Ring-Pass-Not." We always have the choice to cement positive patterns or negative ones. Typically, by this age and stage, we are no longer trying to "keep it together," the pattern has likely jelled.

Between fifty-six and sixty we begin to pass over into advanced, and, for some, "old" age, completing the second revolution of Saturn. For the last 2,000 years we viewed everything through the filter of Pisces. Since it is such a sensitive sign, we experienced much pain and suffering in relation to the cycles of the constrictive planet Saturn.

Age manifests differently in the Age of Aquarius. The filter is changing, so our experience does too. As the traditional ruler of Aquarius, Saturn feels right at home now. Its constrictive nature works well with the sign of crystals. Saturn now manifests as disciplined choices we make consciously that assist us to more gracefully embrace the aging process, so pain will not be as painful, and aging won't make us as old.

Saturn is associated with the father, and the mother is aligned with the Moon. These two planets rule Capricorn and Cancer, respectively. We see there is a relationship between the twenty-eight- year cycle of Saturn and the twenty-eight-day cycle of the Moon.

URANUS CYCLES

Every eighty-four years, the current approximate lifespan of many people, Uranus travels around the Sun. It spends seven years in each sign, bringing release and surprises, as it breaks down the structures and limitations brought about by Saturn. Aquarius is presently ruled by Uranus, but before its discovery, Saturn held that position.

Another connection between Uranus and Saturn will become clear in our study of the great cycle of Tarot, in a subsequent volume, which begins with The Fool, Uranus, and ends with Cosmos or The World card, Saturn. The Tarot shows us that the cycle is perpetual, as The Fool follows Cosmos/The World, beginning the cycle anew. Our expansion is not limited by the completion of any one cycle.

Uranus' axis runs horizontally, compared to the other planets in our system, which orient on the vertical axis. This is very unusual, and the planet represents unusual events and beings. In 1781, Uranus was discovered through the use of the telescope, a scientific instrument invented about one-hundred years earlier. Uranus, through its ruling sign Aquarius, rules technology and the stars!

Only once a planet is known, does its influence begin to manifest in our lives. Uranus brings unexpected energy into creation. No one expected to find this planet, and no one had any idea what modern technology would bring.

In the symbolism of the Tarot, there is no eighth chakra to assign to this planet, no eighth day of the week. Uranus is outside of any traditional system of seven. However, the Kabbalah speaks of three additional energies and they are assigned to the three outer planets: Uranus, Neptune and Pluto. As mentioned previously, they are the three Elemental Mothers of Creation: Air-Uranus, Water-Neptune and Fire-Pluto.

NEPTUNE CYCLES

Neptune takes 165 Earth years to go around the Sun, approximately two lifetimes, spending about fourteen years in each sign. As we will not experience all that Neptune has to offer us in just one incarnation, it makes things a bit mysterious, as though a curtain is half-closed.

Neptune's energy manifests as dream-like illusions, as well as spiritual realities. It is the Mother of Water and its actions tend to cleanse and wash away unneeded patterns. Neptune, in Roman mythology, is the god of the sea, and this energy is at the root of unconsciousness. Underlying the unconscious, we have the superconscious! Once we become conscious of the whole, we are no longer conscious of the parts.

As we move further away from the Sun, the last planets are not personal, but generational. As it moves so slowly through the signs, everyone born within an eighteen-year period will have Neptune in the same sign. This perpetually creates a new generational consciousness. Examining Pluto, along with Uranus and Neptune, we get a more accurate picture of these overlapping cycles.

PLUTO CYCLES

Pluto, is it a planet, or isn't it? When the astrological system was devised, no one knew Pluto, Neptune, or Uranus existed. So how can we know Pluto's attributes? We shall ask the Romans, who got it from the Greeks.

Ancient mythology has named the planets after various gods and goddesses. We can better understand the planets, by studying the ancient stories. Though the planets are not considered gods, which is debatable, their symbolism stems from the same source as the myths.

The god Pluto ruled the underworld and the afterlife. The planet is certainly in a very dark place, if not the underworld, certainly the outer-world of deep space. The Sun, at the center of our solar system, is the source and sustainer of life. Pluto's orbit is the farthest away from the Life Source, and thus represents death.

The path of Pluto around the Sun is so long, its transit covers three lifetimes, or 248 years. Murder is an involved expression of Plutonian energy. It would take a full Pluto cycle (248 years) for the opportunity to arise to potentially balance the Plutonian aspect of that karma. Even then, one might still choose to perpetuate the pattern. Considering Mercury, the planet of conscious thought, which has a much shorter cycle, we can see then that it is possible to resolve negative thinking almost instantaneously. This gives us some perspective on karmic cycles.

Generationally, David was born, along with many baby boomers, when Pluto was in Leo. Leo rules the heart and produced the "Love Generation." Men began wearing long hair, reminiscent of a lion's mane. People "dropped out," creating their own "kingdom." It has been said that this generation is self-absorbed, which is another Leo trait.

> ***Pluto in the Signs:***
>
> 1939-1957: Leo
> 1957-1972: Virgo
> 1972-1984: Libra
> 1984-1995: Scorpio
> 1995-2008: Sagittarius
> 2008-2023: Capricorn

At this writing, Pluto is halfway through its transit of Capricorn. Though most astrologers focus on where the planets are today, examining the "astrological weather," there is a delayed effect created by the outer planets. On a deeper level, although Pluto may be in Capricorn at present, those born under this influence will not manifest these energies in the world until adulthood. This creates "generational streams" of energy, moving through the lifetimes of everyone on our planet. We may easily recognize the external differences, but it is important to recognize what underlies these contrasts.

RETURNS

Imagine all the planets are pointing cans of spray-paint at the Earth. The paint is pumped out in a tight series of now, now, now, etc. Using Jupiter as an example (it spends one year in each sign), picture it traveling through Aries and spraying Earth with a can of bright red paint. Everyone born that year would be energetically "red." It would be called "The Red Year."

The next year, Jupiter enters the sign Taurus, and changes the color to red-orange and commences to spray. Anyone born during that year would have a red-orange energetic glow. The "red" people now get a coating of red-orange paint, so the two colors merge. This continues through all twelve signs and the full color scale.

Twelve years later, Jupiter reenters Aries, again picking up the red paint. The "red" people are energetically retouched with the red paint of their birth. This is called a "return." These "red" people have been sprayed with every color of the zodiac, and now get a fresh coat of their "birth color" again.

Rather than yearly events, the planets spray us continually, not with paint, but with their energy. This gives everyone a different "base coat." Even if two people are born on the same day, their location may be different, which would change the nature of the energy. We see reality through the filter of our past experiences. Because everyone's soul, history, and experiences are different, the same astrological event affects each person differently.

PLANETARY CYCLES

Each planet takes a different amount of time to go around the Sun, giving each planet its own individual rhythm, or frequency. These different planetary rhythms, oscillations, or vibrations, are all happening at the same time. It's all about frequency. How frequently does a planet finish its cycle? In the microcosm they are called biorhythms, in the macrocosm they are planetary rhythms.

We all live our lives by the Solar cycles. We count years and days. We use a Solar calendar. The monthly cycle of the Moon also impacts us cyclically, some are more affected by it than others.

When we study planetary cycles, we find the slower the cycle, the more impact it carries. We can only experience a limited number of these cycles during an incarnation. Imagine a lifespan of ninety years. This means that in this life we experience ninety Sun cycles. Divide one lifetime into ninety parts, each of these is 1/90 the total impact that the Sun will have on us.

Consider the Moon. In these same 90 years, we will experience almost 1,200 Lunar cycles. We can see that 1/1,200 is a smaller number. On the slower side, we will experience only seven and a half Jupiter cycles, three Saturn cycles, and only one transit of Uranus. Neptune will take two lifetimes, and Pluto will take three.

Imagine the Moon telling us something 1,200 times. It takes 1,200 times to get our attention. On the other hand, Uranus only has one shot in a lifetime. Which will be more intense?

Our two planets of expansive and restrictive energy, Jupiter and Saturn, give us something that we can work with. Jupiter's cycle is twelve years. Our Jupiter birth-day returns at 12, 24, 36, 48, 60, 72, and 84 years. We can become aware of these years and note shifts of energy or transformation that occur at these times throughout our life. Saturn's returns occur at 28-30, 58-60, and 88-90 years. These are milestones that highlight opportunity for significant transformation in our lives.

THE SOLAR SYSTEM WITHIN

The planets (wandering stars) don't move in a circular path, but rather one that is elliptical, in a loose spiral around the Sun. Each planet's orbit is at times nearer or farther from the Sun, and a bit above or below the ecliptic, or the Sun's apparent path during the year. Consider if we were to walk a mile, we may move a few inches to the left or right. Our head would move a little up and down, due to our stride. In each case the variations are relatively subtle.

As above, so below. We will apply the same image of the planetary orbits to the solar system within us. (Note the circle placement is not exactly to scale in the reference image.)

With the Sun at the center of our solar system, we will place it at the center of our human system, the heart, ruled by the Sun's sign, Leo, here represented by the red circle.

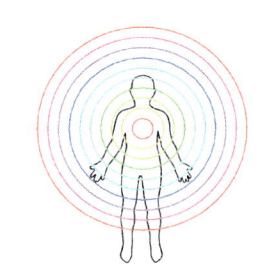

From the Earth's viewpoint the Moon is the second brightest object in the sky, as such, we will place it in our body model next to the Sun. The Moon rules the breasts and stomach, through Cancer. The orange circle, just outside the red Heart Sun, connects the stomach and breasts.

In fact, the closest planet to the Sun is Mercury, but we will place it just beyond the Moon, represented in pale green. The rest of the planets all fall in (3-dimensional) order. Mercury circles through the lungs and arms through Gemini, and the small intestine, ruled by Virgo.

The circle of Venus' orbit follows, crossing over the throat and shoulders of Taurus above the heart; below, it runs through the lower back and kidneys of Libra.

The orbit of Mars touches the head of Aries. On the bottom, it shares with Pluto rulership over the sexual/creative center.

Now Jupiter's circle passes over the thighs of Sagittarius at its nadir. Above, it goes beyond the head, as do the rest of the planets. We are moving beyond the traditional seven chakra system. What does this mean? Jupiter aligns with the energy field above us, as one layer of our aura. Jupiter, ruler of religion, moves through the "Halos of the Saints."

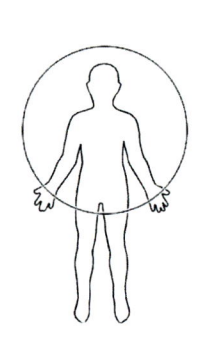

Just beyond Jupiter's orbit a circle passes through the knees, associated with Capricorn, which is governed by Saturn.

Another circle, representing Uranus, ruled by Aquarius, passes over the ankles and above our heads. It also permeates our electrical body, as it is the planet of electricity. As Aquarius is ruler of our current age, we see an electronics/cyber expansion happening all around us.

The next ring, aligned with Neptune's orbit, claims the feet, ruled by Pisces, which circles a still higher center above us. Neptune's energy is "other worldly," so it may sometimes be hard to get a handle on it. Neptune rules the ocean, which is vast and mysterious, the deep holds many secrets. Neptune is also associated with the illusory, including our fantasy life. We can easily get caught in the web of *maya* or illusion, if we are not rooted in what is real, which means that which is eternal.

The final concentric circle represents the last planet, Pluto. It touches us not. Perhaps, this is why some say Pluto is not a planet? Pluto's orbit actually intersects Neptune's in a few places, which gives Pluto some Neptunian energy, and vice versa. It touches our feet at times. Pluto takes a very long time to move around the Sun, 248 Earth years. That's more than three of our lifetimes! It rules generations, moving through each sign for an average of twenty years. The energy of Pluto always serves, in some way, as the catalyst for our most powerful transformation.

Explore the *Auric Meditation* below. Allow your consciousness to drift beyond the perimeters of your own physical body, as you sense the energies of five heavenly bodies. We invite you to listen to the guided meditation in the recording, *Ten Gates into the Garden: Spiritual Exercises and Meditations*, for a deeper, more expansive experience.

Auric Meditation

Our intent in the Planetary Auric Meditation is to visualize five astrological energy fields, operating beyond the periphery of our own auric field, that impact us energetically. How may we access them? We begin by sitting comfortably with the spine straight, close the eyes, and attend to the breath. Consciously slow it down. Trace each inhalation and each exhalation as you gradually enter into a state of focused meditation.

As you continue to breathe, sense, feel, visualize, or imagine an energy right above the head. This we will refer to as the "Jupiter field." Notice what you sense. Is there anything up there? You may not be able to see anything, but can you feel something? Humanity continually ponders the questions, "What is beyond or above us?" "Is there a heaven above or a hell below?" These larger questions, and other like them, are addressed through the energy of Jupiter, expressed in religion and philosophy.

Jupiter is the planet of expansion. Become present to your awareness moving out beyond your own physical form. Continue to extend your awareness out in all directions, limitless. Allow this energy to envelop you in its benevolence. Feel the abundance of the Universe cradling you in its totality. Know that you are supported and sustained by the All That Is.

As we move out further, we detect the "Saturn field." If there is difficulty sensing Saturn, remember the planet represents limitation, constriction, and obstacles. As we contemplate this energy, we are learning patience, and why the ancients called this planet, "The Ring Pass Not." Our discipline supports the persistence, patience, and practice, also ruled by Saturn, we must employ to move beyond all limitation. Saturn says, "Thou must fulfill!" Note how this field feels compared to Jupiter's field.

As we move out further, we detect the "Saturn field." If there is difficulty sensing Saturn, remember the planet represents limitation, constriction, and obstacles. As we contemplate this energy, we are learning patience, and why the ancients called this planet, "The Ring Pass Not." Our discipline supports the persistence, patience, and practice, also ruled by Saturn, we must employ to move beyond all limitation. Saturn says, "Thou must fulfill!" Note how this field feels compared to Jupiter's field.

We move now to the unlimited freedom of the "Uranian field," which comes from the fulfillment of Saturn's lessons of limitation, and the balancing of our karma. Become conscious of the electromagnetic essence of your being, the activation of both positive and negative poles, the expression of Yang and Yin moving through your chakras and meridians as Life Force. Within this energy, we sense what it feels like to have broken the ring, the wheel of bondage to the Earth we experience again and again through reincarnation. Be present to the vibration of this field. How does its resonance differ from that of Saturn and Jupiter? What has been activated within you?

> **Auric Meditation, Cont'd**
>
> Beyond the Uranian energetic field, we dissolve into the cosmic ocean of Neptune. This is the storehouse of bliss, opening us up to an awareness of Universal Consciousness. It may take lifetimes to reach this state of consciousness, but know it is there. Here the ego has been sublimated in the Divine. Once the of wheel birth and death has been transcended, incarnation is no longer needed. The ego ceases its hold. All personal identity falls away. We are one with ALL. Our life-stream flows into the sea. Neptune is the Holy Spirit of our solar system. We tap into this whenever we perform a selfless act or when we put other's needs before our own. The fruit of selfless service is *moksha*, bliss! This is why it is better to give than to receive. What is the essence of this Neptunian energy as it vibrates through you?
>
> What lies beyond that? Pluto. Where can this planet of transformation take us? Once we merge with the Divine, we move beyond the 3rd dimension. Pluto, through Scorpio, rules death, and we now die to the material plane, the pattern of life and death we have experienced through many incarnations. We must leap into the abyss, knowing that we are always evolving into something greater. We transcend physical birth and enter the greater cycle of cosmic birth. Allow this dynamic energy to permeate your being. Open and allow the transformation to occur. You have nothing to lose.

THE FOUR ASTROLOGICAL ELEMENTS

Each of the twelve rays, or the twelve energies of the circle, manifest through one of four elements: Fire, Earth, Air, and Water. The ancient Greeks believed everything was made up of a combination of these four elements. We may well have been conditioned to believe that this is simplistic thinking.

Yet, we understand that our very DNA structure is made up of four parts. Quantum physics tells of four fundamental forces that make up creation: Gravitational, Electro-Magnetic, Strong Nuclear, and Weak Nuclear. The elements are the four building blocks of our being: Fire (energy/Spirit), Earth (matter/form), Air (mind/consciousness), and Water (emotion/feeling). Let's look more closely at each.

Fire Signs: The Fire Trinity

Each of the four elements manifest in each of three modes. If we gaze into a candle flame, we notice three distinct colors: red, yellow and blue. These colors also correspond to the three fire signs. Aries, is the red flame, Leo, the yellow, and Sagittarius is blue.

In Aries, the leading, or cardinal-fire, it manifests in its wildest state, bright red, burning where it will. This fire is in its primal state, uncontrolled. When we see this kind of fire, we call "911."

In Leo, the flame becomes fixed in one place. Now it is brought under control, manifesting as a match, a candle, or fireplace, for example. It could be the burner on the stove, or in a furnace. Leo is ruled by the Sun, a large yellow, fixed flame. Now that the fire is contained, we can be creative and do something with it.

The blue flame corresponds to the mutable mode of Sagittarius. This is the flame of transformation, lifting us up above matter. It is the fire of new ideas that incinerate old concepts.

Within our being we may relate the red fire with anger, passion and aggression. The Sun's yellow flame is our heart and manifests as creativity and desire. The blue flame is the fire of mind, religion and philosophy.

Earth Signs: The Earth Trinity

The Earth signs show possession of things in Taurus, taking care of them through Virgo, and putting them to use with Capricorn.

Capricorn, the blue wedge, is cardinal-earth, which plans and sets the goal. Taurus, the red-orange section, is fixed-earth, and manifests that goal in the physical, and the mutable-earth sign Virgo, the yellow-green piece of the pie, cleans up afterward.

Capricorn is a sign of leadership, a sign of position and power. The one in charge certainly initiates the actions to be taken. Taurus, as fixed-earth, establishes these actions in the third dimension. Now mutable Virgo can work with what is manifested.

Air Signs: The Air Trinity

Libra, the sign ushering in autumn, here represented by the green wedge, is cardinal-air. As the sign of balance, its symbol is the scales. The word Libra means "book," in Latin. When we combine it with its opposite sign, Aries, we get the word libraries, repositories for many books.

This "book" also refers to the script we wrote before incarnation, which is why Libra is a leading sign. The goal of the script is to bring the soul into balance.

Aquarius, designated here as the purple wedge, is fixed-air, and rules knowing, as crystal clear thought. Through the act of balancing, we are led to knowing.

Finally, Gemini, the orange piece of the pie, rules the conscious mind of thought. As this is the air sign of dissolution, we can see how we may over-think things, defusing any pure knowing that is there. A noted Gemini, Bob Dylan said, "Don't think twice, it's all right."

The energies of the signs operate, regardless of the order we move through them. We can see that by arranging them differently, we learn different things. In Air, we think (Gemini), we balance the thought (Libra), and then we come to a clear knowing (Aquarius). God knows all the combinations.

Water Signs: The Water Trinity

The element Water offers another cycle. The leading-water sign, Cancer, rules springs, fountains and streams, pictured here as yellow-orange. This is the start of the water cycle, as it bubbles up from the ground, eventually creating a stream that flows here and there.

By the time we get to the fixed-water sign, Scorpio, represented as green-blue, the stream has dug deep, becoming a powerful river. Its path is fixed in the earth. It is very difficult to change the course of a river.

As with fixed-fire, fixed-water, in the form of rivers, lakes and ponds, brings many gifts. Humans have learned to harness the power that water holds. With the use of great generators, we convert the water-power into electricity.

In Pisces, the fuchsia wedge, we complete the cycle, in order to begin it again. The mutable state of the Water element is the ocean. The river flows into the ocean and is subsumed. Its individual traits no longer exist. It has merged with the great sea. As a mode of dissolution, the ocean eventually dis-corporates anything tossed in. In another few thousand years, the Titanic will be no more.

The ocean even dissolves itself as its enormous surface area assists evaporation. It becomes the source of most of the water that returns to us as rain, maintaining the cycle of water.

Within ourselves, we may be overly sensitive, protecting the new growth inside. We may be fixed with strong undercurrents of emotion that drive us to act, or we may tap into our compassion, selflessly helping others.

THE THREE ASTROLOGICAL MODES

Astrologically, each of the four elements of the zodiac (Fire, Earth, Air, and Water) manifest in one of three modes. There is a holy trinity of energy within each of the four elements, the forces of which express in different ways.

Cardinal Signs

The first mode is referred to as cardinal, or leading. These signs lead off each of the four seasons. This represents, in the traditional [...] he Father, Creator of All. In [...] strological year begins in the [...] the nights, in our yearly cycle [...], as the Sun enters the cardi-

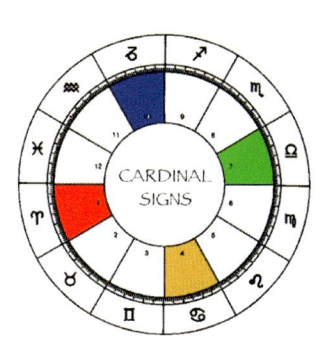

[...] me, bringing new vegetation up through the earth. The [...] ken from the sleep of winter.

[...] the Sun enters the cardinal-water sign, Cancer. The life-[...] nment for the growth that unfolds during these months. [...] are of summer growth spurts.

[...] ng-air sign, Libra. The element Air represents the mind, [...] gns with the beginning of the school year in the fall.

[...] use our mind to prepare for what the season brings. In [...] ght determine life or death, as the environment can be deadly in winter. The cardinal-earth sign, Capricorn, leads off winter. We use the element Earth to symbolize this time, as even liquid water becomes solid during the winter months.

Fixed Signs

The second mode of this cosmic triangle is referred to as fixed. This is the mode of establishment and sustainment, aligned with *Vishnu* in Hinduism, where the cardinal creation is preserved. Most people are focused in this realm of awareness. Fixed energy holds the creation together.

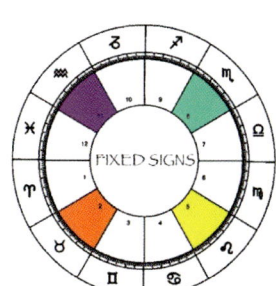

In Esoteric Christianity, the *Father-Mother* energy has created the world, and the Sun/Son becomes the solid foundation of creation. The Sun is the center of our solar system and is the physical manifestation of the Great Central Sun, the point of origin of all spiritual-physical creation. It is what Jesus referred to as the "cornerstone" rejected by the builders. This means that we overlook or reject our true foundation, which is Spirit, rather than matter. The Self is the rock, on which we build a solid house.

"The stone which the builders rejected has become the chief cornerstone."

Psalm 118:22 NKJV

The four fixed signs dwell in the middle of each season, and also correspond to each of the four elements. Taurus is fixed-earth. Leo is fixed-fire. Water is fixed in Scorpio, and the sign of fixed-air is Aquarius.

We will see these four fixed elements appear again and again in our studies. Visions of these energies appear in both the Old and New Testaments. They are described as a bull (Taurus), a lion (Leo), an eagle (Scorpio), and a man (Aquarius).

Mutable Signs

The final mode is mutable. It is the energy that dissolves away all forms, so that the new might be created. The last third of our trinity ends each of the four seasons.

Creation brings Spirit into manifestation. It remains polarized for a time, eventually disintegrating, dissolving back into Spirit. This mode is associated with the Holy Spirit of the Christian Trinity and Shiva in the Hindu.

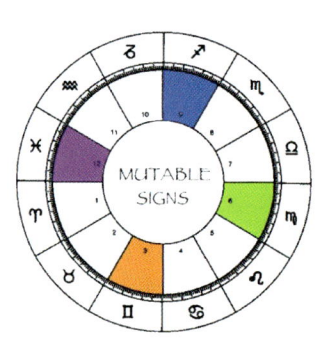

The four mutable signs are Gemini, mutable-air, completing spring; Virgo, mutable-earth, which closes out summer; Sagittarius, mutable-fire, which concludes the fall, and Pisces, mutable-water, which is the last sign of winter. As these signs all bring dissolution, they open the way to reality as the illusions disappear.

Pisces is the fish. The opposite sign, Virgo, governs wheat, in general, and loaves of bread, specifically. Wheat requires no cross pollination, which is why it is aligned with the sign of virginity. The energies of these two signs, representing selfless-service, respectively, were utilized when Jesus fed 5,000 with just a few loaves and fishes. The other polarity of Gemini and Sagittarius shows the connection between the higher and lower minds. We move from mundane thinking to deep philosophical thought.

THE YEARLY ASTROLOGICAL CYCLE

Aries

We begin the cycle with spring and the cardinal-fire sign Aries, which represents the flame that reawakens nature. It's a time of new beginnings, in many respects. The cycle of the Tarot begins with The Fool card. As we start the year with Aries, we celebrate April Fool's Day.

In the human body, Aries corresponds to the head. Generally, most people are born head first. Within the head, Aries is the brain and the sense of sight. During Aries, we celebrate

Easter, when women and girls have traditionally donned Easter bonnets on their heads. The Easter egg is also a symbol of new life.

In the Christian Mysteries, Jesus took full advantage of the influx of power, at this time, to rise from the dead.

Along with Easter, we also celebrate the Jewish Passover, at this time. This holiday recalls the time when Moses led the Jews out of the bondage they experienced in Egypt. This Exodus came at the beginning of the Age of Aries, some 4,000 years ago. Even today they blow the Shofar, the horn of a ram, in worship.

In Aries, the Sun reaches its exaltation. This means as the solar energy moves through the beginning of any cycle, it is raised to its height of power. Whenever we begin a new project, the most intense energy is at the beginning, when we actually "get it going."

If one fires up the charcoal grill, first one soaks the coals with starter fluid, before throwing in the match, creating an intense initial burn, to get the whole thing going. We need more energy to jump-start something than to maintain its operation. If we have ever hand-pumped water, we know that initially we need more energy to get it going.

Aries' symbol is the ram. The glyph is reminiscent of the ram's horns, jutting out from its head. Additionally, the symbol resembles a nose and eyebrows, again alluding to the head. This glyph can also represent a new sprout rising from the earth.

The color aligned with Aries is red, which is the start of the lower end of the visible light spectrum. The red planet, Mars, is said to be the ruler of Aries.

When we speak of "rulers," we are referring to a concentrated, focused manifestation of a specific energy. The signs manifest the energy more generally, creating a magnetic field in which the energies operate. The planets act more as triggers, creating specific energetic patterns within and across the "magnetic fields" of the signs.

Keep in mind that the signs and the constellations are two separate things. There is a constellation called Aries. Two thousand years ago the constellation, Aries, and the sign, Aries, were in the same place. The patterns of the stars were "seen" as various animals and gods creating a mythology used to explain events on Earth.

The constellations that formed the zodiac were used to construct a system to help people understand the cycle of the year. It was the cycle's reality that was reflected by the symbols in the sky. It served as a cosmic mirror, used to help humanity grasp the bigger picture. The bottom line is the stars, out there, millions of miles away, don't cause things to happen to us. However, as part of the whole, they serve as a reflection of what we are creating for ourselves.

It is impossible to say, absolutely, that the planets and stars have no direct effect on us at all. If there were no stars, we would not be discussing astrology. In fact, once we get a more complete understanding of the universe, we will find there is nothing in creation that does not affect us, as we are one with the creation. Since we are one with the universe, anything happening anywhere, at any time, is also happening to us.

As Mars is the ruler of Aries, it is very comfortable in its home sign. Opposite Aries is Libra, the home of Venus. When Venus is in Aries, farthest from home, it does not function to its full potential. Venus is The Empress in the Tarot, and Aries is The Emperor. In other words, the energy of the feminine Venus is in Aries, the sign of the masculine. Here the divine feminine is overshadowed by the martial energy that is counter to its nature.

In today's society, we see gender roles changing, becoming more fluid. Up until now, and still to a great degree, women have come up against powerful resistance when they have tried to make their own way in the world. When Venus operates in Taurus and Libra, the signs she rules, she is able to work creatively through the subconscious and the power of suggestion to influence the world.

We have said that the Sun is exalted in Aries. The planet Saturn, however, is in its fall in this sign. Saturn in Aries can manifest as a tyrant, as one who is severe and merciless. As with any traits, these can surely be overcome. With Saturn in Aries, it is typically more difficult to do so. Wisdom does, generally, come with maturity, to keep the personal will in balance.

The key phrase for Aries is "I Am." It is pure being, the Eternal Flame of Life. When Moses asked who God was, God answered, "I Am that I Am."

Taurus

From Aries we move to Taurus, the second of the twelve parts that make up the whole cycle. We move from leading-fire smack into fixed-earth. We find the most volatile energy applying itself to the most solid of forms. Isn't this how anything begins? We apply our energy to bring about some change in matter. Everything begins with a thought (energy). We pick up a pencil. We blast a tunnel through a mountain. We walk across the room. Energy moves matter.

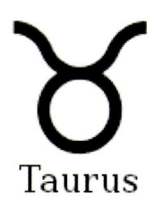

To the right is the symbol for Taurus. The picture is typically regarded as the head of a bull, the most common symbolic depiction of Taurus. Incidentally, the Spanish word for bull is "*toro.*"

As Aries rules the head, Taurus governs the neck and throat. The symbol depicts the chin resting over a circle, representing the throat chakra. The energy of Venus, ruler of Taurus, resides in the throat chakra. Our throat gives us the ability to speak and sing. The throat is an upper womb, through which we birth our thoughts in the form of words.

When we turn our focus within, we hear the inner word, as represented in The Hierophant, the card aligned with the sign Taurus. We use our words to express what we find of value. What we value, we typically want to possess. The sign, Taurus, therefore, rules that which we value, both materially and spiritually, as well as our personal possessions, money and resources.

The color assigned to Taurus is red-orange. This sign is ruled by Venus, guardian of music and art. She is queen of the vegetable kingdom. As we move through spring, the Earth begins to give rise to the lush green of new growth. The color associated with Venus is green, and is the complement of Mars' red. Within Taurus, we celebrate Earth Day. We may also recall Mother Earth at Mother's Day.

As the Sun is exalted in Aries, Taurus is the exaltation of the Moon. The Moon is the most changeable light in the sky, going through its phases every twenty-eight days. The Moon deals with the emotions, also a changeable energy. In Taurus, a fixed sign, the Moon's fluctuation finds some grounding and stability in the realm of matter. The bull is a symbol of fertility, while the Moon presides over the womb and gestation.

Uranus has its fall in Taurus, undoing some of the stability of the earth sign. In the Tarot, Uranus is represented by The Fool, who's letter Aleph, means bull or ox. The Fool is about to lower in vibration, or "fall" down to Earth (Taurus).

The key phrase for this sign is "I Have." What do we have? We have a body, a form, the vehicle through which the energy of Aries moves to propel us through our experience.

Gemini

We experience birth in Aries, the first sign, and we become aware of the physical plane in Taurus. As we begin to make sense of it all, we begin to have thoughts about our external environment. Thus, the key phrase for Gemini is "I Think."

Here, we enter the realm of mind. The ruler of this sign is Mercury, the planet that orbits the most swiftly around the Sun. In Roman mythology, he was the messenger of the gods. A messenger's function is to communicate information, and Mercury is the sign of communication. The faster the mind, theoretically, the easier communication becomes.

Jupiter is in its detriment in Gemini. Here, expansive Jupiter is hemmed in by the mundane thoughts of the lower mind. Jupiter governs the Higher Mind, associated with religion and philosophy. Jupiter wants to fly freely into the realms of loftier ideas and ideals.

In the Garden of Eden story, from the Bible, God created (Aries/Fire) from the clay (Taurus/Earth) Adam and Eve (Gemini, the twins). In the Tarot, the card for Gemini, the Lovers, shows Adam and Eve in the garden. As Gemini spans most of June, perhaps this is a reason for so many weddings during that month.

The symbol for Gemini looks like the Roman numeral two (II), representing the twins. In the body, these twins are our two arms, as well as our two lungs, which is apt, since Gemini is an Air sign. Air is symbolic of the mind. The twins are the conscious (Adam) and subconscious minds (Eve).

Our conscious mind, in conjunction with the subconscious, allows us to imagine from multiple perspectives; therefore, we have the ability to see all sides of a situation. Our mind has the capacity to contemplate something from so many vantage points that we must eventually learn to discriminate between ideas.

This multiplicity of perspective can stress the need for a more holistic view of reality. If a group of us were sitting in a circle, and one of us were to stand in the center and keep perfectly still, no one would be able to see that individual. Each of us would only be able to see a part of the person in the center. Everyone would have a totally different point of view. Some of us would not be able to see the being's face, the back of the head and body would be obscured from view for others. Each of us would have a different perspective, and none would have a complete picture.

95

Would any of us see more, or better, than anyone else? Would any of our viewpoints be more correct? Again, no one would be able to see the entirety of the whole.

Astrology uses a circle to represent the whole. We may put whatever we wish into the center. Though there are more, from the astrological perspective, and for simplicity's sake, we'll assume there are twelve different ways to look at anything. Are some views better? Each one is only one-twelfth of reality.

This highlights the difficulty we run into when identify with only one sign or another. The goal is to become all twelve. If we really desire the truth, we must look at our experience from all twelve directions. Then we must synthesize the twelve into a single vision. Is this too much for our minds to handle? We hope so. Ultimately, we must transcend our mind to do this work. We want to be the whole pie, rather than just one sliver!

The color associated with the vibratory rate of Gemini is orange. There are no planets exalted in Gemini. Could this mean that just thinking does not empower anything? Master Jesus said,

"Take no thought for your life."
Matthew 6:25 KJV

Cancer

The fourth sign, Cancer, brings forth the Water element as cardinal-water. Our need for water is expressed through Cancer's key phrase, "I Feel." We need to balance out all of Gemini's thinking with some feeling. In Aries, the creative fire burned. In Taurus, the passive earth received. In Gemini, we activated creative thought. Now, in Cancer, we must become receptive, like water, so that we might feel. When the thinking of Gemini is combined with the feeling of Cancer, our words become more compassionate and potent.

The sign Cancer is ruled by the Moon, associated with the divine feminine and the mother archetype. The Moon's magnetic pull on the Earth affects the waters of this planet. Our personal planet, the body, is also mostly water, and thus impacted by the cyclic nature of the Moon's energy.

The Mother is the source of all form. The form we currently dwell in was developed in our mother's womb. In the esoteric teachings, it is said, before Creation, we all existed in a Cosmic Womb. Cosmically, the Mother births all of creation into being. The Chariot card, associated with the sign Cancer, represents the physical form we manifest in moving out into the world.

The Moon's twenty-eight-day cycle correlates to a woman's menstrual cycle. With Jupiter exalted in Cancer, and as the largest planet in our system, it indicates growth and expansion, something experienced throughout pregnancy. Jupiter is known as the "Greater Fortune." Blessings for all mothers! Mars has its fall in Cancer, as the active, martial energy has no traction in the receptive, watery realm of the Moon.

Cancer's symbol, the crab, presents the idea of a home and a hard, protective shell. Cancer is also the womb, a protected house for the fetus. It is the archetypal Mother energy. Saturn governs its polar opposite sign Capricorn, and is said to be in detriment in Cancer. The Father energy, as manifest in Saturn, cannot experience pregnancy first hand, and therefore remains detached to some degree. Cancer is very sensitive, while Saturn sees emotions as of little practical use.

Cancer's glyph, to the right, is reminiscent of the breasts, as well as the stomach, both of which offer sustenance. As Cancer rules the Mother principle, the breasts serve to feed and nourish the newborn. The stomach allows us to receive food to nourish every cell in the body.

The glyph shows two spirals of energy, whirling in opposite directions. The nature of the emotions is such, sometimes one way, sometimes another. As Cancer is a water sign, we might be reminded of the story of Jesus and the woman at the well in which the Master spoke of two types of water, the physical, which offers a temporary quenching, and *living* waters that when taken one would never thirst. (*John 4:6-15 KJV*) There are also two types of feeling, one working through the senses, the other intuitive.

In the astrological color scale, Cancer, orange-yellow, falls between the orange of Gemini and the yellow of the next sign, Leo. The thoughts of Gemini create the forms of Cancer. These are thought-forms, resulting in the birth of the next sign, Leo.

As we begin to feel, to become much more sensitive, we may need to strengthen our outer shell, our atmosphere. Even as the Earth has an atmosphere, so do we. We are told that the Earth's atmosphere protects us from many "dangerous" forms of radiation, as well as smaller chunks of matter flying through space.

In our own life, we may at times feel the need to protect ourselves from "bad vibes" or "negative energy." We can begin to strengthen our energetic field, or aura, through meditation and various spiritual exercises. Though, eventually, we will realize that we are the source of these "disturbances."

The Hindu tradition speaks of a beam of Light, called the *Antahkarana*, that connects our physical form through the crown chakra to our Higher Self. We might see it as a Cosmic umbilical cord that connects us to the Source of our sustainment. Beyond the Higher Self, the *Antahkarana* links us with our Supreme Self, and still beyond that to our divine Presence, the I AM.

Explore the *Egg of Light Exercise* below, to begin to awaken to the Higher aspects of our being. We recommend you experience the meditation using the available audio recording, *Ten Gates into the Garden: Spiritual Exercises and Meditations.*

Egg of Light Exercise

Through our powers of visualization, the following exercise can help us deflect another's energy vibration of which we wish to remain free. In the exercise, when we speak of the Light of Christ, we are referring to the Spiritual Sun at the center of our Solar System.

We are not the source of this exercise, as it has been in practice for a very long time. (We use the illusion of time, so that you may have the illusion of perspective.)

The purpose of this exercise is for us to become not only acquainted with the use of visualization and our own imaging of objects and Light, but it also brings us to a state where we are totally surrounded by the Christ Light. This is exercise has nothing to do with "Christian" religion.

Step 1: Sit in a relaxed position in a straight-backed chair, or on a meditation cushion. With eyes closed, visualize yourself within an oval-shaped egg, which is filled with the White Light of the Christ. (In many ancient writings, the egg always represented the one who had attained. The egg, traditionally used as a symbol of birth, contains the potential for all things.)

Step 2: Draw the Light of the Sun into the egg form, through the top of the head, and center it in the Heart. Fill the oval with so much Light that you can see and feel its brightness. In fact, it is possible after 3 or 4 days of practice to see the Light when sitting in a darkened room. (Be aware that many highly evolved beings have never "seen" it. Our aim is to develop our faculties of focus and knowing, not the senses.)

Step 3: Image yourself occupying an ovoid space in the center of this Egg of Light you are creating. In performing this exercise, one should feel a terrific uplift and exhilaration which will improve the health and general condition of the individual.

You will especially note the exhilaration in this exercise, if you practice it within two to three days of the approaching full-moon phase and just after the full moon.

This exercise should be taken seriously. This and the other spiritual exercises contained in this volume are an opportunity to attain fundamental self-unfoldment and mastery. Consistent and honest effort in using this exercise will bring you into the fullness of your reality. The more we practice, the greater will be our devotional aspects and the more real will be the transformation within our entire being. It will quicken and hone our spiritual mentality and bring other gifts of the Spirit, like greater intuition, and, most of all, the realization of our increasing Cosmic Consciousness.

Leo

Now that we have worked with the Light of the Sun in the *Egg of Light Exercise*, let's look at the sign the Sun rules, Leo. Many are familiar with Leo's symbol, the Lion. The glyph looks like a lion's head, with its huge mane falling to its shoulders. The symbol is also reminiscent of a heart, Leo's home in our body. As the lion is the king of beasts, the heart is the king of organs.

Leo is fixed-fire, the second fire sign, where we progress the "I Am" of Aries to the "I Will" of Leo. We move from being, to acting, as we activate our being. Leo is, therefore, a sign of creativity. Leo also rules acting, as well as the ego. Perhaps, this explains why some actors are described as having outsized egos.

Seriously, one needs the ego, in order to express the will. The key is, as always, balance. It's not the size of the ego, or the will, but the balance between them. This lies at the very source of the creative principle.

As Leo corresponds to the heart, it is the sign of love and romance. As it follows the sign Cancer, the teaching is that romantic love must have its foundation in our feeling life. We must be sensitive to each other and be willing to protect our mate. In life, we often leave the home of Cancer for the call of romantic love.

Lions mate for life. It is not some fickle "puppy-love" that moves from partner to partner. We should never confuse casual sex or infatuation with love. Our goal is not to fall in love, but rather to be lifted up by it.

Leo also rules children, often the result of romantic love. The Sun, ruler of Leo, is pictured in the Tarot as a child, or children. As the Sun "lives" in this sign, Leo's color is yellow. No planets have their fall in Leo.

Pluto is said to be exalted in Leo, which brings about creative transformation. Pluto was in Leo, when the individuals called the "Love generation" were born, who brought great changes in consciousness, during the 1960s.

Saturn is in its detriment, as it rules Capricorn, the darkest time of the year. (Northern Hemisphere) Leo, which spans the height of summer, is ruled by the Sun, the Source of Light.

99

Virgo

Virgo is the sign of the virgin, and as mutable-earth is the second earth sign, following Taurus. We progress from the "I Have" of Taurus and see just what we really do have in Virgo's key phrase "I Analyze." Virgo breaks things down to their smallest units. In the body, Virgo governs the intestines, whose job it is to further break down what we have swallowed into the stomach, ruled by Cancer, through the throat, aligned with Taurus. The body is able to absorb the nutrients it needs for optimal functionality, by breaking down complex forms into simpler ones.

Virgo serves the same function in the mind, giving us the ability to break down complex ideas or experiences into smaller bits of information, so we can better process and assimilate them. Our schools are an out-picturing of this same process, and the school year begins in late August or early September, at the onset of Virgo.

Diet, nutrition, service, work, and healing are all associated with Virgo. A fundamental astrological teaching points to the connection between our diet and disease. If we are what we eat, do we really want to be a dead animal? So many appear content to eat chemically laden, processed foods that are devoid of Life Force, making no connection to the fact that roughly one in four people in America currently die from the effects of cancer.

As mentioned earlier, Virgo is associated with wheat, which reproduces without cross pollination, so it is considered a "virginal" food. Bread has been called the "staff of life." In the Tarot, Virgo is pictured, as the celibate Hermit, holding a staff. As Virgo rules work, we celebrate Labor Day during this sign.

Virgo shares the planet Mercury with Gemini. So how can a planet represent more than one sign?

In the last age, humankind was only aware of seven lights in the sky; these were the Sun, Moon, Mercury, Venus, Mars, Jupiter and Saturn. Applying seven planets to cover twelve signs was a mental exercise in itself. In many mystical systems, the One becomes the Three. Subsequently, the Three manifest the Seven, which are then completed in the Twelve. Ultimately, the Twelve, again, give birth to the One. Perhaps, at this point, this information may be producing more questions than answers. When we study the science of numbers, in Chapter 6, it will begin to make greater sense.

Virgo

Mercury rotates much slower than the Earth. It spins on its axis every fifty-nine Earth days. Mercury orbits the Sun more swiftly than the Earth does. As such, one "day" on Mercury is 2/3 the length of its year, which is eighty-eight Earth days long. In other words, three days on Mercury require two full revolutions around the Sun to complete. The relationship between the numbers two and three, as it relates to Mercury's rotation and revolution, mirrors the relationship between the energies of the High Priestess (card 2) and the Empress (card 3). Mercury carries the energies of the High Priestess and Empress in potential, in the way Adam (conscious mind) carries Eve (both the "virginal" subconscious and "creative" subconscious) in potential, before her creation. Refer to the illustration of Mercury's glyph at the bottom of page 68.

Now back to this unusual planet's dual rulership. The energy of Mercury, as it relates to Gemini, is more focused on itself, whereas Mercury's energetic relationship to Virgo, has it focused on others. Gemini, with its relationship to the conscious mind, is the sign of communication. Conversely, Virgo, as it relates to health and service, has an affinity with the subconscious mind. Whereas the school year begins during Virgo, it ends when the Sun moves into Gemini.

Mercury, the ruler of Gemini, rules the hands, which are used for communication. We can sign, make other hand gestures, or communicate through writing, keyboarding, or texting. These activities are associated with the side facing the Sun. The Virgo side, facing the other planets aligns with Virgo, and activates the hands' ability to heal and serve.

Virgo, ruled by Mercury, is also its sign of exaltation. It is believed that the true ruler of Virgo is Vulcan, a yet undiscovered planet. Vulcan, in Roman mythology, worked the forge, as blacksmith to the gods. Vulcan is believed to orbit between Mercury and the Sun, so we can intuit that his forge is the Sun itself!

The color associated with Virgo is yellow-green. Its glyph represents virginity. The symbol will make more sense, when we look at it in relationship to the glyph for Scorpio.

Virgo and Scorpio's glyphs are virtually identical, except that there is an enclosed loop to the right of the "M" in Virgo's glyph, symbolizing a girl's intact hymen, before she has had vaginal intercourse, while the "M" aligned with Scorpio's glyph, the sign ruling sex, has an open and active arrow pointing to the right, indicative of a phallus. In the Tarot, Venus, representing the Empress card, is depicted as pregnant, a difficult task for a virgin, and so we find Venus in its fall in Virgo.

Libra

As we move into the second half of the zodiac, we find these signs have a strong relationship with their opposing signs. The first sign of autumn is Libra, and its polar opposite is Aries, the first sign of spring.

The "I Am" of Aries is polarized with the "We Are" of Libra. Aries is individuality, while Libra is partnership. The glyph for Libra represents the scales of balance.

Libra symbolizes the partnership between the first half of the zodiac with the second half. We began with Aries at sunrise on the first day of spring. With Libra, we begin the journey home at sunset, on the first day of autumn.

As the sign of the scales, Libra represents balance, depicted on the Justice card, associated with this sign. We are balancing the first half of the cycle with the last. Libra is, therefore, the sign of karma, or the *Law of Cause and Effect*. The planet associated with karma is Saturn, which has its exaltation in Libra, and is the sign where karma's effect begins. It is the nadir of our bungee jump, the lowest point, at which the energy changes polarity, and we bounce back up toward the sky, returning to the Source or Primal Cause.

The *Law of Cause and Effect* is much more complex than we might imagine. In most cases, each effect produced becomes another cause. Every thought we think, every word we speak, or action we take, creates these chains, which are continually multiplying ad infinitum. These are the chains that bind us to this planet, limiting our real freedom. Libra simply shows us the solution lies in balance.

When the seesaw is perfectly balanced at the center, its ups and downs cease. So, in order to find balance, we must discover our own center. To reach the center, we must let go of the extremes. Be. Being is freeing!

As Libra is the sign of marriage and partnerships, we may extrapolate that all relationships are karmic. They serve the expansion of consciousness, and the evolution of the soul.

The glyph is reminiscent of a scale, and it can also be seen as a sunset. In the body, Libra rules the kidneys. Additionally, it rules the lower back, also alluded to in the symbol. The kidneys filter the blood to keep the body in a state of balance.

Not only is Venus the planetary ruler of Taurus, it also governs the sign Libra. Venus is a goddess of love, which is a basic ingredient for the partnership of marriage. Green is Venus' and Libra's color, the color complement of red Aries. These colors are used in many Christmas designs, and represent the balance of the masculine and feminine energies, as expressed in the pagan celebration of Yule.

Saturn, the primary planet associated with karma, through its message, "Thou must fulfill," is raised to its height of power, or exaltation in Libra. Its focus is the result, or effect, of all cause, which is finding the balance in the scales.

As cardinal-air, the second air sign, Libra brings Gemini's thoughts ("I Think") into balance. In Libra, the thoughts are transcribed into books (*libras*). When we combine the opposite signs Libra and Aries together, we get libraries. Time spent with books in libraries moves us in the direction of the last air sign, Aquarius whose key phrase is "I Know."

As we earlier observed the difficulties facing Venus in Aries, we find the same situation reversed with Mars in Libra. Here Mars is in detriment. When we say detriment, it does not imply "bad" or "wrong." It is simply a debilitation, so it is hard to apply any of the planets' inherent abilities in a productive way. It is as if we put someone who is a concert pianist in a room with no piano. They are in no way harmed by this, they are simply unable to do what they do best.

Again, as gender roles continue to become more fluid, and the divine masculine energy aligns more equally with the divine feminine and vice versa, the way the Libra/Aries and Venus/Mars polarities play out will necessarily change accordingly.

Scorpio

Once we weigh our soul upon the karmic scale, we see what is needed for balance. In Scorpio, we get rid of the dross. In the body, Scorpio rules elimination.

As a triple sign, Scorpio is complex, and can manifest in any or all of its three energetic expressions. The un-regenerated Scorpio is symbolized by a scorpion. These deadly creatures inject their poison through their tails. This creature represents the deceptive, sneaky, lower nature from which we all eventually must evolve. Scorpio's key phrase is, "I Desire," which, in the energy vibration of the scorpion, manifests as selfish desire.

Scorpio's second energetic expression is represented by the serpent, the Kundalini. The serpent's bite is just as deadly as the scorpion's sting. The difference is one of heads or tails. A snake strikes head on. As our own Creative Life Force raises up along the spine, we might have a "snake-bite experience," which is not a physical bite, but rather one experienced in a dream or meditation. Kundalini is a deep subject we will cover in greater detail in a subsequent chapter.

The snake is also a symbol for sex, due to its phallic shape. The misconception that the snake, in the Garden of Eden story from the Bible, represents sexual temptation has caused many to view sex as evil. The Catholic Church distorted the original symbolism and perpetuated the belief that women are evil for tempting men into sex, and therefore sin. Even today, this attitude still remains active for many, whether unconsciously or consciously. In fundamentalist religious sects, women must veil themselves in various ways. In certain Islamic countries, for example, women are required to cover their flesh, so as not to "tempt" men to sexual desire.

The third symbol associated with Scorpio is the eagle. As a symbol for the United States, it indicates that the founding fathers intended this country to be one of transformation, where we might manifest our highest potential. The eagle is a symbol for sight and clear vision, as this raptor is able, while soaring through the sky, to see a rabbit from miles away. Scorpio also rules the third eye, located near the pineal gland, which resides at the center of the brain.

There is a strong connection between sex and spiritual sight. Again, due to the depth of information on this subject, we will investigate this concept further in the chapter: Kundalini and the Chakras.

Scorpio is also symbolized by the mythical phoenix, which continually renews itself. It burns off impurities on the fire within, eternally to be reborn out of its own ashes. This energy of renewal gives Scorpio its transformative abilities. As we learn to redirect the powerful sexual energy up the spine, our consciousness is greatly transformed.

The triple progression of Halloween to All Saints' Day, followed by All Souls' Day, occurs during Scorpio. This triune of holy days indicates the transformative nature of the sign, as we evolve from our "monster" or masked (hidden) self to the saintly being of our soul.

The color-energy of Scorpio is green-blue, and has its complement in Taurus' orange-red, its opposite sign. Gray, a symbolic color of wisdom, is achieved by combining complementary colors.

Scorpio also rules death. In Scorpio, death and sex are two sides of the same energy. Sex creates the body by which we might have experience on Earth. Death offers us a portal back home. Every death is a birth into a higher plane of existence. The Death card, in the Tarot, aligns with Scorpio, and represents the death or transformation of the false ego, where we turn from a materially based focus toward a spiritual one.

The sensitivity and feeling we developed in Cancer are prerequisites for healthy sexual experience that awaken in the energies of Scorpio, fixed-water. In the first Water sign, Cancer, we experience feeling and emotion. We experience these feelings at the surface level of our personality. The second Water sign, Scorpio, opens us to the mystical experience of sex, through which we experience a new depth of feeling, as we unite with the "other."

As Taurus governs what we possess, its polar opposite, Scorpio, governs other people's possessions, which may relate to our partner's resources, financial and otherwise, or an inheritance.

Scorpio used to share Mars' rulership with Aries. With the discovery of Pluto, this distant and tiny planet now rules Scorpio. Astrologically and musically speaking, since there are only seven natural notes in the Western musical scale, Pluto is the higher octave of Mars. In the Western scale, we use the seven whole notes, A through G. To play the note above G, we must play the A again, at a higher octave. The root word *oct*, as in octopus or octagon, means "eight."

As Scorpio, ruled by Pluto, is the eighth sign, it is the higher octave of Aries, the first sign, ruled by Mars. The lower octave manifests through Aries as the warrior, conquering the world around us. In Scorpio, the higher octave, under Pluto, the war is now fought secretly. It's an inner battle for control, rather than an outer one. A younger soul interprets Armageddon, jihad, or holy war as an external battle. The more evolved soul knows it is an inner battle between one's own Higher and lower nature.

Pluto is a planet of transformation. Just look at how, through no activity of its own, scientists transformed it into a dwarf planet, and, even now, it may be transforming back into a planet. Seriously, though, just as a snake sheds its skin and the phoenix drops its body, know that transformation only changes the form. Who we truly are always remains unchanged.

Uranus is exalted in Scorpio, while the Moon experiences its fall in this sign. The electrical discoveries of Uranus are surely transforming the world through technology; however, the miracle of birth is not well placed in the valley of death.

Let's look at an interesting progression through the signs. We are born in Cancer, sign of the womb, the mother, the family, and the home. In Leo, we go through our first seven years, ideally, just playing and being children. In Virgo, we go out into the world to school, and, ultimately, begin our work life. Then in Libra, now that we have a good education and employment, we may choose to get married, which has, traditionally, been seen as a requirement before sex is experienced in Scorpio.

Astrology offers us an energetic pattern that demonstrates that sex should come after marriage. The Church says the same thing. As we enter further into the new Aquarian Age, these patterns no longer apply. Look at it without the interference of church and state. Libra simply implies partnership. The teaching then becomes, if we want to experience sexual union, there must be someone with whom to unite. Whoever that is becomes our consenting partner at the time of that consummation. Indeed, as we progress further into the "New Age," many more old, outmoded patterns will continue to dissolve.

Let's examine the symbols of the last three signs we have studied.

♍ ♎ ♏
Virgo Libra Scorpio

On the left side of the scales we have the sign of the maiden, virginity, Virgo. On the right, we have Scorpio, the sign associated with sex. As noted previously, these two glyphs are similar in shape. We highlighted that Virgo's glyph indicates the female's intact hymen. The Scorpio glyph shows the male genitals in action. These symbols, as they relate to human sexuality, are weighed against each other. It is our responsibility to achieve balance, once we enter the potent energetic realm of sex.

Sagittarius

As resurrection follows death, Sagittarius follows Scorpio. The key phrase here is "I Perceive," or "I See." We are now able to use the in-sight we developed in Scorpio.

Sagittarius vibrates as blue, while its polar opposite energy signature is the orange of Gemini. Sagittarius' love is philosophy, at the other end of the spectrum to Gemini's focus on thinking. The symbol for Sagittarius is the centaur, half man, half horse. The horse denotes long distance travel, which is governed by this sign.

Sagittarius' glyph is a bow and arrow. As an archer, the centaur shoots his arrows heavenward. Again, this represents the wide open, expanded mind, which allows our ideas, born in Gemini, to fly to new heights of consciousness. Thus, Sagittarius is also a sign of religion and higher learning.

The region of the body the glyph alludes to may take a little more imagination. Imagine the diagonal line that enters the point of the arrow represents the femur or thigh bone inserting into the hip socket, while the crossbeam signifies the knee. As such, the part of the body Sagittarius rules is the thighs. The powerful muscles here are necessary for us to travel through the world, as we walk, skip, run, leap and climb. When this astrological system was initially devised, walking was the main source of transportation, for the general public.

Jupiter is Sagittarius' planetary ruler. In the Tarot, it is symbolized as the Wheel of Fortune. The wheel became instrumental in revolutionizing travel. Jupiter rules the liver, which is adversely impacted by rich foods, fats and sugars, also governed by Sagittarius.

Whereas, Venus is called the "Lesser Fortune," Jupiter, as mentioned earlier, is referred to as the "Greater Fortune," and is the largest planet in our system. Other than the Sun and Moon, Venus and Jupiter are the brightest lights in the sky. For the ancients, the smallest planet in their awareness was Mercury, ruler of Gemini, the opposite sign of Sagittarius. When Mercury travels through the energy of Jupiter, it is in detriment. The smallest can get lost in the largest. There are no planetary exhalations of falls in Sagittarius.

This sign appears in the cosmic cycle after the experience of death, through Scorpio. It stands to reason that we find religion and philosophy focusing, in large part, on what happens after we die.

Sagittarius is the sign of optimism and joviality, as well as the sign of reward. It falls during the time of the year when we celebrate the harvest and Thanksgiving, the reward received after months of toil in the fields.

Sagittarius' mutable-fire completes the fire trinity. It takes that creative power of Leo and expands it from the One (Aries) to the many. This sign ignites the fire of the mind. A candle flame is tricolored. The red flame denotes Aries, the yellow flame is Leo, and the blue flame aligns with Sagittarius.

Capricorn

Whereas Sagittarius is a sign of expansion, Capricorn is a sign of contraction. It brings structure to the Higher Mind. Its energy provides discipline, and also creates hierarchal structures and government.

The ruler of Capricorn is Saturn, the only visible planet surrounded by a ring, which Galileo first observed through his telescope in the early seventeenth century. As such, it became known as the "Ring-Pass-Not," and was thought to be the outer boundary of our Solar system, which parallels the skin, our own personal outer limit.

We can observe how Capricorn's structure works in our physical body, as the sign rules the skeletal system. It also governs the teeth, another concentrated part of our anatomy. An additional essential limitation we surely appreciate is our skin. It limits our organs to the body, rather than allowing them to expand out all over the floor.

The image to the right is a reminder that Capricorn also rules the knees. The glyph is even reminiscent of a kneecap. We use our knees to climb up to a higher position, manifesting as ambition, goals, planning and patience. Though Capricorn is a sign of completion, where we achieve our goals. The Buddha teaches that being overly goal oriented, attached to the results of our actions, is a path that leads to suffering.

Capricorn's symbol is the mountain goat. Actually, it is half goat and half fish. This shows us how Capricorn energy can present in great extremes. The goat is able to climb up a sheer face of the mountain, while fish dive deep to the bottom of the seas. We may view the symbol as representing both the heights and the depths of experience.

Now that we have graduated from our school of higher learning in Sagittarius, we move into the realm of profession. The key phrase for Capricorn is "I Use." Now we are able to put to use what we have learned. The triad of the Earth element takes the possessions of Taurus that are analyzed and cared for by Virgo and puts them to their best use in Capricorn.

Leadership is another attribute of this sign. A good leader delegates tasks that utilize people's skills and talents in the most effective ways. Through an organizational framework, one person may affect many. Consider the chain of command structure of the military, for example, in which a few words from one person at the top can move an entire army.

When we progress to this point in our spiritual development, it becomes very easy to control all the various systems of our body. There are many stories of yogi's, who have amazing control of their physiology, and are able to stop their own hearts in deep meditation. Some people have the ability to walk over hot coals. The fakir rises from his bed of nails with no puncture wounds or blood dripping from his flesh. Our body was not meant to control or limit us.

In the Northern Hemisphere, Capricorn begins winter, with the shortest day of the year. At the darkest time, many religions acknowledge the return of the light in celebrations such as Yule, Christmas, and Chanukah.

Mars is exalted in Capricorn because it makes the best "use" of the martial energy. The Tarot symbolically paints Capricorn as The Devil, equating it with the sign that falls during the time of year with the greatest darkness. It also taps Mars for the fires of hell. The concept of the devil is actually just a veil, for there is truly no such thing. The teaching is that the devil is God viewed through the eyes of the ignorant.

Capricorn, sign of the Father energy, complements Cancer, the sign of the Mother energy. We evolve from inside the womb of Cancer, to become a leader of the free world, in Capricorn. Many presidents and world leaders are born under the influence of this sign. As a womb, Cancer is also a cave in the mountain of Capricorn. Capricorn's color is indigo.

Aquarius

It would have seemed that Capricorn was the conclusion of the cycle. So, what's beyond perfect? Everything else.

The glyph for this sign is an old symbol for water and Aquarius is known as the "water-bearer," as imaged in the constellation. Aquarius is an energy that bears the waters of consciousness. The glyph is also reminiscent of a sign wave, which is apt, because Aquarius also rules electricity and vibration. Additionally, it rules the aura, part of our electrical or energetic body.

Aquarius is the sign of friends, groups and associations, among whom we can stand as equals. This energy is also expressed through altruism, so now the focus shifts away from "my, me and mine," and instead is directed toward others. We have cycled through the previous sign of system and use, where we acquired the tools to help the rest of humanity. President Roosevelt, who was an Aquarian, used the structure of government to create programs for the needy, during a time when government focused more effort toward helping the people.

Aquarius' key phrase is "I Know," and represents crystal clear thought. In Aquarius, we complete the trinity of Air. The many thoughts of Gemini, balanced by Libra, are now known in Aquarius.

In addition to crystal clear thought, Aquarius rules all crystals, and, more fundamentally, all crystalline structure. In Capricorn, we began the process of crystallization, in Aquarius it is complete. As these are the first two signs of winter, it is the time when rain turns to snow and ice, in the form of water crystals.

As elements become crystallized, like when coal is transformed into diamonds, many become transparent, so light may pass through them. As we take on our crystalline form in this age, we also allow the light to transmit through us.

The gemstones aligned with Aquarius are quartz and aquamarine. As we move more and more into the Aquarian Age, the as yet unknown properties of this stone will be revealed.

In the physical body, Aquarius aligns with the ankles. As the knees enable us to climb up or down, the ankles enable us to rotate left and right, which allows us to expand our horizons. The color associated with Aquarius is purple.

Leo, the opposite sign to Aquarius, is ruled by the Sun, which is a star. The Sun is in detriment in Aquarius, which rules groups, and is all the stars! The Leo Sun is associated with ego and individuality. When we look at all the stars, we see how they all work together as a group, where ego and individuality become less important. Yet, Aquarians appear to be some of the most individualistic people on the planet. True Aquarians care little about what anyone thinks of them, so they don't dress or act to fit in. Considering that every flake of snow is different, it's strange that so many of us are conditioned to conform. There are no planets in exaltation or fall in this sign.

The ruler of Aquarius is the planet Uranus. In the last age, Saturn also ruled Aquarius, which made sense, since Saturn is a planet of restriction, and therefore crystallization. With the discovery of Uranus, it was then designated ruler of Aquarius, because it more accurately represents the freedom and unorthodoxy associated with Aquarius. Uranus is uniquely different from the other planets in our solar system, in that its axis runs perpendicular to the Sun.

If we imagine we are lying on our back at Uranus' North Pole, and looking straight up, we would see, out in space, a bright star, which is our Sun. As the planet Uranus rotates on its axis, we would see all the stars and planets moving in circles around the Sun. As we, on Uranus, revolve around the Sun, it appears, from our perspective, that the Sun traces a spiral path, circling ever wider. If we speed up the journey, using time lapse, it makes it easier to see the apparent path of the Sun, which would leave a trail through space.

One year on Uranus is equivalent to one lifetime on Earth, approximately eighty-four years. The Solar spiral we are observing moves very fast, Uranus completes one rotation, or a day, every seventeen hours. Seventeen is also the number of The Star card in the Tarot, ruled by Uranus.

During our eighty-four-year flight, we will see the Sun's spiral continue to increase for twenty-one years until it is circling us around the horizon. Then, for the next forty-two years, it is nighttime on the North Pole, while the Sun apparently travels in the direction of the South Pole, eventually making its way back again to the equator. It is Uranus that is moving, however, so it is an optical illusion that the Sun appears to travel across the sky.

Finally, the Sun peaks over the horizon, as it spins 360 degrees around the equator. For the next twenty-one years its spiral diminishes, returning back to the center point above our heads, where we began. This continues until the Sun goes nova. What we end up with is a planet that flips its polarity back and forth every Uranian year. Uranus rules electricity and what we have just described is a representation of alternating current.

Now we can see why Aquarians are often viewed as so unusual. Though, from their viewpoint, we are the odd ones.

This planetary magnetic oscillation creates an alternating sexual being. This may be why the concept of gender is changing so rapidly in this Aquarian Age. In truth, we are neither male nor female. There is no sex in heaven. Sex, or union, assumes separation, and there is no separation in the non-physical realm.

Pisces

Pisces means fish. The glyph symbolizes two fish tied together, but attempting to swim in opposite directions, which may explain the indecisiveness associated with this sign. Pisces is also the ocean that contains the fish. Pisces isn't just one ocean like the Pacific or Indian, it represents all of them, which cover most of the Earth's surface. This Piscean ocean is everywhere, touching every coast of each landmass. Perhaps this explains Pisces' indecisiveness. If we're already everywhere, where could we possibly go?

Pisces also rules the Ocean of Cosmic Consciousness. It is a state within which all separateness dissolves, where we merge with the Infinite. As this is the last part of the cycle before the wheel turns again to Aries, we may compare it to the last thing we do during our daily cycle. We sleep and dream.

Pisces is also the sign of the collective unconscious. This is the Ocean of Consciousness that is our Source, as well as our goal. Is it not said that all life began in the sea? When we gaze at the night sky, we know all the stars are an expression of Aquarian energy. Now we also know the ocean of space the stars swim through is Pisces.

Pisces' polar opposite is Virgo, which takes everything apart, reducing it to its smallest component parts. In Pisces, we merge, putting the pieces back together. Virgo is mathematics, while Pisces is poetry.

In the physical body, Pisces rules the feet, which is a little cosmic joke, since fish have no feet. The feet support and carry the whole body around, reinforcing the idea of selflessness and sacrifice, associated with the sign Pisces. Sacrifice? What do we sacrifice? We give up our sense of separateness. The feet know they are not separate from the body, so sacrifice is a non-issue. Did Jesus make a sacrifice, when he died on the cross? Only if he believed he was separate from the rest of humanity.

The vibrational affinity with Pisces is violet, and its key phrase is, "I Believe." Belief is at the root of so-called "faith-based" religions. These are what some would call the "true believers." As we move out of the Piscean Age and into the Aquarian Age, we must leave our beliefs behind. We are transitioning from believing to knowing, in order to keep evolving through the zodiac.

The feet stand under us, and so they symbolize our understanding. Pisces is a sign of understanding, because it contains all the signs. They have all flowed into this cosmic ocean. We also gain a more complete understanding of reality, whenever we sacrifice our illusion of separateness.

Pisces is also the sign of the spiritual path. If we consider a path in a meadow or in a forest, it's clear nobody has taken out a path-making machine and cleared the way. Paths are created by the feet that walk them. The path depicted in The Moon card, aligned with the sign Pisces, represents the evolutionary path of our soul.

As we begin to practice the exercises in this volume, unlearn the untruths, and use the tools of intention and prayer, we are able to carve out a path for ourselves. As others begin to see the beneficial results of our evolutionary process, and, perhaps, follow our positive example, we will have then become a path-maker, a way-shower.

In the school of Christian initiation, Pisces is baptism, which is an initiation through which we may "walk a new path." We let go of past limitations, and we accept the cleansing, so we can begin anew.

Pisces, as mutable-water, is the final sign of the Water Trinity. Bursting forth from underground, the newborn spring wells up and begins to flow through the energy of Cancer. As the stream's flow increases, it grows to become the powerful, deep river of Scorpio. Finally, the water reaches the sea, merging with the All in Pisces. This image progression also symbolizes the individual soul merging back into the Oneness of God.

Pisces is the most receptive sign of the twelve. Humans have been depositing things into the ocean for centuries, ships, garbage, warheads, and more. The ocean accepts it all, whatever comes along. It is the epitome of total receptivity.

In Aquarius, we began our humanitarian work, as we moved into the realm of selfless service. Now, we finally go beyond our ego or false self and merge. With Pisces, the astrological year is ending. This last sign of winter is one of dissolution. The deck is cleared for nature to begin again in spring. As the sign of Cosmic-Consciousness, all twelve signs flow into Pisces, connecting all life.

TERRESTRIAL & CELESTIAL BODIES

Our bodies are an amalgamation of all twelve signs. Just as the energies of all the signs are expressed in the physical body, we, at our essence, are a fusion of all the signs. We are not merely a "piece of the pie." Our goal is to integrate all aspects of our being, and reunite with Self, the Source of all Creation, rather than getting too caught up in the creation itself.

A baby in the uterus curled in on itself in the fetal position, with the spine facing out, and the crown of the head facing down, illustrates the process of involution, Spirit coming into matter. The grown adult with spine curving in the opposite direction, the front of the body opening out into space, crown facing up, where the toes almost touch the head is superimposed on the zodiac.

Here each body part aligns with the sign that rules it. For example, the head aligns with Aries, Taurus aligns with the neck and shoulders, etc., all the way around to Pisces, which is opposite the feet. This is the representation of evolution, matter returning to Spirit. As we evolve, we turn ourselves inside-out, allowing the inner Divinity to manifest in the outer world.

The ancient Israelites were divided into twelve tribes, but they were all one people. Our focus of study is Holistic Astrology, as we are looking at the whole picture. If we had to watch a movie frame by frame, we would lose all sense of the film in its entirety, and it would make no sense. When we become a holy person, we are becoming a whole person.

Let us begin at the end with another story.

> *There was a group of Zen Monks arguing over a cat. They were fighting over in which end of the monastery the cat should sleep. The Abbot of the Monastery walked in on them and immediately grabbed the cat. He held a sword over the animal asking, "Can anyone say anything good about this cat?" The monks fell silent. The cat was slain.*
>
> *Later that day the cook came in and asked what had happened. The Abbot recounted the event to him. The cook immediately placed his sandals on top of his head and walked out. The Abbot called to him, "Too bad you weren't here earlier. You would have saved the cat!"*

Ponder this for a moment. What comes to mind?

Earlier in the chapter, we studied the circle of the zodiac, the cycle of the year. All cycles repeat. From the waters of Pisces arise the fires of Aries, as each year winter becomes spring again. Left to itself, the Earth will revolve around the Sun for millions of years more. The Moon will continue to circle our planet, affecting the tides as long as the oceans remain. The cycle of the year, moves us through the body from the head down to the feet and back again to the head. In reality, there is no end.

The cook was simply putting forth this idea, by placing his sandals on his head. He was demonstrating that the cycle is eternal, that there is no such thing as death. The head and the feet are connected in this eternal turning of the wheel. This awareness would have saved the cat, because in reality, there is no end, there is no death. When we know that the cat has eternal life, it becomes impossible to kill it. The form may change, but nothing is destroyed, consciousness is eternal. Once we can grasp the reality of this, we become greatly empowered.

ASTROLOGICAL MODIFIERS

How can we use astrology to modify our behavior to our benefit? Each sign of the zodiac has three basic modifiers, the following sign, the previous sign, and the opposite sign. Let's look at how this works more closely. We are not merely exploring our own sign; rather, we are investigating the energies of all the signs expressed in everyone.

Aries Modifications

We will begin with the first sign, Aries, the warrior, primal, red fire. We need power to begin any cycle. When that power turns into anger or rage, we now have energy expressions of this sign that can well be unproductive. These qualities lead to stress, which results in system burn-out.

When we find ourselves in an angry state, we may use any of three modifiers. The sign that follows Aries is **Taurus**, fixed-earth, solid ground, physicality. Leading-fire hits fixed-earth. We may use the grounding, physical Taurean energy, by punching a pillow, hitting our bed with it repeatedly, or screaming primally into it. To transmute the anger energy, we may also simply go for a vigorous walk, run, practice yoga, tai chi or qigong. Any form of physical activity will be a productive way to cleanse.

The second modifier is the previous sign, **Pisces**. In Pisces, we touch the universal, we access our compassion, and we sacrifice our sense of separation. We are able to let go of the anger, because, in the Cosmic view, it becomes meaningless. As we are the All in All, ultimately, we can only be angry with ourselves.

The third modifier is **Libra**, the opposite sign to Aries. In the "we are" realm of Libra, we consider the perspective of the other person with whom we are angry, we put ourselves in their shoes (Pisces). We understand that the angry energy we put out will ultimately return to us, since Libra rules karma.

Libra is symbolized by the scales, so this energy brings balance to our being. We cannot be angry, when we are in balance. The term "righteous anger" is often used by those trying to justify their actions. (righteous means "right use") You may ask, "What about when Jesus threw the money changers out of the Temple?" Jesus may have emitted a force that appeared to be anger, in that situation, but he was not personally angry. When he left the Temple, he left the incident behind him. It was in the past. When we are present in the moment, we remain free of any negative energy.

Sometimes a guru will yell at a beloved student, blasting them with energy, to help them let go of false patterns. It is an act of love, not anger.

Taurus Modifications

When Taurus, fixed-earth, is our starting point, this energy may manifest as stubbornly holding on to outmoded patterns of thought, emotion, or behavior. We might feel stuck or fixed in one place, unable to move forward, when patterns have become ingrained in our being.

What happens when we apply the following sign, **Gemini**, as a curative? Gemini is the sign of the conscious mind and thought, so first it is wise to "think" about the situation, to work it through in the mind. Additionally, Gemini governs communication and counseling, so it may help to "talk it out" with a trusted friend, mentor, or therapist. As we work in the realm of mind, it becomes easier to try out possible solutions in our head, to examine various actions we might take and then look at the possible results. This process opens the door to fresh ideas. When we don't allow our emotions to sway our vision, we operate through pure, non-judgmental mind.

We may also go back to the previous sign, **Aries**, and use the power of the will to release ourselves from the old, unproductive patterning. We may speak of "lighting a fire" under someone to get them going, but it may be wasted energy, because no one will change unless they desire it. The right use of our energy is to reignite or stoke the fire within our Heart to shift our own patterning.

No emotion, in and of itself, is negative. Anger is a force that can be a powerful catalyst for change. We can use that very anger we were previously trying to modify to alter our situation for the better. The anger energy motivates a change in our own consciousness that expresses as "I'm not going to take it anymore!" We transmute the stagnant energy that was previously binding us and we move on, free to be.

Scorpio is the opposite sign of Taurus. It may appear that sex is one of the greatest motivators in the world. If it were not, there would be no life on the planet. Sex is constantly used in advertising. It is everywhere. Scorpio rules desire. It motivates us to act. Again, if we don't desire change, it is impossible to effect it.

We have learned that Scorpio is a river. A river is always moving. If it is blocked, it flows around or over any obstructions. Learn to flow…or die. Scorpio rules death, one sure-fire way to get us un-stuck. Death works in one of two ways. Either we die or someone else dies. If we die, no problem, we automatically break free.

When someone else dies, it can cause us to take a look at our own life and what we have accomplished. Death may be a catalyst for us to take some impulsive action. We know a woman who married a man twice her age, impulsively, when her brother was killed. It was a short marriage, long enough to produce one male child, which she thought would rebalance the family. These are extreme experiences, as Scorpio is an extreme sign.

Gemini Modifications

Gemini's key phrase is "I think," which is a very useful tool, but it can also become a hindrance. We might find ourselves over-thinking, or getting *lost* in thought. We may live totally in our heads. Perhaps our communication habits have become unbalanced, driving our friends away with our constant chatter.

We can work on this energy imbalance through the next sign **Cancer**, the sign of feeling. As we begin to feel more, we think less. Cancer rules the Mother energy and the home. The mother feels or intuits the needs of her children. In a healthy mother-child relationship, much is communicated in silence.

We may also apply the previous sign **Taurus**, by practicing Zen meditation, or silent contemplation. Rock (Taurus) gardens (Venus) are used for this purpose. We focus on a stone, letting all thought fall away. The stillness of Taurus brings quiet to the mind. As Venus, ruler of Taurus, governs music, we may find listening to relaxing music can aid in quieting the mind.

Sitting across the astrological wheel is the opposite sign, **Sagittarius**, which is ruled by Jupiter, the largest planet in our solar system. As such, when we focus on the big picture, the tiny details (thoughts) can be put aside for a time.

Since Gemini is the twins, there are two types of thought, that which is produced through the lower or ego mind, and thought conceived in the Higher Mind. Gemini is our everyday thinking, the thoughts that most people have all the time. Sagittarius rules philosophical thought, which is transpersonal. When we engage in more expansive thought, we are dealing with universal ideas, looking at the principles underlying Creation. Philosophy derives from the Greek root, meaning "love of wisdom." Gemini is knowledge; Sagittarius is wisdom.

The difference, it is said, is that while knowledge informs us that a tomato is a fruit, wisdom tells us not to put tomato sauce on a bowl of ice cream.

Cancer Modifications

We continue, now, with the modification of Cancer energy. This is a sign that rules the heights and depths of emotion. There are many who experience depression, an unproductive Cancerian energy. When we find ourselves experiencing symptoms of depression, we can progress the energy to **Leo**, the next sign.

The key here is to remember our true nature. When we are enmeshed in depression, or any other unproductive emotional state, we can get so caught up in the experience that we forget who we really are. We identify ourselves as the "state" of being, rather than realizing that we are Life, or "being," that is presently qualified by a particular emotional state. We can say, "I am depressed," or we can realize that we are currently experiencing symptoms of depression. Only when this is clear, are we able to take action and change our circumstances.

Leo is ruled by the Sun, so another treatment for depression is light therapy. Everything seems brighter when the Sun is shining, and this offers a clue to the effectiveness of light to alleviate such conditions as Seasonal Affective Disorder, SAD.

The stomach is ruled by Cancer; as such, it is where one's experience of depression may be centered or felt most readily. That is why so many overeat or stop eating altogether, when they are depressed.

Cancer is a receptive sign, so when we are depressed, typically our focus is turned inwardly. As we move to the energy of Leo, we center ourselves in the Heart. We activate the Sun within, which ignites Self-Love. We recognize that we are Love and begin to send that energy out to others. Now we have changed the polarity of the unproductive energy expression. When we love our Self, we are able to love those around us. Centered in Self, the highest aspect of our being, and focusing our attention on others, we are less likely to remain depressed.

Explore the *Transmutation of Energy Exercise*, below, which can assist in the transmutation of energy.

> **Transmutation of Energy Exercise**
>
> When we feel any sort of unproductive energy expression in the stomach region, or any other area of the body, we place our hands over it. Slowly, we pull the stagnant energy up to the heart center on an inhalation, and then anchor it there with our exhalation. This may be repeated for as long as it takes to sense a shift in the quality of the energy. Love will dissolve all the unproductive energy. Loving our enemies also applies to "inner" enemies.

We may also return to **Gemini** to work on our feelings. As Gemini rules communication, we find that talking through a problem helps significantly. We get depressed, because we push things down deep inside. What we do not express becomes depressed.

When we have an issue with a family member, it's easy to let things "stew" until later. Because they are part of the family, we know we will see them many more times. There is no urgency to resolve the conflict. When we finally sit down with them and communicate how we feel, the depression is lessened. There may be anger, but we now know how to transform that.

A depression in the ground creates a place where water may gather after a rain. Our own depressions can also hold emotions. Water left to stand becomes stagnant and toxic. Emotions are energy-in-motion. We must allow the energy to move, in order to remain in balance.

The opposite sign from Cancer is **Capricorn**. When we create a structure or discipline to follow, there is no space for the depression to exist. If our day is structured, we can only experience what we allow into that structure. This principle is used in addiction recovery. Participants in Alcoholics Anonymous create a repeatable daily structure, living "one day at a time."

Capricorn also rules maturity, so as we become more emotionally mature, our depression will occur less frequently.

Leo Modifications

Leo is ruled by the Sun, a bright star in the center of our solar system. It also represents a bright focal point in ourselves, the Heart. We want to allow this inner Sun, or Heart Light, to radiate light and love to all around us, regardless of their nature. The Sun does not choose a select few planets on which to shine its light, yet we tend to narrowly choose who we love, based on family ties and personal preferences. Problems arise due to our mis-alignment with the Sun energy within us, which, esoterically, is the Sun/Son of God, the Christos. Personal preferences arise out of ego mind, the great center of imbalance in the world. Here we refer to the false-ego, that with which most people identify.

How do we modify the ego? The natural movement is toward the next sign, **Virgo**. Here, we have the energy expression of purity, diet, and service. Virgo is the sign associated with nuns and monks, generally not known for having outsized egos. By purifying the false-ego, we find the true Ego, the individualized expression of God within us. The ego creates an awareness of our self-identity, a sense of separateness and limitation. Will we identify with the thoughts, emotions, memories and flesh associated with the four lower bodies, or the limitless, divine spark within?

Virgo gives us the path of selfless service, expressed through helping and healing. When all our energy is directed toward those around us, we stop feeding the ego. As the energy moves out from our center, our light expands and grows. In the last age of Pisces, Virgo, its opposite sign, was the path to God.

How does diet relate to the ego? We look again at personal preference. When we change our diet, we may need to give up foods we love. If we are trying to lose weight, we eat less sugar and fat, main ingredients in so many yummy but nutrient and Life Force void foods. Maybe we are moving toward a vegetarian or vegan diet. Purifying the physical body creates a more balanced inner environment, a clearer channel, through which the divine Life Force may operate. False-ego does not like being told what to do. It doesn't like change. It doesn't like discipline.

We can modify Leo through the energy of the previous sign, **Cancer**. Leo is the sign of children, and Cancer is the sign of the mother. Who's in charge? Will the children run about, doing whatever they want, or does the compassionate, nurturing mother hold the reins? In this day and age, father may take on the role of mother. The energy has more to do with the role of nurturer, not the gender. We are all mothers of the false-ego, as we each have created our own. They are not inborn.

Cancer is a sensitive, emotional sign. True Ego is sensitive to others, aware of its own connection to all Life. People on "ego-trips" are focused on themselves and are insensitive to others. We cannot modify the ego by thinking about the ego, which only feeds it. Be a Mother to all.

Leo's opposite sign is **Aquarius**. As Leo represents a star, (from movie star to celestial star) Aquarius represents all the stars, the group consciousness. Ego does not fare so well in this environment. To work well within a group, we must leave the ego at the door. We must be willing to loosen our hold on our individually.

Aquarius rules the internet, a connected group of individuals. Through this medium, many transcend their physical attributes, as it doesn't matter what one looks like. Our age, race, gender, weight, and such, are irrelevant. Our consciousness becomes our face. There are places on the internet where false ego thrives. Yet, combining knowledge from many sources is the Aquarian ideal. Group consciousness outweighs individual consciousness, in this instance.

When the planetary ruler of a sign transits (passes through) its opposite sign, it is far from home and weak in influence. Astrologically it is called detriment. Here the Sun, ruler of Leo is in detriment while passing through Aquarius. We can see around us that the Sun is much more powerful in the middle of the summer (Leo) than the middle of winter (Aquarius).

Virgo Modifications

We have said that Virgo rules work, diet and health. We can get out of balance, when we become a workaholic. We believe that the more we do, work, and accomplish, the better off we are. We forget about moderation, some Yin to balance the Yang. If we stopped sleeping so we could get more done, we would wind up dead. Our physical body, as with all things, runs on a cycle. Our body needs an "off" time, it needs sleep. Still, many are not actually "off" when they are asleep and wake exhausted. Cultivating waking down-time, moments of stillness and contemplation or meditation, is just as essential as sleep. Even our soul requires an "off time" for growth. On this side we call it death, on the other side it is birth.

The workaholic Virgo might share the burden of activities or responsibilities with a mate or partner. One must, however, be willing to ask for help. This choice is in alignment with the next sign, **Libra**, a means to balance out the workload. Virgo energy can create a cleaning fanatic or germaphobe, resulting in a spotless but unlivable home, a "Don't touch anything!" energy pervades the house. Out of consideration for the others living with them, they must be able to let some things go. The other person's needs and feelings become more important than one's own compulsiveness.

We know overwork can run down our immune system. On the other hand, inactivity can also lead to stagnation and illness. Again, balance, found in the next sign, Libra, is the answer to bringing Virgo, the sign ruling health, into alignment.

One may take a break from the work life, by moving back into the fun of **Leo**, the previous sign, and create a balance between work and play. Leo rules children, masters of play, who make it nearly impossible to keep everything in its proper place. Leo also rules love, which warms up the cool, mental world of Virgo.

The Sun rules Leo, and we find it easier to clean a room, when the light is on. It's easier to cleanse our mind of limiting patterns, when the Light of Truth is shined into it. This is the work of the teacher or guru, who is able to see our limiting blocks and can help to remove them. We do not recommend taking advice from those who dwell in the darkness of depression or negative attitudes.

The opposite sign, **Pisces**, gives universal vision, affording us the understanding that those little cleaning details may be unneeded. We, again, can see the forest rather than focusing on the trees. Pisces puts back together what Virgo has separated out. All the signs flow into Pisces, the sea. Einstein was born during Pisces and was able to grasp the whole picture of energy and matter.

As a mystical sign, associated with sleep and the collective unconscious, it creates a space where Virgo can rest and relax. We are modifying the left-brain energies of Virgo with the right brain energies of Pisces.

Every energy we experience has a modifying energy; though, actually, there are no real opposites, only a polarization of the same energy. These opposite signs create the six great polarities. True modification comes by finding the mean, the center point of these opposing forces. For example, Capricorn, traditionally represents the Father, while Cancer is the Mother. "Parent" is a particular focus of energy, while "Father" and "Mother" express the polarity.

In a functional marriage or partnership, each modifies the other, ideally by eliciting the partner's productive qualities to come forth from within the individual. This greater balance may then manifest in any children a couple may choose to parent.

Now it's your turn to explore modifying the remaining signs, using the prompts on the following page. With the given clues, identify attributes for the last six signs, which may need adjustment, and then work through them using the other three modifying signs. When we are told the answers, we acquire knowledge. When we are given the opportunity to figure out how it works, we gain understanding.

> **Astrological Modifiers, cont'd**
>
> **Libra Modifications:** Sign of balance, marriage and partnership.
> Following Sign Scorpio: sex, death, transformation, partner's resources.
> Previous Sign Virgo: health, work, and diet.
> Opposite Sign Aries: "I Am," self-identity, vision, new beginnings.
>
> **Scorpio Modifications:** Sign of sex, death and transformation.
> Following Sign Sagittarius: resurrection, religion, philosophy.
> (Some religions encourage one to raise the vibration of the sexual energy)
> Previous Sign Libra: marriage and partnership, collaboration, karma.
> Opposite Sign Taurus: possessions, values and the inner word.
>
> **Sagittarius Modifications:** Sign of higher mind, optimism, beliefs, over-expansion.
> Following Sign Capricorn: systems, structure, discipline.
> Previous Sign Scorpio: degeneration, generation, regeneration, inward focus, occult.
> Opposite Sign Gemini: conscious mind, communication, siblings.
>
> **Capricorn Modifications:** Sign of limitation and bondage.
> Following Sign Aquarius: group focuses, interconnectivity, altruism.
> Previous Sign Sagittarius: optimism, expansion, philosophy, travel.
> Opposite Sign Cancer: home, family, compassion, feeling.
>
> **Aquarius Modifications:** Sign of groups, causes, friends, aims and goals.
> Following Sign Pisces: leadership, discipline, patience, right use of energy.
> Previous Sign Capricorn: compassion, softening, dissolution of all forms.
> Opposite Sign Leo: heart energy of Love, creativity, self-expression.
>
> **Pisces Modifications:** Sign of the collective unconscious, self-sacrifice, faith, belief.
> Following Sign Aries: initiating energy, action, new beginnings.
> Previous Sign Aquarius: knowing, emotional detachment, disrupting the status quo.
> Opposite sign Virgo: analysis, service, health, work.

In subsequent works, we will look at how this technique can be used to help progress a person. For now, the keys to the evolution of our soul in this lifetime are found in the sign opposite our Sun sign. As we discover the qualities of the sign of our opposite polarity, we can begin to incorporate them into our life. This is spiritual stretching. In order to become who we really are, we must access and integrate that which we think we are not.

ASTROLOGICAL HOUSES

Throughout the course of a life, we enter many houses. When we walk into someone's home, we enter into their energy. Every house feels different to one degree or another. Each has a different layout, unique furniture, colors, even a distinct smell. Most of us grow up living in only one house, then we move out, and, at some point, occupy a home of our own. We make it our own.

Even a dorm room's energy will reflect the student's energy signature. Each adds their own flair of individuality amongst the institutional furniture. We feel differently when we are in a noisy or a quiet house. A clean and neat house has a different feel than one in which chaos reigns. We learn to conform to the general rules of each house in which we live or visit, such as removing our shoes when we enter.

Around the world there are many different customs, languages, atmospheres. We can look at astrological houses in the same way. Planets act differently, depending on which house they occupy.

The signs move around the Earth every twenty-four hours. The Sun moves through the signs every 365 days. The houses never move, but they do expand and contract, based on their degree of latitude. The farther the location from the equator, the greater the distortion becomes. At the equator, day and night are always twelve hours long. Around the North and South Poles we experience midnight Sun, at which time the Sun never sets for months at a time. Six months later it remains below the horizon. This phenomenon illustrates the distortion of which we speak.

In an astrological chart, the sign ruling a house is located on the cusp at the entrance of that particular house. Most houses contain two or three signs, which affect the energy of the house. Some signs may rule over more than one house, if the chart contains an interception, where two signs do not fall on any cusp on the chart. In this case, two other signs take on greater influence, because they each fall on the cusps of an additional house.

There are twelve houses, each corresponding to one of the twelve signs. They occupy areas of the sky, above and below the Earth. The first house always begins at the eastern horizon and moves down the circle in a counter-clockwise direction. The opposite house, the seventh, is always on and just above the western horizon. When we see a beautiful sunset, we are looking through the seventh house. The seventh sign, Libra, at home in the seventh house, is ruled by Venus, the planetary energy that governs beauty and art.

Houses one, two and three begin in the East at the horizon and move counter clock-wise up through the lower right quadrant of the wheel to the western horizon, where we travel through four, five and six. Houses seven through twelve continue around the top half of the circle, returning to the eastern horizon.

When we know our time of birth, it's easy to figure out in which house our Sun resides. Between 6:00 and 8:00 am, the Sun is in the twelfth house. If we were born between 8:00 and 10:00 am, we would find the Sun in the eleventh house. Then the Sun moves across the tenth house to the top of the chart, arriving at noon. To figure out where any of the other planets are, we need to have our birth chart erected. The houses represent times, and areas of focus, through which energy is activated in our life.

As an example, Virgo, the sixth sign of health, corresponds to the sixth house of the chart. This area will give us information regarding our health. If we found Jupiter in that house, we might focus on the liver (ruled by Jupiter), and look at the sign it's in, as well as Jupiter's relationship with the other planets. Positively, as Jupiter is a planet of healing, it could indicate an ability to heal others.

The Sun sign represents how we, fundamentally, see and experience our self. By contrast, the rising sign indicates how others see us. In Hindu Astrology, the sign on the eastern horizon, the rising sign, has the greatest significance in the chart. It is said that this is where our Spirit touches matter, in this the first house. We find clues for understanding in the first sign, Aries. In the yearly cycle, Aries brings spring, while in the daily house cycle it is sunrise.

First House: Home of Aries, ruled by Mars

Let's tour the neighborhood. The first house we approach has a big, red door. As we enter, we notice there is a lot of activity. In fact, they're working on the house right now. Saws, hammers, and drills indicate a project is underway. The house is very warm and dry. As we survey the scene, we notice some architectural drawings being used in the new construction. In the corner we can see a surveyors' pole and a pair of binoculars.

Second House: Home of Taurus, ruled by Venus

The second house we visit is in a swanky neighborhood. The lawn outside is immaculate. As we enter there is a thick, plush, green carpet and art on all the walls. Rather than the din of saws and hammers, we hear wonderful classical music playing. There are many treasures to behold, as in a museum. The house is a little cooler and a bit more humid than the first but feels very stable and well grounded.

Third House: Home of Gemini, ruled by Mercury

Now we'll investigate the house next-door. It's nice and bright, we can feel air circulating throughout the house. We see a TV, a number of smart phones, and other communication devices strewn about. The house is filled with many books. We see a pile of newspapers stacked in the corner. Walking around, off a long hallway, there are many children's bedrooms, where the siblings and neighbor children are at play. Some of the children are engaged with the various media, while others play educational games.

Fourth House: Home of Cancer, ruled by the Moon

As we enter the fourth house, wonderful smells and aromas from the kitchen stimulate our appetite. There is a big family kitchen, where the mom is cooking dinner. We sense the energy of emotions pervading the space. We discover there is even a safe room within the house. There is a large family room with a bowl of fruit on a table, and a terrarium housing a family of turtles.

Fifth House: Home of Leo, ruled by the Sun

The fifth house we visit has been converted into a daycare center. There are dozens of children playing with toys or reading. The children are rehearsing a play, which they will present later. We feel uplifted. The happy children make us smile. There is a yellow glow coming from the fireplace in the next room.

Sixth House: Home of Virgo, ruled by Mercury

The sixth house is cool and exceptionally clean and sterile. The decor is mostly black and white. A doctor lives here, who also has an office suite attached, for their practice. They employ a nurse, a nun, who lives nearby. This house also contains many books about diet and health. There is a child in another room focused on some math homework.

Seventh House: Home of Libra, ruled by Venus

The seventh house is inhabited by newlyweds. In the front yard, there is a beautiful garden filled with colorful flowers. The interior walls are covered with artwork. There is a wonderful feeling of partnership in this house. A large picture-window facing west frames a magnificent sunset. A freshly baked kidney pie cools on the kitchen counter.

Eighth House: Home of Scorpio, ruled by Pluto

The eighth house we visit has a black wreath on the front door. Inside the family is mourning for a deceased loved one. The energy is very intense. All the lights in the house are turned off and the mirrors are covered. Looking out the back window, in the yard, we see two teenagers locked in passionate embrace. Given a tour of the house, we discover there are a number of hidden rooms, which makes the house much larger than it appears. There are many pictures depicting saints, decorating the walls, and an egg made of the stone serpentine is displayed on a table.

Ninth House: Home of Sagittarius, ruled by Jupiter

The ninth house is quite a distance away and takes a while to get to. It sits on a very large, heavily wooded property. There is a field with a horse running free. When we arrive, we see many people preparing for a festival. They were gathering fruits and vegetables from the garden and bringing them into the house. The atmosphere is very jovial. Everyone is laughing and enjoying themselves. As we explore, we find many college degrees displayed, and a case full of athletic trophies.

Tenth House: Home of Capricorn, ruled by Saturn

The tenth house is a stately manor and we must wait to be buzzed in the front gate. We see a lofty spire on the top floor that seems to reach the sky. We walk up a steep stone stairway to the door, and are ushered in by the butler, who proceeds to show us around. The house is very old but orderly. Many rooms are hidden behind closed doors. The walls are covered with pictures of politicians and business men.

Eleventh House: Home of Aquarius, ruled by Uranus

The eleventh house is a very unusual, modern place. It is evening when we approach, and the house is awash in light. The trees are filled with tiny spot lights bringing brilliance to the night. The interior is decorated with modern art. There is a community meeting going on in the living room, where a lot of people, who seem to know each other, are getting along quite well. They all communicate verbally, and simultaneously send each other texts and emails.

Twelfth House: Home of Pisces, ruled by Neptune

The twelfth house is the oldest on the block. It is dark, damp, and a bit dusty. It is filled with ancient artifacts and looks like a museum. Many generations have lived here. As we walk the property, we notice a koi pond, and stop to watch the fish. When we return to the house, we become strangely tired, affected by the heaviness in the air.

The soul chooses to inhabit a physical form for a period of time, for the purpose of evolving through experience. The houses in which planets are placed indicate areas of our life where we have activated energies to support us in our evolutionary process, or that require our focus and balancing in this lifetime. We can see in which realms our karmic merit or gifts and talents are manifesting, and those where harmonizing is required, so we may transcend our karmic debt or limitations.

Don't be confused. Although we just associated the houses with their native signs to show their natures, the signs continually move around the circle. Each sign can be on the cusp of any house, depending on the time of day. Our rising sign is always that which is ascending on the eastern horizon, the first house, at the time of our birth.

Remember, the astrological chart shows us more of who we are truly not, than who we really are! We are not the person hearing or reading this. That's just who we think we are. The greater part of who we are is non-physical.

The text box below contains a select list of key words associated with each of the astrological houses.

Houses: Select Key Words

First House: Physical appearance & body, vitality, how we express and strive for significance in the world, how others see us, our, how we see the world.

Second House: Values, possessions, resources, earned income, finances.

Third House: The conscious mind, communication & media, speaking & writing, early life & education, immediate environment, neighbors, siblings.

Fourth House: Home, land & family goods, family, parent who primarily nurtures family, psychological foundations & early patterning, emotional security, end of life conditions.

Fifth House: Creative energy expression, children, love affairs, risk taking, gambling, sports, recreation.

Sixth House: Work life, co-workers & employees, school, health, service, self-improvement, small animals & pets.

Seventh House: Marriage, partnership, one on one relationships, dealings with the public, legal issues, open adversaries.

Eighth House: Sexuality, death, transformation, hidden issues, inheritance, other people's money, debt.

Ninth House: Higher mind, higher education, publishing, philosophy, views & beliefs, spiritual growth, expansion, long distance travel, in-laws.

Tenth House: Profession, ambition & prestige, public standing & reputation, community relations, dominant parent, or one who has more dealings outside of home, authority figures.

Eleventh House: Friends, associates, groups, organizations, humanitarian causes, goals, aspirations, unexpected circumstances.

Twelfth House: Past lives, subconscious mind, collective unconscious, older karma, hidden adversaries, confinement, solitude, the divine and higher realms.

ASTROLOGICAL ASPECTS

We hear stories of con men who are always trying to "work the angle" on a situation. Astrological aspects show the various angles formed between planets in relationship to one another, when viewed from Earth. There is also a cosmic correlation between God's angels and God's angles.

We illustrate aspects on a chart using various straight lines that connect the planets. We use the following glyphs to identify these angles.

Conjunctions

A conjunction occurs when two planets appear to be in the same place on the wheel. Their energies blend creating a new energy. Sometimes there are many planets apparently close, when three or more planetary energies blend, it is termed a *stellium*. When a planet is very tightly conjunct the Sun, it is called "combust." If Venus, for example, appears next to the Sun, and we wanted to look at it, it would become invisible due to the Sun's brightness. So, the Sun's influence would obscure those Venusian aspects in our life.

The symbol is the circle of the zodiac with a line pointing to the eighth house, the house of Scorpio. The act of sex always requires a conjunction.

Oppositions

An opposition is a 180-degree angle, one half the 360 degrees in the zodiacal circle. To explain the energy of an opposition, imagine two planets are on opposite sides of the Earth, both sending us information simultaneously. Imagine two people trying to get our attention while we stand between them. The opposition can produce tension, which can be useful too, if we are stringing a clothesline. There has to be pull from both directions or the line goes slack.

When we are dealing with opposite energies, or with people on each side, an energy line is created. We can only resolve seeming opposites by experiencing the actual oneness that contains the polarity. Hot and cold may be opposites, when each is experienced separately, but when we look at the bigger picture, we see temperature manifesting at differing degrees.

How the energies manifest depends on which planets are in opposition, and how strong or weak they are. Planets are strong in their home sign and sign of exaltation. They are strongest when in angular houses (house one, four, seven, and ten). We also want to consider what areas of our life are symbolically opposed. (individuality/partnership; values/desires; conscious mind/ superconscious mind, etc.)

Trines

If we take the three people out of opposition and place them at the points of an equilateral triangle, a have a more functional arrangement. Each of them can see the other two at the same time. Energy can flow more easily among them. This aspect is called a trine and is created when planets are 120 degrees from one another. In the wheel of the zodiac, all the signs of each element trine one another. Aries (fire) trines Leo (fire) and Sagittarius (fire), for example.

We might think that the trine is better than the opposition because there is less tension, but this isn't always the case. If things flow too easily, we may take them for granted or squander opportunity. It could be that the tension of the opposition is so difficult that it prompts us to act. This may be the very thing we need. We get to choose how we work with these various expressions of energy.

Squares

A square is a 90-degree angle, half the angle of the opposition. Traditionally, squares indicate where the lessons of this life are to be experienced. It can be difficult to "turn the corner" on a problem. Imagine walking; we can see what's ahead, we know where we have just been, but when we turn a corner, we must reorient ourselves. Energy in a square can get hung up in corners. It can become more challenging to make right use of the energy.

As discussed earlier in the chapter, each element has a triune nature. The fire signs are Aries, Leo, and Sagittarius. Earth signs are Taurus, Virgo, and Capricorn. Water manifests through Cancer, Scorpio, and Pisces, while the air signs are Gemini, Libra, and Aquarius.

Each mode (cardinal, fixed, mutable) covers four signs that may manifest as squares in a chart. The initiating energies of the cardinal signs begin the seasons as Aries, Cancer, Libra, and Capricorn. The fixed signs, Taurus, Leo, Scorpio and Aquarius, occur during the middle of each season, sustaining or fixing the energy to hold everything together. The mutable signs, Gemini, Virgo, Sagittarius, and Pisces, end each season. They allow for the dissolution of their season's energy that it may be reborn anew. The cycle is unceasing.

We have seen charts with a grand cross, which contains four planets all squaring and opposing each other. In each case, the person felt as though they were boxed in and opposed at every turn, and were thus motivated to undergo a complete transformation. We have also read charts for people who had no squares or opposition; they were very unmotivated to do anything.

Semi-Squares

The previous aspects are known as the major aspects, implying there are also minor aspects. We have seen that half an opposition (180 degrees) is a square (90 degrees). Now, half a square (45 degrees) is called a semi-square. Its tension is not as great, but neither is its harmony.

Sextiles

Half of a trine (120 degrees) is called a sextile and is an angle of 60 degrees. Like the trine, it indicates a good flow of energy between the planets involved. Every sign is sextile to the second sign away on either side.

Aries will sextile Gemini and Aquarius. Taurus will sextile Cancer and Pisces. Gemini has a sextile with Leo and Aries. Fire signs sextile Air signs. Water signs sextile Earth signs. Air signs sextile Fire signs. Earth signs sextile Water signs.

Semi-Sextiles

Half a sextile is a semi-sextile, showing an angle of 30 degrees. Every sign is semi-sextile to the signs before and after it. This aspect can indicate opportunities that go unnoticed.

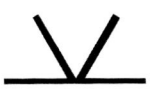

PUTTING IT ALL TOGETHER

The Cosmic Theatre

Commenting on the cosmic drama of life, Shakespeare said, "All the world's a stage, and all the men and women merely players." The houses are the various sets within which the play takes place. The signs are the various colored gels that qualify the lights, creating the mood in which the play is viewed. The planets are the actors playing specific characters, while the aspects are the relationships the characters form with each other.

Time & Space

Astrology is the science of time and space, and this is all we need to construct a chart. They distinguish the difference between one person's life and another. We are each just slices of the same cosmic spiral; we are all parts of the same whole.

Time for Relationships

Everything in astrology is about relationship, the relationship between one time and another time. It's the relationship between the space/time continuum of our birth and the same continuum of the present.

When we celebrate our birthday, we are celebrating the relationship between our date of birth and the day on the calendar. However, there was another relationship yesterday and there will be yet another one tomorrow. These relationships, such as birthdays, are celebrating the cycle of the Earth's return to the place it was at birth, in relationship to the Sun. In reality, it is never in the same place, as the Sun is continually moving through space, which creates a spiral orbit with all the planets. The Sun revolves around the great wheel of our galaxy, which is also moving. Wheels within wheels.

We too experience the different cycles of all the other planets. We are, however, usually not aware of them. We can use the science of astrology to become aware.

Astrology is not our only resource. We can get along fine without it. We may, however, develop our awareness to the point where all these cycles operate intuitively. We become aware of all the cycles of time, because we are the cycles of time. It's all going on within us.

The Birth Chart

What is a birth-chart anyway? The natal or birth chart is a symbolic picture of our soul's focus for this lifetime. It reveals potentialities, based on the electro-magnetic vibration template of the planetary energies at the time of birth. Does this sound like a limitation? It is no more limiting than our genes or DNA.

The chart doesn't make us who we are, it just shows us who we are, or the nature of our soul consciousness, at the time of our birth. It shows potential, the talents and productive patterns that are available to us in this life, as well as the obstacles and pitfalls we might experience, as a result of patterns of restriction we are manifesting. Additionally, it reveals how they are likely to play out, should we do nothing to shift the course. In this regard, it focuses our awareness on the lessons we have incarnated to learn.

The birth chart can indicate we have chosen a life in which we actively live out a new cycle of growth, one of sustaining what already exists, or one in which we gather and prepare for new soul evolution. We can get a sense of our potentialities for work and career by examining our natal chart. We may begin to discern the relationships we draw to ourselves and how they are serving our growth and soul evolution.

Each of us has the capacity to ignite the beneficial energies, and to transmute those that are not aligned with our greater good. The chart serves as a useful tool that shows guide posts and stumbling blocks that can further us along or block our soul's progression. The chart becomes a "treasure map" that offers clues to help us discover life's riches that lie dormant beneath the surface, just waiting to be unearthed and put to beneficial use.

These levels of awareness are not exclusively astrological. Anyone with perfected sight may access them. Our inner guidance will always offer the best advice we can receive. It's more productive to spend time developing our inner abilities than to spend years trying to master astrology. This is the fourth lifetime David has consciously been using astrology to aid in counseling others.

We rarely look at our own charts. If anything, we'll use them to look back at an event that has taken place, to gain more insight into the workings of creation. We never try to predict anything for ourselves. We'd rather be surprised. Well, actually, we would rather be the surprise. We already know the ending, it has already happened.

CHAPTER 5

Meditation

MEDITATION IS NOT WHAT YOU THINK

We are born into a world of constant activity, continually bombarded with bits of information. Consumerism demands our attention. Endless messages pour into our subconscious. We become lost in the maze of society. We become distracted and forget what is here, focusing on what is there. We are conditioned to believe happiness is gained by external means and buying certain products will bring us that happiness. We forget who we are. We forget why we are here. All we focus on are thoughts and feelings.

Our mind's activity is often overlooked, because of its constancy; that is, it's always there. When David was a child, he had a grandfather clock that stood in the hall of his home. As the large pendulum swung back and forth, it loudly ticked off the seconds, sending its rhythmic pattern through the house. He heard it constantly, in the background, whenever he was home.

One day he noticed something odd. He had been inside the whole day and could not hear the clock's tick tock. It was working fine, but he couldn't detect the sound. He walked up to it, trying to hear the tick tock, but only perceived silence.

There was nothing wrong with his hearing, he could discern other sounds around him. He figured that his brain had somehow canceled out the sound, ignoring it because of its repetitiveness. He thought, knowing that, he should be able to hear it. He couldn't. He tried for ten or fifteen minutes, and eventually gave up.

The next day after he came home from school, he heard the clock again. Then he tried to make the noise disappear, again with no results. He had just come inside from a different environment, a different world of sound, so he could easily perceive the clock.

In the same way, we are not aware of the activity of our mind until we can experience a different state of consciousness. This is what meditation offers us. Philosopher Alan Watts said, "Our minds participate in a compulsive repetition of words, calculations, and symbols." We lose ourselves in the forest of thought. We live, as the fish, unable to see the water. Our same ever-present mental chatter even begins to seem normal. Meditation can create a bridge over the river of thought.

SILENCE

Create space in your schedule for this spiritual experiment. Make a practice of complete silence. If we can maintain it for a day, our awareness will begin to blossom. The first thing we notice is how much energy we put into thinking about what we are going to say. Some of us even practice conversations over and over in our minds, before we speak with someone.

We see this replayed over and over on TV, or in movies. We may see a nervous kid or adult, going over and over what they will say, before calling someone for a date, speaking with the boss, or preparing for a confrontation. We all do this on a lessor scale all the time. We become aware of it during silence. Quieting the incessant, internal monologue is the first step in quieting the mind.

We can do another exercise in self-discipline: simply refrain from using certain words. For example, stop swearing, completely. Don't curse, even if you stub your toe, or fall off a cliff. This may take some effort to master.

In the early 1900s, novices in the order of the Silver Star, founded by the English occultist, Aleister Crowley, were forbidden to use the word "I." Whenever they said it, they would have to cut their arm with a razor blade. The consequence was clearly extreme, but these people were taking the exercise very seriously.

These next few stories illustrate the power of silence.

Silence - 1965

Silence. We rarely think about it. We rarely practice it. Is there nothing we're missing? Have we missed our fill of emptiness?

David's first experience with silence was in 1965. He was working on quieting his mind. Here he recounts this experience in detail.

> *Growing up, my mind was extremely noisy. I thought so much I seldom fell asleep before 3am, even as a young child. I thought about everything, over and over, each time exploring deeper levels of information.*

I would continually over-think things. It was as though I had a number of talk-radio stations playing all at once. (Perhaps this was the seed of my habit, many years later, of playing numerous records simultaneously, when I was a disk jockey in San Diego.) My mind was overflowing with thoughts.

After graduating high school, I moved into a spiritual community. Most people called it a hippie-house, but I didn't. Among many things, I practiced yoga and tried to learn to meditate. I only realized how noisy my mind was, when I tried to quiet it.

We learned mantric meditation. Mantras are words repeated over and over. The words, of any language, can be chanted aloud or repeated silently within. We chanted in Sanskrit.

In spiritual work, new and unfamiliar words are often used to eliminate attachment to old meanings and concepts, which only incur more thought. The first mantra I ever received had no meaning at all that I could discern.

For fifteen minutes each day, I quietly sat with my eyes closed, repeating this meaningless sound over and over, day after day, after day.

Here are a few things to consider. Firstly, there was the repetition of my daily practice. As I sat in the same place at the same time each day, a pattern formed. A little discipline entered my life. My mind began to budge a little from its usual mode of incessant chatter. The mind would, not so willingly at first, give me fifteen minutes, knowing it had 23 hours and 45 minutes to do as it pleased.

This was challenging for me and took months to show any result. I did this work 50+ years ago. Since then, the energy on the Earth has been evolving and rapidly raising in vibration. As such, results are typically much quicker today.

Another thing operating was intent. I intended to meditate. Practicing every day showed my subconscious mind I was serious. It became inclined to aid me. It became a natural event and part of my makeup. The duration of my meditations increased, as my rebellious mind and body relaxed. (There's nothing more disruptive to calmness than a lot of bodily sensations.)

I then reached a small plateau. There are times in meditation it appears we are making great strides, and others when nothing at all seems to be happening. (I use the words "appears" and "seems" because in reality, these states of growth are always present; it is the removal of our limitations that reveal them.) In other words, our mind is naturally clear, it's our attachment to thought that keep us from experiencing clarity. Our consciousness is naturally whole. It is the thoughts that divide it up. We strive for alignment with the One-Mind, whole and complete.

My meditations expanded, though still at a basic level. As my adventures continued, I found myself on the "other side," California, that is; I grew up on Long Island. My spiritual striving became more focused, as all else became more peripheral. I had "dropped out" of the civilized world. There was less and less to think about.

My meditations grew deeper still. I began using a different mantra, Om. My first contact with the word Om was in high school, reading "Siddhartha," by Herman Hesse. I had no idea what it meant, though it planted a seed.

Later, I learned Om is a Sanskrit word, which means the Omnipresent and Omnipotent Source of all unmanifest and manifest existence. It is Light. The vibration of the word is the sound of Light. It is the word spoken by God in the creation stories. It is the sound of the universe, the "background noise" scientists have detected, the resounding mmm.

I began chanting Om silently, not just for a few minutes, but all the time. I inevitably fell into thought a lot at first, but I kept working at it. Before long, I found myself talking less, as I became progressively emptier and clearer. Thoughts would come, I would acknowledge them, then they would go. All that remained was Om recycling in my mind.

Sometime later, I traveled north of San Francisco, to Mendocino, to visit an older, distant cousin, who made jewelry. When I arrived, he gave me a silver pendant he had made. It was the Om. I had told him nothing previously of my inner thoughts or lack of them. I wore it from then on; it was a special treasure.

I continued with my discipline, emptying the mind and filling it with the sound of Om, until eventually my thoughts ceased. Actually, they never truly ceased, but became really quiet, no longer disruptive. So, I was basically reduced to Om, though my mind was still not quiet. It was filled with Om. I had been releasing everything but that sound. It was a tool. The work was done. It was time to let go of the tool.

I was standing on the street curb, when this thought occurred to me. I removed the pendant, held on to the cord and swung it forcefully into a parking meter on the sidewalk. It flew apart into myriad pieces. My mind was quiet; no, it was empty, void. It had broken apart as well.

Then a most curious thing happened. The trees began Om-ing! The ground below my feet was chanting this cosmic word! All around me, everything joined the chorus. My consciousness turned inside out and expanded in all directions. I was in the middle of a three-dimensional mandala, becoming one with the One. Then there was no I anymore, just the Infinite Glory and Joy of Creation. The empty mind was overflowing.

Silence - Easter

Years later, David had quite a different experience of silence. The following is his recollection.

By day, I worked as a grounds-keeper at Southern Methodist University, in Dallas. Behind this veil, I was a brother in a mystical Holy Order, living as a missionary. Easter was approaching.

In our spiritual practice, we worked the Christian Mysteries, so Easter was an important holiday (holy day) for us. Our spiritual disciplines brought true liberation, although they appeared to be limiting.

During lent we kept silence from dinner until dawn, meditating for three hours each night. During Holy Week (the week preceding Easter Sunday), we kept total silence, and ended with a three day fast of only water.

I want to be honest and express I wasn't a very productive worker. My job was to take care of the fine arts building. I began my day running a nail over a grindstone, which was attached to a stick I used to pick up all the cigarette butts and paper strewn around campus. There was so much time to do so little that I began some alchemical grounds keeping.

This means that working on one level produces results on another. As below, so above. This alchemical transference can work no matter what we are doing. It comes down to knowing what we are doing. Are we vacuuming the rug or are we cleaning our subconscious? Are we scraping the wallpaper off the wall or scraping sediment off our soul? I was picking up the scattered trash around the grounds, but I was really picking trashy thoughts from my mind.

Any work can be a deeper work. I took my work to different places. I developed martial arts techniques, when spearing cigarette butts. I learned the Zen of raking. I learned to listen and talk to the plants. I had little to do. So, I began to do little. I spent more time inside the building reading or talking to students. I was an ineffective worker.

I worked during Holy Week. I told two of the other gardeners whom I had befriended I was practicing silence in observance. I hadn't found it necessary to let anyone else know.

Up until that point I had never had any run-ins with the boss. On Good Friday, he cut me to pieces. That morning everyone was getting ready for work. I sharpened my nail-on-a-stick. The walls were metal, the ceiling was high and the air was hot. There was an audience of at least twenty-five. The boss called me over.

He knew I was a Brother, but if anything, that was a strike against me. He let out a string of curses intermingled with comments on my rotten work ethic. It poured from his mouth for five minutes. His face contorted and sweat dripped to the floor. It was hot. I just stood there silently looking at him. He raged on. I was at peace.

He finally finished and I just nodded, acknowledging his talk. I really hadn't heard any of it, although I did get the gist. I just sent him Love and Light, and the negative stuff never touched me. The power of silence… Later, my friends, who had witnessed the whole incident, told me about the boss's reaction.

I guess it kind of blew his mind. He said he had never in all his life chewed someone out who never said a word back. He couldn't believe I had just stood there without defending myself, that I just stood there and smiled back. Because I didn't react, he was hit with himself.

In simplicity there is great potency. The less we do the greater impact we have. David wasn't just standing there; he was allowing the Love of God to pour through. We can do nothing, and nothing happens, or we could not do anything and allow all things to happen.

When we do nothing, it's still an action, a "doing." When we don't do anything, there is no action. It's not as subtle as it appears. Do we clear our mind or allow our mind to be clear? When we do things, it's based on the false assumption that there is an "us" that is separate from everything else. The illusion is there is a "doer" separate from the "doing." This is frustrating to the "earth mind" that accepts individuality without question.

Can we imagine all the cells in the body acting individually? They would be "doing" something all right, but we, as the whole, would not be able to get anything done. When the cells work as a whole system, however, allowing us to act through them, (like walking across the room) things happen.

We are silencing the false ego. We are silencing the lies. We are silencing the distractions. This is inner work. We are not getting up and turning off the TV. We are going within and turning off the TV. This is the power of silence.

It's really a great accomplishment, to be able to get beyond this forest of thought. We not only begin to see our own repetitive mental patterns, but we become aware how many of these patterns aren't even ours.

Have you ever had the experience of getting a song get "stuck" in your head? Some part of the brain keeps singing it over and over. The more energy we exert to remove it, the more it hangs in place. The mind acts like a child who is fixated on something. The more we tell the child they can't have the candy, the more they scream. In parenting, we learn the art of redirection. We bring the child's attention to something else.

We do the same in meditation. We turn the attention of the mind toward something else. If we are told, "Don't think about elephants," it's impossible not to, because the subconscious just hears "elephants." In order that we not think of them, the subconscious deduces that elephants must be present, so it manifests them in the imagination.

We can redirect the mind with sound. We learn to listen. We learn to listen to sound without telling ourselves about it. Listen without looking for meaning, as we would listen to classical or ambient music. Feel the sound. Experience it.

LISTENING

Sound is the basis of all creation. It vibrates at the foundation of the cosmos. We create the reality around us with our words and our thoughts. The issue is, what we are perceiving is not really reality, it's just our concept of reality. If we wish to experience true reality, we must become receptive to it. When we think or speak, we are activating, we are creating. When we listen, in meditation, we surrender, we relax, we receive, which builds upon our ability to concentrate. In concentration, we contain and contract our focus; in meditation, we release and expand our focus. In concentration, we focus; in meditation, we are focused upon.

Explore the *Listening Exercise*, on the following page. We recommend you experience the meditation using the available audio recording, *Ten Gates into the Garden: Spiritual Exercises and Meditations*.

> **Listening Exercise**
>
> Sit in a relaxed position, with your spine straight. Don't push or force anything. Simply relax. Now close your eyes and listen.
>
> Listen to everything, the ambient sounds, people talking, vehicles outside, mechanical noises, birds, whatever enters in. Be open and receptive.
>
> Expand the sphere of your awareness. Listen in all directions at once. How far is it possible to detect sound? What is the hearing radius? Listen, without talking to yourself. Refrain from judging, analyzing, or labeling "that noise is a bird," or "that noise is a car."
>
> Simply listen.

BREATH

Breath is the underpinning of virtually all meditation practices. It is the Life Stream that fuels all the physiologic functions of our body. Breath is the vehicle for *prana* or *qi*, the Life Force, that supports and sustains all existence.

Breath is the gateway between inner and outer. It is an expression of both yin and yang. Our inhalation is a passive experience, one in which we release, to receive the inflow of the Cosmic Current. The exhalation is active, as we unconsciously or consciously contract the abdominal muscles to help expel the spent air.

Our breath, thoughts, and emotions are intimately related. The breath can become very erratic, when we are upset, as an indication that the sympathetic nervous system has kicked into gear and we have activated the "fight, flight or freeze" response. As we gain control of the breath and slow it down, we activate the parasympathetic nervous system, which moves us into the "relaxation" response, where we can "rest and digest," the mode in which all healing occurs. That is why meditation is such a potent practice.

Whereas thoughts can be highly charged by our emotions, the breath itself remains neutral. It may be temporarily influenced by the current condition of our mental and emotional bodies, but slowing the breath enables us to subdue the *monkey mind* and any extreme emotions. As we learn mind control and harmonize the emotions, our breathing pattern naturally deepens and slows down. Ideally, this slower, richer expression of breath becomes our default rhythm. When this occurs, we reap innumerable benefits.

Our meditation practice organically leads us to consider the breath. When we direct our focus within, it is the one constant we can use as a means to bring our awareness back to the present moment. The breath is the tether to the eternal now.

> **Conscious Breathing**
>
> Focus on the breath. Gently inhale and exhale through the nose. Allow the belly to be soft, as you inhale, releasing the abdominal muscles. Imagine a balloon expanding in the lower abdomen with each in breath. With the exhalation, gently contract the abdominal wall, forcing the air out. Explore this sensation for several cycles of breath. Now imagine the balloon is filled with helium and begins rising from the base of the spine to the tops of the shoulders, as the breath fills from the bottom of the torso up. Keep the shoulders relaxed, as the breath rises. As you gently contract the abdominal wall, with the exhalation, visualize the balloon turning to lead and descending down to the base of the spine, through the legs and feet to the core of the Earth. Then, with soft belly, allow the body to inhale on its own.
>
> Continue with this rhythm and visualization. Don't force. Don't push. Relax. Feel the effects of the breath internally. Notice how the slower rhythm of breath impacts the mental and emotional bodies as well.
>
> Now move your consciousness to the nostrils. Feel the currents of air pass over the outer rims of the nostrils, as the breath enters and leaves the body. Note the subtle sensation. Simply focus on the breath.
>
> This breath meditation can be done anywhere at any time. If you ever get lost or spaced-out in meditation, you can use this as a centering exercise.

KABBALAH

In esoteric Hebrew wisdom, the letter *Tzaddi* is used to symbolize meditation. The symbol represents a fish hook. In this practice of meditation, we float on the sea of the subconscious mind. We fish. Our bait for this fishing expedition becomes the subject of our meditation.

We have learned to focus our consciousness; now we may apply it. We put forth the intention to meditate on "divine Love," for example. Let it sink into the waters of the subconscious. It will draw to it ideas, visions, feelings that have an affinity with the bait, "divine Love." We only need to listen and observe. As the information bubbles up from the subconscious mind, it is pulled up into the conscious mind.

We can bait our "meditation hook" with anything we wish. Our own subconscious mind is connected to the collective subconscious, the vast storehouse of ideas created by the thoughts of humans throughout all time.

Another type of meditation consists of the repeating of a word or *mantra*, like Om, as David described in his earlier recollection. Begin by saying it out loud, over and over. Gradually allow the volume to diminish until it is a whisper. Now mouth the word with no audible sound until you are only thinking the word. Hear it in your mind. Allow the thought to go deeper and deeper, quieter and quieter, until there is no more thought. You are in a meditative state.

> **Om Mantra**
>
> We will now use the mantra OM, also spelled AUM. AUM is the seed sound, containing all sound within it. It starts at the back of the throat, moves through the middle of the mouth, and comes forth to the closed lips, resonating through the nose. Refrain from attaching any meaning to it. Don't think, just feel.
>
> Now try chanting AUM in time with a gong, bell, bowl or drum. Repeat it again and again. Attempt to sustain the mantra for 5 minutes. As you continue practicing this mediation, you can extend the timing longer.

Sound is a powerful tool. Many music recordings are designed specifically for meditation. Be sure to use relaxing music with no words. We recommend you experience the meditations in this chapter, using the available audio recording, *Ten Gates into the Garden: Spiritual Exercises and Meditations*.

When we were in the womb, there was nothing to see. As we were fed through the umbilical cord, there was nothing to taste, nothing to smell. We may have touched our own body or the interior of our mother, as we floated in the sea of amniotic fluid, but without much to compare the sensations to, they would not register for long. We do, however, hear, and discern between sounds. Our first sense to be fully activated and integrated!

We might imagine the fetus is in a meditative state, having no words with which to think, awareness without thought. Hearing is also said to be the last sense to leave us at death. Mothers talk to their unborn and prayers are read to the dead. This is especially true in Tibetan Buddhism, as the *"Tibetan Book of the Dead"* is read to the corpse to help the soul with its transition to the non-physical realm again.

In walking meditations, if the mind is clear, physical activity will not disturb it, but complete focus is needed to avoid the distractions.

INSTRUMENTS OF MEDITATION

We can choose a drum, gong, bell or bowl and allow the sound to lead us deeply into meditation. Quartz crystal bowls are powerful meditative tools, based on the singing bowls of Tibet and India, which are made of the seven sacred metals that we hold, symbolically, within our chakra system.

Drums, bowls, gongs, and bells are all circularly shaped, and have been used since their creation as spiritual tools. The sound created by these various instruments is also circular. Visualize a still pond. When we tone the instrument, we imagine a stone breaking the surface of the water, creating concentric rings, waves of sound emanating from the point of immersion. The sound continues to vibrate until at last, the pool is still once more.

If we look at a bell from below, we see the circle as the rim and a dot in the center as the clacker (at rest). Look familiar? See the dot as Self and the circle as the world. When one has detached from the outer, having found the "Pearl of Great Price," the "Rock of Ages," the "Philosopher's Stone," one is still and at peace. From this central point of our being, when we touch creation, it is the clapper hitting the rim, creating sound. (The sound of one hand clapping?) Spirit touches matter. Sound is the unifier. It touches everything. It connects everything.

We, as God-beings, are also given the power to create sound. When we manifest our own sound in meditation, we call it a *mantra*. As mentioned previously, a *mantra* is a sound we repeat over and over, silently or aloud.

Mantra meditation is at the foundation of Transcendental Meditation or TM, brought to the West, by Maharishi Mahesh Yogi, in the 1960s, with much support from The Beatles and The Beach Boys, among others. The root of the word "transcendental" is transcend, which means "trance end," the end of the illusion that has entranced us. We awaken from the sleep of ignorance.

TM basically involves repeating a specific mantra given by the teacher. The mantras in TM are typically in Sanskrit, the spiritual language of Vedic scripture. When we are not told the meaning of the mantra, we can't create a false belief around the word. The word is to be kept secret from others, as this greatly increases its potency and eliminates any spiritual dilution.

Spiritual dilution happens when we have a spiritual experience then tell others about it. This may cause a number of unwanted effects. First of all, our experience is our own, something only we felt that left an impression on us. An impression is a change in our form, caused by our reaction to an "outside" force. We may try to leave an impression in a ball of clay, by applying force. The impression cannot be made unless the clay is soft and receptive.

No one can do anything to us, unless we accept it, which is our own choice. This is a very basic rule. When David's boss was chewing him out, he didn't resist, so he wasn't affected.

When we tell a friend about our experience, we begin to translate that experience into a mental picture, in order to communicate it in words. Then our friend creates a picture, based on our description of that picture. Our friend is now attempting to understand our experience, without having experienced it. This is the root of the false concept.

For example, let's say that in meditation, our consciousness was lifted up to a more subtle and higher vibration. Using our spiritual sight, we become aware of an energy field around someone in the room, we might describe as their aura.

Since people listen in accord with their own limited awareness and experience, the one to whom we describe our experience may imagine we used our physical eyes, and we saw physical light around Ms. X's head. They might even begin to think there is something special about Ms. X.

Centuries ago, artists painted images of holy people with golden halos encircling their heads. People viewing such a painting today may think there were people back then actually walking around with halos. As a result, one might discount a truly spiritual person, because they don't "fit that description." We understand the "vision" has more to do with our ability to perceive the aura than it has to do with the one at whom we are looking.

Another distortion may occur, if someone hears about our vision and wants to see the same thing. They end up striving to recreate what we experienced through their own limited understanding. Since they don't really know what we saw, they end up at a dead end. We can, however, convey our experience to a real spiritual teacher, as they will not dilute or misunderstand it.

Candles

Candles offer another focal point for meditation. The triple flame candle meditation exercise, on the next page, has several levels. It begins more like a concentration exercise, as concentration is the foundation for meditation. If there is difficulty concentrating, review Chapter 1: Concentration.

Explore the *Triple Flame Candle Meditation* on the following page, as a means to enhance your ability to sustain a single point of focus.

> **Triple Flame Candle Meditation**
>
> ***In preparation you will need a candle and matches, or a lighter.***
>
> Sit upright in an uncluttered area, place the candle on a table at heart level and light it. Now begin to gaze at the flame. Look closely. Observe there are three distinct little flames at the tip of the one flame. Discern the three colors, red, yellow, and blue, which make up the one flame. These are the colors of the three astrological fire signs (Aries, Leo, Sagittarius).
>
> The next level of the meditation involves amplifying and diminishing the flame. Be sure you are seated away from any breeze or draft. With a flame, we are dealing with very little friction, so a great deal of inherent resistance is eliminated. It is much easier to move a flame with the mind than it is to move a rock. Gaze into the flame, breathe deeply and rhythmically. Now imagine yourself merging with the flame. See yourself fully engulfed in the flame. With each inhalation visualize the flame expanding. Will it to expand. With each exhalation visualize the flame diminishing. Will it to diminish. Continue the flow of breath, willing the flame to expand and diminish with each cycle of breath.
>
> Now we will move more deeply into the inner work. Rather than using a real candle, now visualize the flame burning brightly at the top of the head. The intention in this meditation is to still the flame completely. Any thought that arises will cause the flame to flicker. This practice is easiest when the mind is quiet. Remain with the meditation for as long as you are able. Be patient with yourself if thoughts flow in. Bring your awareness back to the breath and to the image of the flame hovering above the head.
>
> Once the lower level flame practices are mastered, we continue by visualizing the flame floating on a waveless expanse of water. Any thought makes the flame dance. Still the flame's movement, by detaching from any thought that arises.
>
> The intention is also to still the water completely. It becomes a clear reflecting pool for the flame. Just as the quality of the flame reflects our thoughts, the water reflects the emotions. Allow the surface to become smooth as glass. This may take years to master. Start now. This practice illuminates the mind with Light.

Contemplation of the Elements

The next spiritual exercise in our studies is called the Element Breaths. It is our adaptation of a foundation practice of Sufism, in which one concentrates on the elements Earth, Water, Fire and Air. Similar practices can be found in wisdom traditions throughout the world. The version this adaptation is said to have its roots in the Greek Mystery Schools, and has since been passed down from Sufi teacher to student for thousands of years.

The potent practice on the following pages may, for some, feel unusually familiar. Used as a daily ritual, it cultivates vital energy and a greater sense of inner balance. Beginning with concentration on the breath, the *Purification of the Elements* gradually deepens into a practice of contemplation. It is an excellent foundation for meditation. Ideally, one would practice this in the early morning, and it is best experienced standing barefoot, or sitting in contact with the earth. If practicing inside, stand or sit near an open window, if possible.

Purification of the Elements: Contemplation

Close the eyes. Let the belly be soft. Inhale deeply, visualizing the breath entering the body through the base of the spine and filling the torso from the bottom up. Then exhale slowly and completely, gently contracting the abdominal wall, emptying the chamber of the torso from the top of the shoulders into the chest, then the belly, and out through the base of the spine.

Exhale further and further, until there is nothing left to exhale. Then allow the inhalation to occur spontaneously, organically, with no effort, as the abdominal muscles release again. This natural inhalation is very important, so there is no strain on the lungs or muscles in the chest.

Now practice holding the breath for a moment after the inhalation, perhaps for a couple of beats, before you release the exhalation. This is a wonderful way to prepare for the following meditation in the *Purification of the Elements*.

Purification of the Elements: *The Earth Element*

Native American elders have said the main cause of psychological imbalance and physical illness is the loss of a sense of relationship and communion with the Earth. As a way to restore their vitality during long vigils, the early Christian mystics, who lived as hermits for years in the desert, concentrated on the Earth's magnetism.

Either standing or sitting, imagine yourself as a tree with roots growing from the base of the pelvis, legs and the soles of the feet, deeply anchoring you into the Earth. Become present to the support Gaia, the Earth, provides you, both physically and energetically. Sense her great strength and magnetism. Breathe rhythmically in and out through the nose, without forcing. Visualize you are drawing the Earth's magnetism and healing power up from her core, through the feet and legs, and consciously direct Gaia's magnetism to those parts of the body that feel depleted.

Feel the Earth's healing power. You may have sensed this vibration in your feet, when walking barefoot outdoors, or in your hands, while working in the garden.

Begin to sense a subtler phenomenon, a lattice-like, crystalline structure, underlying the denser aspects of the material plane. Feel at this subtle level, the Earth, as a singular organism. Now become aware of her connection to the solar system and the greater galaxy. Your alignment with the Earth connects you to the Moon, other planets, near and far, as well as the Sun, and the most distant stars.

As you inhale, sense yourself as part of the greater whole, and the energy we call Life. Know your body is made of the substance of the Earth, and is subject to the balance, harmony and order of the natural world. As you exhale, release all toxins, and what the body can no longer use back into the earth. Breathe out any fatigue, restlessness, agitation, or disharmony.

Now focus your awareness on the magnetic field of your body. Just as the Earth, as a whole, has a force field similar to a magnet's, so does the physical body. As iron filings align around a magnet, align your own magnetic field to the Earth's. When magnetic power is weak, the iron filings appear chaotic. When the power is strong, the filings align in cohesive, symmetric, harmonic patterns. On each inhalation, imagine the filings arranging themselves in an orderly manner. With the exhalation, feel the body give forth its natural magnetism, harmonizing the atmosphere around you.

Purification of the Elements: *The Water Element*

The breath of the Water element cleanses, purifies, nourishes and cultivates creativity, as we move into the flow. It is also useful to break free from habitual thought patterns, allowing us to move forward through life, flowing gracefully around obstacles, rather than butting up against them or getting entangled in the eddies of negative thought forms.

Inhale through the nose and exhale through the mouth, as though you are releasing a fine stream of water through the mouth, by pursing the lips. Visualize a pure, cool mountain stream. Wade into the water, gradually. Step in and slowly immerse yourself. Feel the water rising from the ankles to the knees, up to the waist, and finally enveloping your chest and heart center. Allow the water to soften any tightness surrounding the heart, dissolving any obstruction there.

Sense the water droplets permeating every cell. A wash of water flows over your body, down the legs, and drips from your fingertips. Focus the awareness on those parts of the body that are out of balance, and those that feel stagnant or constricted. Fill them with Life Force energy and vibrancy with every inhalation, releasing tension and congestion with every exhalation. Feel vitalized and refreshed.

Immersed in this crystal-clear mountain stream, focus on the water's purity. Allow yourself to become the water. Let the generative, nurturing qualities of power, purity, and vibrant Life Force energy flow through you and out into your immediate environment.

Purification of the Elements: *The Fire Element*

The breath of the Fire element is a quickening energy. It ignites the imagination, sparks inspiration, and rouses us, when we feel dull and drowsy, or after a period of intense physical or spiritual practice.

Purse the lips and inhale a thin stream of air through the mouth, hold the breath briefly, then exhale through the nose. Allow the inhalation, like a bellows, to fan the fire centered in the solar plexus, where the ribs splay open. Throughout the inhalation, imagine the glowing embers of the fire becoming brighter and hotter.

Now hold the breath briefly, and move your awareness up to the heart center, the seat of the heart chakra, the home of the Heart Light. This is a sensitive point located several inches above the solar plexus. Exhale out through the heart chakra, visualize a golden stream of sunlight radiating out in all directions.

As you inhale, become present to your soul's desire; your aspirations for expanded awareness, spiritual growth and understanding; your desire to be your authentic self; to create a meaningful, fulfilling life; to stand up for and voice what you believe in.

As you exhale, radiate forth your Heart Light, the personal Sun that resides on the altar of the heart. Feel the intense golden Light permeating every cell within you and into the energetic field around you.

The fire breath helps transmute energies that no longer serve us. Offer up to the fire any self-doubt, unworthiness, judgment, addictive tendencies, or resentments. Avoid making pledges you are unable to keep. Simply offer your clear intention and be open to the purification process.

Rather than focusing on will power to effect change, concentrate on the Fire element, a natural force of disintegration and rebirth. The action of Life, serving as a teacher, activates and incinerates what needs to be burned, which allows our deeper and truer nature to emerge.

> **Purification of the Elements:** *The Air Element*
>
> The breath of the Air element relates to freedom, bliss and transcendence. Visualize yourself as a great eagle perched high on a promontory. Experience the wind blowing through your feathers, permeating all your skin through every pore. Feel the cool, freshness of the mountain air.
>
> Take flight and ride a current of air, soaring upward. Breathe slowly in and out through the mouth. (Be mindful this can dry the throat, so breath slowly and for shorter timings.) As you inhale, allow the breath to loft you. Sense its buoyancy, lifting upward, like a zephyr dancing across a crystal-clear lake.
>
> As you exhale, extend your awareness out beyond the boundaries of the body. Allow your physical, emotional and mental bodies to disperse on the wind, as your consciousness permeates the far reaches of the cosmos. Revel in your sense of expansiveness. You are unlimited, infinite in scope. It may help to visualize yourself soaring through vast, open spaces, such as a mountain canyon, or a starry night sky.
>
> Once you have completed the final purification breath practice, reflect on the overall effect exploring all the Elements has had on your whole being. Each Element Breath practice amplifies different forces and qualities within our being. When we practice all of them together, they create a sense of integration and wholeness. Each Element Breath practice complements and moderates the others. As we attune to our own inner awareness, we intuitively sense which we need to practice to achieve greater balance.

GUIDED MEDITATION

There are many ways to meditate. In guided meditations, we are led, in person or with a recording, on some sort of a journey of discovery. The guide takes the conscious position (doing our thinking for us) so we can take the subconscious one. This may help us experience higher levels of consciousness, if the speaker is at a higher level of consciousness. When we have become more proficient in meditation, external help is no longer needed.

The advantage with this practice, for those who are new to meditation and still developing more mind control, is that by listening to another's voice, the mind has something on which to focus, beyond the breath, mantra, sound vibration, or candle flame. The sound of the voice becomes the focal point. The mind is also occupied with visualization or conjuring the sensorial elements the guide suggests throughout the meditation, which may make it easier to focus the mind. Do we really have any original thoughts? Where do the ideas we think about come from?

We are connected to the global community through our computers and phones, we watch TV and listen to the radio. We read, we listen, we are taught. We create the world we see around us with our minds. We take bits of information from our senses and assemble them to fabricate our sense of reality. There is a truer reality, but we obscure it with our distracting thoughts. There is a unity we may be present to, when our mind is still we may become aware of our consciousness beyond thought. Strive for the empty mind, that it might be filled with that which nourishes the soul. Remember, meditation is not what you think.

Create space in your daily schedule to practice these spiritual exercises. These words and practices are not designed to simply offer information, they are designed to provide us with experience of a new reality, an alchemical transformation. We must do the work, though, if we truly seek personal transformation. As with any physical exercise, we won't feel their benefits, unless we practice them regularly. Explore *The Vision Room*, listening to *Ten Gates into the Garden: Spiritual Exercises and Meditations.*

The Vision Room

Let's journey in guided meditation inside the School of the New Light.

It's the first night of winter; the Moon is full and directly overhead. The ground is snow-covered, reflecting the Moon's bright light.

Walk across the snow to a large dark patch in the middle of a vast field. Approach it and notice a ladder emerging from a hole in the earth. This is a kiva, an underground room, built by the indigenous of the US South-West, for spiritual exploration.

Climb down the ladder; find a place to sit against the clay walls. The room is comfortably warm. Begin to focus on the rhythmic cycles of the breath until your mind becomes quiet and you enter a deeper state of meditation. Now rise and walk to the far corner of the room, from which you see a light radiate. The corner walls open to a pathway, which leads to a tunnel descending further underground.

The path is well lit and safe to walk. Feel the solid ground beneath your feet as you descend deeper and deeper into the earth. Smell the richness of the earth. Hear the echoes of your footsteps as you walk through the tunnel.

Ahead there is an abundance of light. The tunnel opens to an enormous cavern. Down below, there is a great golden pyramid, radiating golden light, rising from the earth in the center of the cavern.

Approach the pyramid, walking to a passageway out of which a brilliant orange light pours. Walk through the doorway. Feel the orange light pervading your whole being. Attune yourself to its vibration. Harmonize your physical, emotional, mental and spiritual bodies with the light.

A long hallway stretches out before you. Throughout the corridor there are portals leading to different classrooms. Walk to the room at the end of the hall from which emanates a dark blue light. This is the Room of Vision. Outside the room is a box filled with violet, silk scarves. Take one and drape it over your head before you enter.

Enter and be seated on the long bench flanking the room. Breathe deeply and rhythmically to quiet the thoughts. Your vision begins to emerge through the scarf. Release all expectation. Simply open yourself fully to receive your vision. Refrain from judging what comes forth. Be fully present to what is.

Descend stone steps before you toward the pyramid. Down, down, down, deeper and deeper in to the

When the vision is complete, the light in the room begins to change to golden white. Now you may rise and leave the Room of Vision. Place the violet scarf back in the box. Walk down the corridor to the doorway out into the cavern. Cross the cavern floor toward the stone staircase.

Gradually, make your way, rising higher with each step. At the top reenter the tunnel that leads up, each step brings you higher and higher until you reach the kiva room again. Walk to the ladder and begin to climb up, up, making your way to the surface. Allow the moonlight to wash over you, and the brisk air to begin to rouse you from your meditation.

Remaining in stillness, slowly open your eyes. (We suggest you immediately write down your vision for easy recall.)

CHAPTER 6

Foundation Work

REALITY IS PERSPECTIVE

To live as a so-called "normal" person in this world, there are a number of false beliefs we are asked to accept. Primarily, we are asked to accept that we all die. Additionally, we are asked to accept that others are responsible for our suffering. We are also asked to accept we need money to live. Finally, we are asked to accept the idea that if we think we are God, we are crazy.

We all see the Sun move across the sky each day. We know, intellectually, what we are observing is really the Earth revolving on its axis. In our "real," daily life, however, we still perceive the Sun rise and set.

The difference is, fundamentally, our point of view. The reality we experience is based solely on our perspective. If we want to know what is really happening, we need to develop a God-centered view. We would, indeed, feel the Earth's spin, if we moved our awareness from the personal to a transpersonal experience of life.

Everyone around us is having a personal life. In school, we teach children how to have a personal life. TV stresses the personal, because it's the person who is buying the sponsors' products. Our churches and governments want us to live a personal life, so they may influence, direct, and control it. If we are God, what or who could possibly influence us? Who or what could have power over us, if we are God?

Society wants us to have a personal life to perpetuate the illusion: the game of "us-and-them"; the game of "ours-and-theirs"; the dating game; the marriage game; the family game; the work game. There are many games being played out on Earth. There are many distractions to keep us from the truth of our Self. We are God! Yes, we are God, but we have forgotten.

As human beings, at this time in the great cycle, we are a composite of truth and error. We are made up of our true Self and our false self. The false self is who we think we are. The true

Self is who we are afraid to be. When we say, "We are God," we are speaking of the true Self, who we really are. Problems arise when our false ego begins to think it is God.

The root of our difficulty lies in the fact that the false self is our own creation, which, albeit distorted, is based on the true Self's reflection. Our true Self presents for us a framework on which we erect our concepts, ideas, and imaginings. As an example, Self correctly informs us we are in human form at this time. We experience a physical body, thoughts and feelings. Self tells us it is all our own projection. Self tells us we are in a world of effects, and our true Source dwells within. The false self, aware of this projection, then creates a self-image based solely on the reflection, rather than developing a self-identity founded on the Self within. This is where ego takes over.

When we re-create ourselves in our own image, we create the trap in which we now find ourselves. We create an image for ourselves that cannot possibly express the full nature of our being. This inevitably leads to frustration and the resulting depression, born out of a deep underlying sense that what we are doing with our lives, compared to what we could be doing, is so little.

We are divine Spirit, manifesting in the material world. We are infinite beings living under the illusion of limitation. It is an illusion, created by a misunderstanding, fed to us since birth. We try to live in this reflected world, yet we wonder why things are so confusing.

Look at the world. We live in a field of cause and effect. The suffering we see is an effect. The wars, the sickness, the starvation are all effects. What is the cause of these problems? It's the false ego-centered life.

CHANGE YOUR FOCUS, CHANGE YOUR LIFE

Jesus told us there are just two guiding principles: we are to love God with all our heart, mind, strength and soul, and we are to love our neighbor as our self. *(Mark 12:30-31 KJV)*

When we are caught in ego mind, we may well behave selfishly. For so long, the economic engine of capitalism has encouraged the "me first," "dog eat dog" attitude, all in service of perpetuating the "industrial machine."

Advertisers try to convince us their products will make us happier, healthier, more popular and attractive, better dressed, more successful, powerful and admired.

Look at your hand. Imagine each of the fingers trying to impress the others. Imagine each of your fingers trying to impress you. Do you think you would still be able to use your hand, if each finger was vying for special attention and consideration?

We also believe we are different people, like separate fingers, with no real connection at the root. We are actually here to work together, not compare and compete.

The spiritual path is contrary to the world. When our focus is God, we are Self-centered, or centered in Self. Let's take the "me first" attitude and turn it around, and instead try "me (false ego) last." This orientation opens us up to altruism, compassion, and loving kindness.

When we change our focus, an amazing thing happens. We recover all the energy we had been expending trying to get ahead. All the worldly ambition, the striving, conniving, lying and cheating, all fall away. We become amazed at how much time and effort we spend trying to achieve a position that ultimately only ever leads to old age, sickness and death.

Who will look after us, if we don't look after ourselves? For example, simply because she was selflessly caring for others, with no attachment to the false ego, did so many people look after Mother Teresa's needs.

In David's earlier hippie days, he lived on the street, always on the edge of poverty. He never had any idea where or when he would eat. So many people were in need and hungry. During that time, he met a man named Father Peter, who carried around only a few simple pots and pans. He fed people.

Father Peter didn't have any money to buy the food, and no stove on which to cook. Yet every night, he cooked dinner. Someone would inevitably show up with a stove. Other folks would bring food to cook, a bag of potatoes. Someone else might put their welfare check into the kitty.

If we want to eat, then we feed others. The cook never starves. If we focus on others, our needs will always be provided for.

The point is not really about focusing on others, but rather to focus less on our self (ego). When we are ego focused, we cut off the flow from Source. We short-circuit the energy.

When Martin Luther, the founder of Lutheranism, walked the spiritual path, he began by focusing on his own inadequacies. He was extremely determined to experience God and follow the path of Jesus.

He was merciless in his own self-discipline. He beat and tortured his physical body. He fasted and lay exposed to the elements, almost till death overcame him. The more he would strive to overcome his humanness, the more frustrated he became. His practices became even more austere. He found no light at the end of the tunnel through which he walked. He saw no way out.

Finally, he met a priest, who gave him true counsel. Perceiving Luther's predicament, the priest assigned Luther the task of teaching Bible classes. Soon his problems disappeared. His focus was no longer on himself and had now shifted to his students. He emerged from the pit of isolation, self-recrimination and self-centeredness.

When we are thinking negatively about ourselves, we are on just as much of an ego trip as those with delusions of grandeur. As we give, so will we receive. We want to learn, so we teach.

FIRST PRINCIPLES

Recall the Master Jesus' instructions. First, we are directed to love God with all our heart. Who does this? If we love God with all our heart, how can we also love our neighbors as ourselves? Haven't we already given our entire heart to God? How can we divide it and still offer it all to God? We can't, unless God, our neighbor, and our Self are all the same being.

Love God with all your mind. The key here is *all*. <u>All</u> of our mind. Are we conscious of our mind, or, more importantly, utilizing even ten percent of it? We can't love God with all of our mind, unless we are actually using all of it.

We must develop the mind completely, in order to love God with all of it. We must love with the conscious, subconscious, and super-conscious aspects of mind. It's really all or nothing. Though it may be easy to love God with just some of our mind, we still remain fractured. In order to love God with all our mind, we are called upon to cultivate Unity Consciousness.

How do we strive to love God with all our strength? Strength is force; it is Fire. We must ignite the inner flame of passion in the heart and keep it stoked with vital breath so the divine Life Force can flow freely through us. In so doing, we give God our full strength.

The mind is consciousness, which aligns with the Element Air. The heart is feeling, which is Water. The combination of Fire, Air and Water are the building blocks of what we call Earth. This is the element invoked when we love God with all our soul.

Earth is the fourth of the essential building blocks of creation. Is it strange that we assign Earth to the soul? The soul is the record of our conscious love-energy. (Air=conscious, Water=love, Fire=energy) It is the amalgamation of the collected essence of our experiences from all our lifetimes. Most of these experiences are the result of interactions we have had on the three-dimensional Earth plane.

Science has revealed there is nothing solid in creation. All we truly are is a collection of atoms, which are mostly empty space. Atoms can be broken into smaller pieces, which are also mostly space. Esoterically, these same elementary building blocks are at work, when we reduce creation first to energy, the element of Fire. All creation is essentially vibration.

When energy moves in a spiral pattern, a magnetic field is created. In a science class, at some point, we likely wrapped a wire around a pencil, connected it to an energy source (battery-Fire) and created a magnet. This magnet represents the second element, Water, which displays attraction and repulsion. This is the arena where feeling is born.

The third building block is Air, which represents consciousness, the observer. It is here, on the stage of the mind, the play, or the drama of our life, is enacted.

When the four building blocks of creation, Water/emotion, Air/mind, Fire/strength and Earth/soul, are each functional and together operating harmoniously, we are able to actualize Jesus' prime directives in our lives.

SENSE OR NON-SENSE?

We might say all creation is a combination of conscious feeling energy, the so-called solid world that appears around us. When we examine this cosmic soup, through our sensory apparatus, a world is created and experienced via these same senses. It is a total fiction. Our senses create the appearance of time and space, and our sensory perceptions create the illusion of separation.

If we take a moment to recall a significant experience in our life, is it not presented in images, sounds and feelings? Do we remember our lives, or just a movie of our lives?

We take in the vibrational information our eyes and ears receive. Then we add smells, and those tangibles we are able to touch. How does the energy move? What feelings are added? What internal dialogue enters the mix?

Now we add the variable of time into the equation. We say we "add" time, because the reality we perceive is never actually lived in "real-time." We always experience it as the past, because by the time our brain has processed the event, it has already happened.

We may, however, have a real-time experience, like during a car accident or an explosion, when things happen so quickly there is no time to process the occurrence. The event transpires, before we can put the experience into some context, or compare it with any previous occurrence. Such a process requires time. This time delay is why we experience most of life in the past.

Often, when we are in the midst of an accident, we actually experience time slowing down. Everything feels as though it is moving in slow motion. We perceive it this way, because we are brushing up against the now. Otherwise, we live in the past.

When we listen to a lecture, it requires time for the speaker to translate the thoughts from their mind into words and vocalize them. A time lapse is also in effect as our ears receive the words and the auditory nerve bundle transmits them to the brain, where they are processed and finally comprehended by our mind. Many processes are happening in very quick succession. Our ears transmit the sound vibrations to the brain, where those sounds are compared with our data bank of previously recognized sounds. Ultimately, the brain processes the sounds, which symbolize words, representative of ideas, into something we can understand.

It takes time for light to leave an overhead fixture and bounce off the speaker's face, travel to our eyes through the optic nerve, and then for the brain to process that sensory input. Eventually, we see what we think is the speaker.

Are we forever then trapped in the past? Is there no escape?

BE HERE NOW

The book by Ram Das, of the same title, was published in the 1960s. The message, 'Be here, now,' is simple, though, perhaps, not so explicit. This practice is the path to the ever unfolding now. It's called the *pathless path*, because in reality, we already are here, now. But where is here, and when is now?

Albert Einstein said if we were to move in any direction and go far enough, we would return to our starting point. We would experience the truth of this theory, if we were able to walk around the planet, because the Earth is a sphere.

Einstein envisioned the same result would be achieved, when he imagined shooting a rocket out into space. He theorized it would keep going and going and finally cycle back from the opposite direction. The nature of the universe is a curve.

So where is here? From wherever we launch the rocket, it will return to that place. Therefore, no matter where we are, we're always in the center of the universe. Everything exists at the center of the universe.

Imagine a large ball with a dot drawn anywhere on its surface. Wherever you place the dot, it will always be in the exact center of the surface area. If space works this way, what about time? Are the end and the beginning of time simultaneous?

Jesus said,

"I am the Alpha and the Omega."
Revelation 23:13 KJV

It might be more aptly written, *I AM, the Alpha and the Omega.* I AM the beginning and the end. Jesus wasn't defining his relative position in the universe, nor was he speaking of himself personally. He was referring to the great I AM, the individualized expression of the Divine, the Christ, in his case, fully manifest in physical form.

When Moses asked the voice emanating from the burning bush what its name was, the voice declared, "I Am That I Am," that which is at the beginning and the end. Pure being. The pure being of now, here.

Here and now is the only place we will ever be. It is the mind that wanders. It is our thinking that tricks us into believing we are somewhere else.

When you are in your center, and I am in my center, we are in the same place, we are one. This concept is the essence of the Hindu greeting, *Namaste*. Now telepathy opens up. Now consciousness is shared. Now bliss is experienced. How can we all be in the same place at the same time?

THE COSMIC RADIO

If we turned on a radio that broadcast on AM, FM, and Short Wave, how many different stations might we pick up? They all already exist in the room right now, taking up no space whatsoever. They can all exist together, because of their varying frequencies.

Each of us has a different frequency. The frequencies of all the people on Earth right now also fit very nicely in the room. There is no congestion. Can we communicate with any of them? Well, as with the radio, we can tune into them, by focusing on just one particular frequency. Each individual's presence feels different.

How do we tune in to a specific vibration? We may have experienced being in a crowded place when we heard our name called out. Most of the time, someone else was being called, but we likely felt a little pull at first. This is because there is an affinity between us and our name. Each lifetime we are assigned a vibrational packet we learn to experience and call our own. Our given name is aligned with this frequency.

NUMEROLOGY

The letters that make up our name, the sounds created when it is spoken, are also vibratory keys to our identity. The science of numerology is used to give us a clear picture of our identity-vibration.

There are a number of these systems, each of which work a bit differently. Every letter in the alphabet is given a corresponding numerical equivalent. By adding up the values of each letter in our name, we end up with a vibratory number.

Numerology Letter Attributions

A=1	J=1	S=1
B=2	K=2	T=2
C=3	L=3	U=3
D=4	M=4	V=4
E=5	N=5	W=5
F=6	O=6	X=6
G=7	P=7	Y=7
H=8	Q=8	Z=8
I=9	R=9	

The simplest and most common system assigns the numbers 1 to A, 2 to B, 3 to C, and so on. Numbers over 9 are reduced to the sum of the numbers for each letter (15 = 1 + 5 = 6). The "Master Numbers," which are 11, 22, 33, 44, 55, and so on, are not reduced.

Explore the charts on the next pages to develop a greater understanding of these basic principles.

Destiny Number

The sum of all the letters in the given name at birth. This Destiny requirement remains with you throughout your life.

- Life's Purpose (who you must become)
- What must be lived up to in this lifetime
- Your field of opportunity
- What you must give of yourself to others and to life
- Your spiritual mission for this lifetime
- Kind of people to meet and work with
- Environment and point of contact with others

Author's First Name: D A V I D
(4+1+4+9+4) = 22 (2+2) = 4

Middle Name: H A R R Y
(8+1+9+9+7) = 34 (3+4) = 7

Last Name: D A V I S
(4+1+4+9+1) = 19 = 10 = 1.

Full Name: (4+7+1) = 12 = 3

Birth Force Number

The sum of the month, day and year you were born.

- What you are really like
- What you are naturally fitted to do
- Talents, capabilities, inclinations
- Source of power and energy to draw upon to meet the responsibility of your Destiny

David's birthdate is June 3, 1948

6 + 3 + 1 + 9 + 4 + 8 = 31 = 4

The Chaldean system appoints different number attributions to the letters.

Chaldean Numerological System

Value	Letters
1.	A, I, J, Q, Y
2.	B, K, R
3.	C, G, L, S
4.	D, M, T
5.	E, H, N, X
6.	U, V, W
7.	O, Z
8.	F, P

Consider the Hebrew numerological system below. The partial alphanumeric list is used in the science of Gematria, in which words in Hebrew texts, such as the Torah and Talmud, that have the same numeric value are related to each other. This system is also associated with the 22 *Major Arcana* of the Tarot, excepting The Fool, which has the value 0.

Gematria Numerological System

A = 1	C (core), K = 20	R = 200
B = 2	L = 30	Sh = 300
G = 3	M = 40	Th,T = 400
D = 4	N = 50	
H (honor) E = 5	S or soft C = 60	
U,V,W = 6	O = 70	
Z = 7	P Ph F = 80	
Ch, H (help) = 8	Ts Tz Cz (Czar) = 90	
Th,T = 9	Q = 100	
I,Y = 10		

Now we can explore the meanings of the Destiny and Birth Force numbers, 3 and 4 in the text box below. Take the opportunity to explore your own Birth Force and Destiny numbers to learn more about the energies of the gifts, talents you are tapping into in this life time, and the self-created limitations you have the opportunity to transcend.

The Meanings of Numbers (Select List of Attributes)

1: **Courage**: initiation, will, action, determination, energy, force, individuality, leadership, originality, masculinity, aggression, dominance, impulsiveness, willfulness, boastfulness, contrariness, cynicism, overly talkative then reticent, egotism.

2: **The Peace Maker**: polarity, reflection, adaptability, receptivity, alternation, wisdom, spiritual influence, partnership, sensitivity, diplomacy, meditation, esthetics, sincerity, femininity, self-consciousness, discord, timidity, slyness, overly detailed, extremist.

3: **Giver of Joy**: inspiration, multiplication, imagination, emotion, creative expression, self-expression, socialization, communication, the path of growth, understanding, optimism, love of pleasure, extravagance, selfishness, overly talkative, scattered energy, unfinished undertakings, moodiness, unforgiving.

4: **Construction**: form, practicality, order, classification, application, concentration, foundation for accomplishment, sense of values, fact oriented, seriousness, exactness, fixed opinions, opposition, stubbornness, lack of imagination, confusion from change.

5: **Progress**: activity, visionary, adventure, investigation, new ideas, curiosity, quick mind, the constructive use of freedom, versatility, resourcefulness, religion, restlessness, discontent, critical, impatient, impulsive, temper, sharp speech, nomadic, lacking in application.

6: **Humanitarian Service**: responsibility, idealism, beauty, truth, justice, unselfishness, harmony, home oriented, conventional, protection, nurturing, reciprocity, balance, sympathy, outspoken, self-righteous, dutiful, obstinacy, slow to make decisions, self-sacrifice, quick to complain.

7: **Understanding**: intelligence, research, observation, analysis, specialist, discrimination, knowledge, science, skill with hands, perfectionist, awareness, dignity, love of solitude, security, victory, occult, pride, repression, suspicion, unreasonableness, lack of generosity, lacking powers of self-expression.

8: **Judgment**: authority, efficiency, executive ability, earned recognition, capability, power seeking, champion of causes, business minded, organization, practical endeavors, rhythm, vibration, logic, demanding, overly energized, tension, forcefulness, self-aggrandizing, overly ambitious.

9: **Forgiveness**: benevolence, fulfillment, completion, wholeness, perfection, love, compassion, impressionable, selflessness, attainment, impersonality, artistic, charitable, dramatic talent, attracts money, jack of all trades, divinely oriented, seeking approval, failure to put talents to good use, irresponsible, possessiveness, fickle in love.

11: **Spiritual Messenger**: conscious creation, intuitive, illumination, passage through, gateway.

22: **The Master Builder**: large endeavors, spiritual leader, master teacher.

Can we change our vibration by changing our name? No, that will only change the vibration of our name. We are who we are, no matter what we are called by others. Our perception of who we are, however, can change, if we believe what others call us. (stupid, ugly, annoying, beautiful, brilliant, funny, etc.). Then we will be accepting their illusion of us over our own understanding of who we are.

Very few of us know our true name, which is the totality of our soul vibration. When we use numerology to understand the vibration of our given name, we are only addressing one aspect of our being, related specifically to our incarnation in this lifetime. When David was a Brother in the Holy Order of MANS, one of his strivings was to become a *nameless wanderer.*

We often forget our name is only a temporary identity, and believe it is who we are, and so we identify with it. This connection can be so strong we may subconsciously respond to a name we had in a previous incarnation.

As a result of this potent vibrational resonance, we can use a person's name to contact them once they have transitioned. Most of us use the Internet a lot. Through a computer, we can personally connect, via email or chat, to any one of millions of people. All we need is their address. This address is a name that is connected to one specific being. In the same way, in the spiritual realms, each name is an address connected to a specific being.

It is obvious many people share the same name. Each one still has a different flavor of vibration, however. So, we must add our knowing to our invocation, and be very clear about with whom we are making contact. We need to feel them, see them, hear them.

Before we attempt to contact loved ones, who have passed into the spiritual realms, our first point of contact must be with the Higher Self, and our spiritual guides. We all have them. Though we usually ignore them, they are present with us, still. This first contact will ensure we are not making ourselves vulnerable to entities on the other side we would rather not encounter.

If everywhere is here, is every time now?

TIME TRAVEL & PREDICTION

We Have All Seen the Future

Let's use our imagination for a bit of creative visualization. It's a beautiful summer day. We are going for a nice, long drive down the freeway. As we travel through the countryside there are long stretches of road, maybe fifteen or twenty miles between exits.

As we drive, we see a bad accident on the opposite side of the highway. The police are there blocking off the road, so they can remove the damaged vehicles. Traffic has already started to back up. We drive on.

One mile later we see traffic on the other side at a standstill. Another few miles down the road we've driven out of range of the back-up. The traffic is moving normally on both sides. All the people happily driving in the opposite direction have no idea what lies ahead, but we do. We know their future.

There are no exits between them and the accident, no way off the road. If everything continues as it is, all of the drivers in the opposite lane will be stuck, maybe for hours. If we could get out of our car and tell them what we know, it would appear as though we had seen their future. Our prediction would be flawless.

All prediction works this way. The future can truly be seen, as long as things continue as they are. Yet, in this age, because we are waking up from our limitations, exercising our free will, and creative power, chances are things will change.

LIGHT & DARK

We watch the hours tick by, as day turns to night. This is our personal illusion. The Earth is experiencing both night and day, at all times, throughout eternity. Time is a perspective. If we look from the Sun's vantage point, through the lens of divine Consciousness, there is only day. The Sun never encounters night, because it is always illuminating the day-side of a planet.

Any experience of darkness in our life is a personal illusion, created whenever we diverge from Christ or Buddha Consciousness, the consciousness of the Sun and our own Divinity.

If our awareness is centered in our own internal Sun, we are always conscious of that Light, and so we are enlightened. From that standpoint, it is impossible to see darkness in others. The Light we carry dissolves any darkness we may encounter.

People may tell us they have problems, or live in darkness, but we know it is not true. There is no doubt they are experiencing problems and clouds of darkness, but it is all their own creation. They run this personal "movie" in their heads and need the darkness to see the movie and fool themselves. Their life's drama is real to them. We know it is only smoke and mirrors.

We can easily forget we are watching a movie; we get so caught up in it, especially if it's a really good movie with lots of emotion, mystery, love, action, drama, tragedy, and so on. At the close of each life, the movie ends and the lights come on, at which point we remember we have only been watching an epic drama. Most people spend their entire life in the theatre, sitting alone in the darkness. Still, it is important to recognize we can learn great lessons from these so-called movies.

These "movie-heads" are sometimes referred to as the *walking dead*. They go through their lives, caught up in their own story, convinced everyone else is watching their movie. If we suggest otherwise, they look at us as if we are crazy. When we become enlightened and approach one of these people, they may manifest an extreme reaction, because our Light is wrecking their movie.

If an usher comes down the aisle with a flashlight, during a film, it might annoy us. For a second, we might remember we are just seeing a picture-story. Imagine what the crowd's reaction might be if all the lights in the theatre were turned on. This analogy may, in part, illuminate why Jesus was killed. Fortunately, the Earth and our consciousness continue to raise in vibration. Now, fortunately, fewer Light Workers are being put to death.

Be the Sun. Shine the light. It's now time to wake up.

CYCLES OF TIME

Though our perception of time is a mental construct, cycles always exist. The illusion springs from the misconception that time moves linearly from past to present to future. The enlightened being sees all parts of the cycle simultaneously. Time is merely a division of the cycle. In reality, there is no division.

A significant cycle ended, relatively recently. It began at the Harmonic Convergence on August 17, 1987. It concluded December 21, 2012, the year the Mayan calendar ended. At that time, our solar system aligned with the center of our galaxy, which takes place about every 26,000 years.

The Mayans believed this alignment would greatly accelerate our human evolution. Certain of our contemporaries believed time travelers from the future would show up in 2012. Many misinterpreted the record, believing it meant the end of time, and thus the end of the world, a misconception based on the assumption that if the calendar ends, time ends.

Some say time ended when Edison recorded his first sounds. Others posit the advent of the photograph, or video, both readily available to us now, stopped time. Beliefs have no limits.

In reality, as we move into higher states of consciousness, the illusion of time begins to lose its hold on us. If there were some leap in the total consciousness of the planet, the concept of time would fall away completely. This is actually already in process, as the Earth's consciousness evolves beyond time, or the 4th dimension, into the 5th dimension.

If we believe something will happen for us in the future, such as the "Second Coming of Christ," for example, we have to wait years for that experience. If, however, we know something profound began, when Jesus took on the Christ Consciousness at his baptism, and continues still, then we are right now in the midst of an eternal unfolding!

THREE REALMS OF WORK

There are three realms we can work within to effectuate change in our lives: our energy, our consciousness, and our feeling.

We are all incredibly powerful beings. We must stop limiting our power! We tie our energy up so easily; yet, most are completely unaware of it. We must accept no limitations. When friends, co-workers, or family members tell us we can't do something, we must not accept the restrictions they would place on us!

They might say, "Oh, you can't do that. No one can do that," or "You're no saint," or "Get real." Then we may say, "Yeah, you're right," or "What was I thinking? Of course, I can't do that," or "I'm only human." The negations the others offer us are only their own sense of limitation projected onto us. We can do anything! We are saints! This is real!

We lock up our energy in so many ways, feeling hurt, anger and revenge, to name a few. In fact, we actually hold onto these energies. They get lodged within our cells and subtle bodies, but we can begin to detect these areas of stagnancy. When we are aware of them, we can then do something to release them. Practices such as qigong, tai chi, and yoga offer us a means by which we may break up and release stagnant energy.

There is so much energy with which to work. In the *Partnered Energy Work* exercise on the following page, we focus on detecting our energy fields. We recommend you experience the exercise using the available audio recording, *Ten Gates into the Garden: Spiritual Exercises and Meditations*. To transmute outmoded patterns in the thought and feeling aspects of being, refer to the *Astrological Modifications* in Chapter 5.

Partnered Energy Work Exercise

Stand one behind the other, both facing the same direction, with a foot or two between you. The person in front will stand (or sit) still and breathe deeply and rhythmically. The person behind begins to synchronize their breathing with their partner. Take three long, slow deep cycles of breath. Allow the one in front to lead. Observe closely and align with their rhythm of breath.

As you both continue breathing, the person in back rubs their hands quickly together, to stimulate the movement of energy and activate the magnetics. Place both hands about an inch above your partner's head, without touching it. Feel the perimeter of the energy body closest to the person's physical body. Now, trace the contours of your partner's form from head to toe, letting the hands move in and out, along the edge of the energy field. Be aware of its shape, density, texture, color, or temperature, if you can detect any.

When you have finished, begin again at the top and feel another of their subtle bodies, further out from the first. Once you have finished dowsing the second body, move the hands farther out to the third. Be open. Refrain from projecting where you think it should be. Simply feel where it is.

When you have finished, convey to your partner what you have discovered. You may have picked up on something unexpected. Share your findings, even if it makes no sense to you. The person who was just dowsed will then communicate to the other what they experienced when their aura was being explored.

Now switch. Change positions, or both turn around. Synchronize your breathing with your subject. Take three deep, rhythmic breaths, attuning with your partner. Rub your hands together and proceed in the same manner. Feel where the energy field stretches out or pulls in. You may feel pockets of denser or higher frequency energy, variations in temperature or texture. You may even receive intuitive knowings.

Feel the second body now. Observe and mentally note any variations or insights. Once more, begin at the top to feel the third body. Be sure to communicate what you learned with your partner, upon completion. They will share their experience, as well.

CHAPTER 7

Kundalini & the Chakras

CYCLES WITHIN CYCLES

"Yea, though I walk through the valley of death, I will fear no evil: for thou art with me; thy rod and thy staff they comfort me."

Psalm 23 KJV

We are given a few potent tools to help us along the spiritual path we walk. If we were to divide the One Power amongst 100 tools, each would carry one-hundredth of the total energy. If we divide the One Power into a handful, each will produce a greater effect.

We are given the "rod" and the "staff." The rod is our word. The staff is the Kundalini, which runs along the central energetic pathway of the spine. Kundalini is also known by the name Serpent Power, and the serpent is a well-used symbol for it, as it exemplifies spiral energy.

We rise each day to move through the cycles of our lives. We move in circles, some larger, some smaller. Our blood circulates, that is, it courses through our bloodstream in circles. We all cycle our breathing, ever inhaling and exhaling. We consume and we excrete. Our brainwaves cycle. Our cells are continually replaced. The majority of the body replaces itself every seven to fifteen years. We do not have the same body we did at birth. That body has died, yet we all are still here, which clearly shows we are not this body we currently inhabit.

We go through cycles of waking and sleeping, of birth and death. We cycle through ages, over and over with each lifetime. We cycle through families. Often, we have been one of our own ancestors. It is not unusual for us to reincarnate in many guises within the same family lineage, in order to get to the root of and transcend energetic patterns inherent in that family tree.

Each of the four elements cycle. We know that ocean water evaporates, falls to land as precipitation, becomes a stream, feeding a river, which eventually flows back to the ocean, only to rise again.

Our planet spins around, recycling every twenty-four hours. The earth makes a yearly cycle around the Sun. We are always in motion, turning around and around.

This is the Great Wheel of Life, the wheel of cause and effect, the wheel of endless incarnation. Have we outgrown the need of going around and around in circles yet? Does every action we take seem to bind us even more? Is there no way off this cosmic merry-go-round?

The job of religion, ideally, is to ease us off this seemingly endless ride. The word religion comes from the Latin *religi, religin, or religre*, "*to tie fast*." To tie fast! To reconnect. Its purpose is to reconnect us with God.

THERE IS NOTHING THAT IS NOT GOD

This wisdom, offered by Satya Sai Baba, teaches us God is everywhere. Either our experience is of God in divine union, or we continue in an eternal holding pattern, which we call the cycle of birth and death. Buddha taught the way to free ourselves from the wheel is through the Eight-fold Path. Jesus' 'way' serves as a door through which we also can transcend the illusion of duality.

The earliest known religion still practiced widely today is Hinduism. Vedanta, a Hindhu philosophy, which derives from *The Vedas*, some of the oldest extant scripture. Veda means "truth" or "wisdom." The ancient Vedantist, Patanjali, through his *Yoga Sutras*, codified the science of yoga. The word yoga means "union." Though its goal is the same, yoga is not a religion.

SHAKTI

Kundalini comes from the root word *Kundali*, which means "coiled." Kundalini herself is a serpent goddess and is known as *Shakti*, the consort of the god *Shiva*. In Hindu mythology, these two engage in a cosmic dance that creates the universe.

The Shiva and Shakti energies are originally stationed at the crown chakra, from where Shakti descends, and then resides at the root. In its un-activated state, the Shakti energy lies, coiled and dormant, wound three and a half times just below the sacral region, at the base of the spine. This is the supreme creative force in the human body. Imagine it as a coiled spring that holds enormous power in potential.

The *"Great Work"* is to awaken this creative energy and lift it up to the crown chakra, just above the skull, where it reunites, once again, with Shiva. As Shakti raises in vibration, it is lifted through the chakras, or energy centers, activating them through all of the four lower bodies (physical, emotional, mental and memory/etheric). As the chakras open more fully, awareness is awakened and consciousness is raised up, as well.

In the Hindu myth, Shakti originally dwells at the top, alongside her consort, and is completely awake. Then, she descends to the base, where she coils around it and falls into deep sleep. This is why the Kundalini needs to be roused. This downward movement symbolizes Spirit descending into matter, the commencement of the cycle of involution. Once Spirit is completely involved in physical form, evolution can begin.

We find reference to the Kundalini in the teachings of many different religions: Hinduism, Buddhism, Taoism, Judaism, Christianity, the First Nations of North America and South America, as well as in the Ancient Egyptian teachings. This concept is also found in fairy tales, such as *"Sleeping Beauty."* Why would we repeatedly see this concept in such diverse religions and cultures?

Myths and stories are created to explain experienced phenomena. Early humans were aware of the awakening of the Life Force within them. They felt the spiraling energy move up the spine, like a snake. This experience then gave rise to the idea of Serpent Power, as demonstrated in the myth of Kundalini Shakti.

These are ancient ideas. In the *Kabbalah*, the mystical teachings of the Hebrews, this energy is represented as a snake and a lightning bolt, which are both spiraling energy. Some report they experience the Kundalini as an electrical current. The lightning bolt demonstrates the energy descending, whereas the serpent illustrates the climb back up. Climb is what an aspirant must do to ascend the "Mountain of Attainment."

JUDEO-CHRISTIAN THEMES

The Garden of Eden

In the biblical story of the Garden of Eden, we are introduced to a serpent that lives up in a tree, which indicates the Kundalini was originally found in the "up" position. Adam and Eve, representing the faculty of our conscious-subconscious awareness, are tempted by this energy.

The Creator tells us, if we partake of the fruit of the tree of the knowledge of good and evil, we will lose our unity with God and enter the world of duality.

When we bit into the apple, our eyes were opened, we came alive to the world of the senses, and we "died" to Spirit. We saw that we were naked and hid, because we thought it "bad." God then "cursed" the snake and brought it down the tree to crawl on the earth. In other words, the Kundalini was brought down to the base, where it coiled up and went to sleep. Many awakened beings view our present reality as merely a dream. The ladder in Jacob's dream, described in the Bible, symbolizes the spine, the path the Kundalini follows.

Jacob's Ladder

Jacob had a dream:

> *"And he dreamed, and behold a ladder set up on the earth, and the top of it reached to heaven: and behold the angels of God ascending and descending on it."*
>
> *Genesis 28:12 KJV*

Exodus

In Ancient Egypt, the mysteries of the Kundalini were taught to the initiates. Moses was brought up under the tutelage of the Egyptian Masters. This is evidenced in the story of Moses, Aaron and the Pharaohs' magicians.

> *7:8 And the LORD spake unto Moses and unto Aaron, saying,*
>
> *7:9 When Pharaoh shall speak unto you, saying, Shew a miracle for you: then thou shalt say unto Aaron, Take thy rod, and cast it before Pharaoh, and it shall become a serpent.*
>
> *7:10 And Moses and Aaron went in unto Pharaoh, and they did so as the LORD had commanded: and Aaron cast down his rod before Pharaoh, and before his servants, and it became a serpent.*
>
> *7:11 Then Pharaoh also called the wise men and the sorcerers: now the magicians of Egypt, they also did in like manner with their enchantments.*
>
> *7:12 For they cast down every man his rod, and they became serpents: but Aaron's rod swallowed up their rods.*
>
> *Exodus 7: 8-12 KJV*

What clues does this story offer us? When Moses was traveling through the desert with the Hebrews for forty years, he was told snakes were biting the people and they were dying. Moses had a serpent made of brass. He lifted it high above the people's heads, up on a long stick. He said if anyone could see it, they would be healed.

In the desert, the people were engaging in behaviors that resonated at the lower end of the energetic spectrum and were being burned (read bitten). If they could see what Moses was showing them by way of example, then they would also be able to lift their serpents up high. As they proceeded to raise their consciousness up and make higher vibrational choices, their troubles ceased and many were healed.

CHRISTIAN MYSTERIES

Later, Jesus told his disciples he would also be lifted up, like Moses' brazen serpent, and anyone who saw him would be saved. It's the same story. We can gain great insight into the crucifixion story, if we keep this in mind. The scourging and the crown of thorns then take on a very new meaning.

The Christian mysteries complete the cycle that began when the serpent was cast down in the Garden. During the crucifixion, Jesus, as the Christ, represents the Kundalini energy that is lifted back up.

In Hebrew Gematria, the word for tempter and messiah have the same numerological vibration. When we fuel lower vibrational thoughts and actions and are drawn in by the pleasures of the lower chakras, the energy is directed down toward the base of the spine. We call this "The Tempter." When our focus is lifted up toward the heights of consciousness, we call this "The Redeemer." How we focus our energy is always what brings us down or lifts us up.

Creating a Myth

Imagine we have come to a planet to help out, where people are steeped in superstition and ignorance. Their consciousness is so low, they are far from understanding the way things work in their world. To help their evolutionary process, we want them to raise their energy up from its lower vibration to its highest expression, so we make up a story or myth that will guide them through a process, to further them along their path of unfoldment.

We tell the people God and heaven are "up" in the sky, and the devil and hell reside "down," deep in the Earth. Up becomes the carrot, while down serves as the stick. If they are "good," they get a nice pat on the head, and if they are "bad," they get a firm spank on the bottom. Well, misunderstandings inevitably arise. As a result, they begin to perceive sex as "bad," because the sexual organs are located "down there." Such misconceptions occur when people take things too literally.

The perception that "good" and "bad" are associated with up and down underlies why they lift their spirits and direct their prayers "up," in an attempt to get closer to God. As the focus of their awareness, and, therefore, their energy, moves closer to the crown chakra, they are actually in greater alignment with God.

Colors become symbolic in our myth. Red, at the lower end of the vibrational spectrum, is associated with the devil, and, as we raise in vibration, we ascend toward "my blue heaven." One can go higher still and work with the violet ray. So, the whole heaven and hell story is just another metaphor for the Kundalini.

THE CHAKRAS

In the seven-chakra system, we have energy centers located at the crown of the head, third eye, throat, heart, solar plexus, sacral region, and at the base of the spine.

The Sanskrit word *chakra* means "wheel." These whirling disks are major energy centers in our subtle etheric, or energetic body. Though they correspond to areas in the physical body, and the energy vortexes resonate there, they are not physical in nature.

They also relate to seven levels of consciousness, each of which expresses on a continuum somewhere between its un-evolved and evolved states. The lower three chakras root us to the material plane of existence, while the upper three connect us to the realm of Spirit, and the heart chakra, at center, serves as a gateway between the two.

Root Chakra: MULADHARA - *"Root Support"*

The root, at the base of the spine and associated with the adrenal glands, is aligned with the earth element, the color red, and reflects our three-dimensional consciousness, and basic need for self-preservation. It is through this center the life-force manifests in the physical world, and is symbolized by the square, and a four petaled lotus. This level of consciousness is the foundation of our experience of the physical plane in which we live.

We receive external vibrational impulses through our sensory apparatus, and translate them into sights, sounds, smells, tastes, temperatures and textures, the building blocks of our materially based consciousness. When we perceive information through the lens of the root chakra, the world appears to us as physical, stable and solid.

As mentioned previously, the base chakra's symbol is the square, that massive foundation at the base of the Great Pyramid, in Egypt. The higher we rise up the pyramid, the smaller the squares become. At the point of the apex the foundation disappears.

Our belief in the physical plane is the cornerstone of our edifice of error. The life we build on this faulty foundation eventually must crumble away to nothing. Otherwise we would be trapped in our false creation for eternity. We feel secure in the physical. It is the nest that holds us as we grow, until we consciously choose to allow our energy to fly up the spine back home to our true foundation, Spirit.

In alchemical symbolism, each chakra is assigned one of the seven sacred metals. Lead is aligned with the root chakra. It was the densest and heaviest of the known elements, at the time of attribution. Interestingly, time is also associated with this energy center.

The expression "lead-bottom" refers to something that is weighted down or sluggish. Our attachment to the material plane may hinder us from directing our focus toward the loftier goal of spiritual upliftment. Men often carry their wallet in a back pocket, near this chakra. The love of money is a state of consciousness that binds us to the material plane. This chakra's planetary affiliation is with Saturn, the "Ring-Pass-Not," which supports the idea of limitation, as well as liberation.

In traditional Catholic Orders, the first vow is poverty, which is needed to disconnect from this root center. Buddhist monks and nuns also take a vow of poverty. Non-attachment, or what is referred to as *aparigraha* in the yogic tradition, cuts the cord. Our initial striving is to detach ourselves from the illusions around us. All ideas of ownership stem from the mind. Poverty is also a state of mind.

This is not to be confused with "poverty consciousness," however. Poverty consciousness is rooted in the belief there is never enough. One truly living the Vow of Poverty holds the consciousness that they lack for nothing. Such a being experiences the Oneness of Creation, which overflows with unlimited abundance.

Card 21 in the Tarot, traditionally called The World, is associated with Muladhara. We are using a new title, "Cosmos." The goal of these lessons is Cosmic, that is Cosmic Consciousness. Otherwise, the path leads us back to the Earth in another cycle of incarnation. The choice is ours. There is no right or wrong with our decision, it depends on where we want to go. If we choose to return to the world, we will get another chance to choose Cosmic Consciousness in the next life. Saturn rules Capricorn, a sign of the depths and the heights of experience.

Sacral Chakra: SVADHISTHANA - "One's Own Abode"

As we travel up Jacob's ladder (the spine), we arrive at the sacral chakra, located in the pelvis at the region of the sacrum. The second chakra is aligned with both the feminine water element (emotion), and to a lesser degree, the masculine, fire (passion) element, and resonates as the color orange. Symbolically, Svadhisthana is represented by a circle over a crescent, surrounded by six lotus petals.

When this chakra is functional, we are able to enjoy life's physical pleasures, to develop a sense of abundance, and feel we are worthy of experiencing good in our lives. It is the seat of the creative impulse, which may result in the birth of a child, an idea, or some other creative manifestation.

This center is intimately linked with our ideas about pleasure and our sense of our own sexuality. The energy flow of the sacral chakra was opened up more fully, during the "Sexual Revolution" of the 1960s, when many were more freely experimenting and exploring their sexuality. Until then, this center, for many, had been closed down by previous generations' patterns of sexual repression.

In the United States, we can trace this sexual repression back to the Puritans. They were a fundamentalist religious group, who believed sex was sinful. Sex, for them, served no other purpose than procreation, or populating the planet.

During the 1960s, the slogan, "Make Love, Not War," served to direct human consciousness from the root up to the second chakra. This sexual awakening countered the ideology of war, typically initiated over material things like territory and resources. Love, at that time, was made manifest, for many, in the act of sexual union. Many today equate love and sex, but when we raise the Creative Life-Force up higher, we recognize the heart center generates an entirely different expression of Love energy.

When our awareness resides in the sacral center, our focus tends to be on ourselves, and we are generally immersed in and operating through the senses, buffeted by our emotions. At the heart center, however, the focus shifts toward others, elevating our vibration. Our love moves from a personal experience to one of Universal Love, a love of humanity. When lifted to the crown, Love becomes Divine.

As the only magnetic energy center, the metals associated with the sacral chakra is iron. Sex is a magnetic force that manifests through the act of coupling and allows the masses a brief taste of the power of Kundalini Shakti. This very potent center brings forth a different state of consciousness, when we are sexually aroused. Its intense power is the force underlying procreation.

The second chakra relates to the desire body. As the physical body lives in the physical world, so the desire body lives in the world of desire. Here we move beyond the physical. Interestingly, as we realize sex is not the "be all and end all," we recognize we have choice. We can either continue on up to the third chakra or retreat back down to the first. The "fundamentalists" would have us go back down to the base and remain caught up in fear and vilifying the human body.

When we raise our energy vibration from the first to the second chakra, a different world opens up. After we pass through puberty we are able to better understand double-entendre. We now "get" the hidden meanings, which are typically sexual in nature.

The chakra system gives us seven inner or "hidden" portals through which we may come to understand ourselves in the worlds of matter and Spirit. Astrology teaches us each of these seven views has twelve basic variations. 12x7=84, the number of years it takes the planet Uranus to circle the Sun. Uranus represents our Spirit, dwelling within the framework of the multi-dimensional Tree of Life. The Hebrew tradition offers that the Bible can be read on seven levels. Whenever our vibration is lifted, through a real spiritual experience, everything takes on new meaning.

The Tarot equates The Tower card (phallic Mars) to the second chakra, which shows the man and woman plummeting into the abyss, when they realize the foundation their life has been built on is faulty. Our work, however, is to create a new foundation rooted in Spirit rather than matter. We achieve this, by raising our vibration. We can continue to generate generations of children, or we can regenerate our consciousness. In the last age, Pisces, one might have moved beyond the sacral center, by taking the monastic route and the second Vow of Chastity.

Solar Plexus Chakra: MANIPURA - "Jewel City"

The next chakra is ruled by the passionate fire element, vibrating as the color yellow. This is our instinctual center, which affects how we interact with others and engage with the world. Our sense of self-worth and self-identity are anchored here. Symbolically, this chakra is depicted as a downward facing triangle, surrounded by ten lotus petals.

A balanced solar plexus chakra is essential to our knowing we are worthy simply by virtue of our being. If this awareness is compromised, it will impact our ability to relate to others in functional ways.

Our feelings of personal power, and our ability to achieve financial independence have their basis here, which are closely aligned with our free access to knowledge through education, and deeply influence our self-esteem, sense of personal power, and freedom of choice.

Our self-image is often greatly impacted by our desire to be well liked or regarded by others. If we are motivated by such needs, we live in the realm of the false self and are ruled by the ego. We are then challenged to release limiting patterns that keep us trapped in our comfort zone and bound to the material plane. If we wish to continue our ascent, we must exercise the power of our will and transcend the need for others' approval, so we may turn our focus toward our soul and Self-realization.

The third chakra is located in the region of the navel, stomach and the nerve plexus of the diaphragm. The energy of this center powers the vital organs, and aids in the digestion of food and ideas.

In the Middle Ages, monks were often depicted in paintings as very round, full-bodied people. In their spiritual pilgrimage, their focus may have stopped at the third center. They were poor and chaste, but they ate well. Traditionally, fasting has been key to moving beyond this level of consciousness.

The metal aligned with this chakra is tin, which was long used in the packaging and preservation of perishable food. Now most "tin" cans are made of aluminum, because it is a less expensive material and can be recycled.

The sacral chakra holds us bound to the wheel of birth and death. The sexual engine continually produces babies. As a way to get off the endless wheel, Buddha taught meditation on the navel, which, just below it, flanks the solar plexus chakra. Through the navel, we are connected to our mother, who was connected to her mother and so on, back to the beginning. In order to develop a functional self-identity, we must be able to cut the psychic umbilical cord connecting us to our mother. If we have not done so, we continue to allow ourselves to be influenced (fed) by our mother's energy.

The navel is a potent energy power center in the body. If we are totally focused on the third chakra, we have transcended the sexual force. By taking vows of celibacy, monks and nuns are helping humanity off the wheel of birth and death, in part, by not contributing to the birth aspect of the continuum. When we eliminate the cause, the effect disappears.

The solar plexus chakra is related to the Wheel of Fortune in the Tarot. Notice the Blue Sphinx, which represents the Self, positioned at the top of the wheel. This indicates Self sits "above" the navel center, its vibration is higher than the energy of the material plane.

When we view reality from this center, we begin to transcend the cycles, transcend time. We start to take "the long view" of things, and the cosmic workings are made visible.

From Matter to Spirit

How do we move our consciousness from one rooted in the material plane toward one that is centered in Spirit? We begin to direct our awareness toward the cycles of breath. The breath is a vehicle for the Life-Force to move to us and through us. We breathe continuously from the moment we emerge from the womb. This primal rhythm aligns us to the greater energetic current of the Cosmos.

As infants, we breathe with the whole body, assuming there are no physical conditions that inhibit its natural function. Babies breathe deeply and rhythmically through the nose, unless they are in a state of distress, like when their nasal passages are blocked due to mucous congestion.

This primal rhythm continues until external conditioning from parents, siblings, family, etc. and life experience begin to train the child away from what comes naturally. The conditioning that affects the breath most profoundly is fear, which is a contractive energy that compresses the cells, and disallows the necessary expansion of the lungs. This is, in part, why breath becomes shallower when we are in "fight or flight" mode.

When we are operating from a fear-based consciousness (ego), our body's systems are perpetually on high alert, which quickly depletes our energy stores. We cannot function well in chronic survival mode. Our systems were not built to withstand this kind of constant stress. It would be like driving a car at 6000 + rpm all the time. The vehicle could not withstand that level of force for very long before it would overheat and break down.

A car has cycles that are functional and so does the body. As we slow the breath down, we minimize "stress points" in the body. Our stress markers, like elevated heart rate, blood pressure, and levels of cortisol and adrenaline diminish, and we move from "fight or flight" mode into the relaxation response, as the sympathetic nervous system is pacified and the parasympathetic nervous system is activated.

The diaphragm, the primary muscle involved in breathing, becomes the springboard that assists us in transcending the lower vibrational energies of the root, sacral, and solar plexus chakras that keep us bound to the material plane. The diaphragm, along with the front and back walls of the body, create a pumping action (both up and down and front to back) in the abdominal cavity, which moves the life-force energy through the whole body. The alternating current of the inhalation and the exhalation powers the "battery" we call the heart, the hub of our energetic system.

This pumping action also works like a bellows to fuel the heart flame, amplifying its light. The heart center then becomes a crucible into which we place all that needs transmuting from a lower vibration to the higher. As we dissolve all that we are not in the Flame of the Heart, all that remains is pure Spirit.

To review conscious breathing, refer back to the chapter 5 on Meditation.

Heart Chakra: ANAHATA - "Unstruck"

Now we arrive at the heart chakra, which vibrates as the color green. It is the center of the human energy system, which functions physically, emotionally and energetically to direct the Life/Love/Light Force through us. This is the locus of unconditional love, compassion, forgiveness, joy, and abiding peace, among the attributes of the Christ and Buddha Consciousness.

The heart is divided into four chambers, the divisions create a natural cross within it. The true Christian path begins here. When we *"take up [our] cross" (Mark 8:34 KJV)* and follow the "Way of the Christ," we have begun to love from the energetic resonance of the heart chakra. At this level of consciousness, our polarity changes.

If we are focused on the lower three chakras, our only desires may be limited to money, sex and food. Once we open the heart center, by awakening the fourth chakra, the energy expands outwardly, moving from the personal to the transpersonal, from ego to soul consciousness, then to Christ/Buddha Consciousness, and ultimately to Cosmic or God Consciousness, the vibration of pure, unconditional Love.

At the forth chakra, the Love energy is amplified. Love increases, as the polarity changes, due to a shift of focus away from the consciousness of the lower three ego-based chakras toward the upper three spiritually attuned energy centers. The golden, solar force or Light Force of the Christ Consciousness also intensifies. The light increases, because the open heart offers no resistance, and the open heart's energetic force now radiates forth unimpeded. The heart chakra is the portal through which we must pass to attain higher levels of consciousness.

Here, should we choose to continue our ascent, we heed the call to "take up [our] cross" (symbolic of the four elements associated with the four lower bodies: physical, emotional, mental and etheric). Again, the emphasis is on taking it up, raising our heart vibration to a higher dimension.

"The Sun [Son] shall rise with healing in its wings."
Malachi 4:2 KJV

Some people are waiting for the Earth's poles to change, either physically or magnetically. The real change happens when our own polarity reverses. This happens when the Kundalini rises above our heart chakra. This is what truly happens when we are "born again," or during an instantaneous conversion, like Paul (Saul) reportedly experienced on the road to Damascus.

The heart chakra is the Sun center. In occult work, the Sun symbolizes the heart. Astrologically, the Sun rules Leo, the Lion. So, when the alchemical formula for "turning lead into gold" calls for some "Red Lion," we are meant to activate our heart center, whose corresponding metal is gold. Turning lead into gold was actually a spiritual practice meant to raise the vital force from the root chakra/lead, to the heart center/gold. Our intent is to raise our vibration from the denser realm of matter to the highest frequency of Love/Light.

The heart chakra is geometrically symbolized by a six-pointed star, created with one upward and one downward facing triangle, surrounded by twelve lotus petals. "As above, so below." In this instance, the downward pointing triangle represents the first three chakras and the upward pointing signifies the throat, third eye, and crown. The star is balanced at center in perfect harmony.

In Tarot, the heart chakra is the Sun card, showing a boy and girl holding hands in front of a stone wall. The wall has five layers of stone, which represent the five senses. The children are "in the garden," while the senses are "walled out." The Sun's Light shines within. The children do not need physical senses to see it. The masculine and feminine energies are in perfect balance, resonating with the vibration of the Cosmic OM, the sound of Light.

Love is the most powerful force in the universe. God is Love. We feel the difference between an open heart and a closed one. Our sense of opened or closed is not related to our physical heart. We are feeling the current state of the heart chakra, through which, when open, a limitless outpouring of divine Love flows.

We have been trained away from experiencing the heart chakra in its pure, open state. Instead, we layer feelings and emotions around the heart, cloaking it in limiting patterns of judgment and false beliefs. We have contained the pure Love Energy, so it will "fit" more comfortably into our personal lives. This only limits our ability to experience the joy, peace, abundance and grace that Love/Light/Life is continually offering us. As we release our judgments and concepts, we begin to feel God's Love flowing through our heart center.

The Christ, Jesus, was an example of God's pure Love manifest in physical form. He taught us we can become such a vessel. Human love has its limitations; divine Love is infinite in expression. As we shift our focus from our conditioned human love to unconditional, Universal Love, we will finally be expressing our Divinity through our humanity, with a truly open heart.

Throat Chakra: VISHUDDHA - "Especially Pure"

The throat center resides in the neck and vibrates as an electric blue. The symbol for the fifth chakra is a sixteen petaled lotus, surrounding a downward facing triangle. It is the seat of our creative expression, and the place from which we speak our thoughts, feelings and ideas with clarity and conviction, fundamental to our personal integrity.

The throat chakra is the Womb of the Word. The white collar a priest wears originally meant the purification of the throat center. When activated, the Word has great creative power. With the heart opened, we are filled with Love. Now we may lift that energy to the throat, our vehicle of outward expression.

Our word carries much more than the basic meaning with which those sounds have been endowed. It holds our will and intent, and carries a frequency, infused with emotion. This vibration reflects the level of Light reverberating through the words. Certain words have a higher vibration and Light quotient, while others are denser and emit less Light. Every word we speak is a subtle seed planted in our own subconscious mind or the subconscious of others.

The Word can be invoked for healing (people heal themselves; we provide energy and opportunity). When the throat chakra is purified and activated, the Word is reborn; we are reborn. The Word is an amazing tool of creativity and communication that brings our intention into manifestation. Additionally, it is an amazing agent of our own salvation.

The Circle of Life

String theory is among the most current scientific thinking about the make-up of matter. When we move beyond the molecular level, atoms are revealed, then sub-atomic particles, until, eventually, we arrive at the smallest theorized foundational substance of matter, the string. These are little looped circles of vibrating energy. A thing's vibration determines its nature. These strings are basic building blocks of creation, and it is likely science will uncover still smaller blocks.

When we influence the strings' vibration, we influence matter. We do this easily with sound vibration. A shift in the mere tone of our voice will have greatly different effects. (We can also change matter with thought vibration, but not at this chakra.) Our words are potent vibratory expressions that determine what we create in our lives, and how we impact the people around us. Our word affects the food when we bless it. As the throat chakra is activated, so is the dynamically creative power of the voice.

The Empress card is associated with the fifth chakra. She represents the womb of creation. From the higher womb of the throat, the word is born as sound. Sound affects creation.

"And God said, 'Let there be light,' and there was light."
Genesis 1:3 KJV

The lower womb is the incubator of the physical body, which is affected by sound, as well as the gateway by which the body fully enters the material realm.

On the Empress card, Venus holds a rod in her lap, crowned with the ancient symbol of Mars, a circle with a cross on top, which points northeast. When we invert the symbol, it becomes Venus - simple polarity. The Emperor, the next card, holds the Venus symbol, only it is depicted upside down. The contrasting symbol held by each is like the small circle of the opposite color that resides within each paisley shape in the yin yang or taiji/tai chi symbol, demonstrating that a thing is always contained within its perceived opposite, the essence of balance.

The sacral chakra (home of the reproductive organs) reverberates with the energy of Mars, while the throat chakra resonates with Venus. When a boy goes through puberty, his voice typically changes and becomes lower. While young girls, going through sexual maturity, may "lose their voice," if they refrain from speaking their minds, in order to fit into an existing limiting social structure of their peers, or society at large. We create with our body (Mars), and with our word. (Venus)

The Door to Heaven

In the Tarot, the Hebrew letter associated with Venus means "door." At once, it both blocks passage and allows entry through a threshold. The Empress' lower womb serves as the portal into the physical plane. The Throat Center is an entryway into the energies of the spiritual world, as the two chakras above the throat become activated. The Empress wears a "string" of seven pearls around her neck, which are sacred to Venus. They represent the seven chakras. The evenly balanced necklace shines white with purity. These are the pearly gates guarding the entrance to heaven. So how are we able to pass through?

The throat is the center of the Adept, who balances the head (mind) and heart at this energy center. The iodine in certain foods activates the thyroid gland, which has its physical locus at the throat center. The early Catholics encouraged people to eat fish on Fridays, a good source of iodine. Alchemy? Indeed!

As mentioned earlier, Friday derives from the Norse goddess Freyja, which means "The Lady." She, like Venus, is the goddess of love, fertility and beauty. As the door to heaven, she shares the rulership of the afterlife with her brother Odin.

Explore the *Figure Eight Practice*, on the following page, to bring balance to the throat center. We recommend you experience the exercise using the available audio recording, *Ten Gates into the Garden: Spiritual Exercises and Meditations.*

> **Figure Eight Practice**
>
> While sitting, direct your attention to the throat. Once focused, with a long, slow exhalation, visualize energy gradually pouring down the front of the throat to the sternum, and continuing evenly down the front of the spine to the root chakra. See the energy flow between the legs, under the base of the spine.
>
> As you inhale, move the energy up the back of the spine, vertebrae by vertebrae. Pause at the throat for several cycles of breath, to refocus the energy. Continue directing the flow up the front of the face, over the forehead to the crown of the head.
>
> While exhaling, visualize the energy flowing over the back of the head to the base of the skull then crossing the spine to the front of the neck. Pause to anchor the energy there of several cycles of breath.
>
> Again, with the exhalation, allow the energy to flow down the front body to the base of the spine. Trace the contours of the body in the mind's eye. Continue the figure eight breath pattern for three full cycles, ending at the throat.
>
> If done correctly, you will have just run an energetic lemniscate, the symbol for infinity. Practice for longer timings in multiples of three. (6,9,12,15 cycles, and so on)

Third Eye Chakra: AJNA - "Command"

As we ascend toward the summit, we must pass through the third-eye chakra, whose symbol is the two petaled lotus, surrounding a downward facing triangle containing the symbol for Om. which vibrates as the color indigo. The High Priestess Tarot card aligns with the Ajna chakra. The sixth chakra is the seat of intuition, our innate intelligence and guidance system, and is related to the attribute, thought. As this center opens, our awareness awakens, and we are able to easily discern our highest good, as we consciously seek wisdom, truth, freedom and meaning in our lives.

The sixth chakra relates to the mind and is located between and just above the eyes on the forehead, aligned with the pineal gland. This center is known as "the place of the skull," our own personal Golgotha, which carries the same meaning. It is where Jesus experienced the crucifixion. Here we experience the death of our false ego consciousness that it may be reborn as divine Consciousness. The death of the ego can be excruciating for the ego.

The heart energy manifests through action. ("How can you say you love me and just sit there?") The throat energy manifests through our word, and the third eye manifests through thought. This is where it may get tricky.

As we raise the vibration of our body, mind and Spirit on this path of initiation, we need to go all the way. Too many times, out of fear, we stop our ascent at the mind. This is where we get hung up on the fear of death. In *Matthew 16:25* and *Luke 17:33 KJV*, both recount Jesus teaching that "whoever shall seek to save his life shall lose it." If we can't get our triune nature past this gate, guess where we are? 6 6 6! (This occurs when we get stuck at chakra number 6 in the physical, emotional and mental bodies. 6x3) This is another meaning of 666, a symbol related to the anti-Christ.

We know the Christ (Light-Presence/Christos) is consciousness aware of itself as the Sun/Son of God. We know the Sun is the Heart. What, then, acts against the heart? The head! Simply put, the mortal mind is the anti-Christ. The true "enemy" is within, rather than without. We slay the beast, by going through the crucifixion, by surrendering our mind (ego) to God. Then our mind is God's mind, and "I and my Father are One."

Quantum Physics Meets The Mind

Quantum physicists have proven the observer always influences the observation. If we think a sub-atomic particle will shoot off to the right, it will. In fact, everything is vibrating and moving so fast in relation to us we can't say where anything really is. Electrons move around the nucleus of an atom at a blur. In the time it would take us to point to an atom, it has already circled its orbit hundreds of thousands of times. We cannot say where these minute particles are, but we find them wherever we think they are.

The mind works in the same way. Whatever we look for we find. This is true of answers to questions and solutions to problems, as well.

> *"Ask, and it shall be given you; seek and ye shall find..."*
> *Matthew 7:7 KJV*

Our vision of reality deludes us, because the supporting evidence is always at hand for whatever we believe. Of course, our focus inevitably impacts the outcome, so we are continually creating all the evidence to support our perception of reality whether we are conscious of it or not.

Because it's our gaze (observation/focus) that creates the outcome, it's easy to see how we can fool ourselves. We create our reality based on what we believe. Our experience is only ever an out-picturing of our current consistent inner vibration, which reflects our core beliefs or conditioned patterning. When we manifest something in our life, it mirrors back to us and reaffirms our belief. We then accept this fabrication as real. Life is a self-fulfilling prophesy.

We paint pictures with our minds on the canvas of creation. We must ask ourselves, "What are the colors that make up our palette?" Are they tainted with conditioned patterns that dominate our ego-based consciousness, so our experience of life is muted and muddy? We could be painting with the pure pigment of divine Consciousness and creating a vibrant, joyful, Light filled existence. The fear of losing control keeps us imprisoned in a drab, lonely landscape, where we feel powerless to effect any change in our experience.

Yet, the solution is simple. All we have to do is lose our mind. We must be willing to hand over the palette we think we chose and apprentice our self (ego) to the Master (Self). When we relinquish our hold on the limiting concepts of what we think reality is, the vastness of Truth reveals its nature to us.

Only One Mind exists. We, however, fence some off, and put down our stake and claim it as "my mind." We erect walls that separate a little bit of the One Mind, calling it ours. Insane? Sanity is. We are either in or out. It may fly in the face of "conventional wisdom," but wouldn't you rather be in-sanity? Walking in Spirit is always a contrary path.

The only thing we can truly lose is what we are not. We are not the mind with which we readily identify. If we can lose our mind while retaining our consciousness, we'll know who we really are! If we get stuck at the third eye center, it can be debilitating, as we get eternally lost in thought. We must continue the great work of awakening and integrate all the energy centers. We are in the process of constructing the "Rainbow Bridge."

Our two eyes enable us to see in 3-D, which makes the external universe appear very real, through the illusion of depth. If we were only using one eye, the illusion would be diminished. The more we accept the three-dimensional illusion as real, the more difficult it is to wake up to Reality. Step back from the *brink of depth* and go within. Focus on being single-minded.

As pictured earlier, this chakra, in Hindu symbology, is drawn with two petals, one on each side of a circle. Within the circle is the symbol for Om, the Sanskrit word, symbolizing the vibration underlying all creation. It represents Light. Jesus taught, just as the Hindus, that this single eye (third eye, often referred to as the first eye) is also the source of Light.

> *"The light of the body is the eye: if, therefore, thine eye be single, thy whole body shall be full of light."*
>
> *Matthew 6:22 KJV*

When we are living in our Light body, we move our awareness from the two petals framing the Ajna chakra symbol (duality) to the central circle where the Om (Unity) resides. If we can overcome the inherent duality of our personal mind (ego), we will finally get the point, which is the Center, the Wholeness, the One.

When the third eye is open, it gazes in no particular direction, since the directions we know are all based on the illusion of the physical plane. If we look in any one direction, we are missing all the others. If we look at anything, we can't see everything. This All-Seeing-Eye is found on the Great Seal of the United States of America. It appears on the one-dollar bill, placed on a pyramid.

Pyramid means fire (funeral *pyre*) in the middle (amid) - Fire in the middle - It is an amplifier of light. This center is also a door to the psychic plane. Psyche means "soul." Now we have awakened the soul and have the potential to embody it fully.

Third Eye Initiation

David's Travelogue: August 16, 2000 Sacred River Retreat, Bali, Indonesia

We enter the scarab room of initiation. It is very small and the eight of us can just squeeze in. We sit along the wall and can't shut the door without someone moving out of the way. The room is candle lit, which increases the heat. It is very close and hot, and sweat immediately begins to drip off my face. We sit cross-legged or in lotus position.

Present are seven men, and Shankari, our spiritual guide. In addition to me (image at right) are Andrew, John, Dewa, James, Wayne, and another David. We begin as always, chanting three Oms. Then, Shankari chants. My eyes are closed, and the voice I hear makes sounds I have never heard before. She is working with sound vibration, multiplied and amplified by the chamber in which we sit.

David in Bali at the Yellow Temple 2000

After a time, we are instructed to raise our arms high above our heads. We are each given a golden ball of light about two feet in diameter. It feels very real. I can see and feel it, though my eyes are still closed. We slowly bring it down to chest level.

For a few days the group has been working with the phrase "I surrender to the power of Love." Repeating this, I put the golden sphere into my heart center. We keep our hands there, as Shankari chants again.

After some time, we are told to place one hand on the sacral center and the other on the heart. We visualize an energy "figure eight" to connect the two centers within. The energy begins to move and establish the connection. We then visualize a snake making the circuit. I do this and visualize it in my mind.

Again, Shankari vocalizes. Later, the other David says that he was wondering what instrument she was using, as it did not sound like a human voice. At times it sounded like the wind or the sound of rushing water.

Within a few seconds of hearing the sound, a small black snake jumped into the circuit. It was not from my mind and startled me. It seemed like the real thing. It stared at me so I would acknowledge it. Then the snake plunged into my heart. I felt no fear. I did not dwell on it.

It moved slower than the thought-form it replaced (my creation), as I tend to spin things very fast in my mind. It continued to move through my heart and sacral center with the same basic figure eight pattern, although each time it entered and exited in a different place. It moved in a three-dimensional spiral pattern.

If the two centers were oranges, it was as though each time it entered through a different segment. The snake began to change color and grow in size, and the chakras began to grow. As I watched, my heart center got bigger and bigger to accommodate the serpent.

It became as thick as a large python, continuing to go through all the different segments. It continued uniting the energy fields of the two centers. I felt my heart completely open up. This was the most open it has been in this lifetime, and all the pain (heartbreak) was gone. My heart was healed, after it was torn apart eleven years prior, when my son was killed in an automobile accident.

As I continued observing the snake (it even gave me a snakes' eye view through the cycle), I sensed Shankari moving through the room. The chanting stopped, and she kneeled before me. With my eyes closed, I felt her press a finger against the third eye point on my forehead for about one minute, then she continued on to the next person. She had opened my third eye. I actually felt as though I had a physical eye above my brow. It is still open. It's not like a physical eye, as it does not face any particular direction. I have 360-degree vision with it. I have much work ahead, I think, to learn how to use it.

The room was called the Scarab Room, because there was a mosaic scarab in the center of the room, maybe two and a half feet long. Later, Shankari said she had her other hand on the scarab's head, when she was opening up our inner eyes. We were initiated into the Brotherhood of the "Sons of the Scarab." Our energies were linked, and I will see how this manifests for us, when we return to our various countries.

Crown Chakra: SAHASRARA - "Thousand Petaled"

Finally, we reach the energetic summit, the seventh chakra, which vibrates as the color violet, and has its locus just above the top of the head. This center is associated with Light. When the energy raises to this level, we easily experience our connection with the All That Is, the Divine. Here we delight in the beauty and bliss of a life, anchored in Spirit, and we know implicitly we are unconditionally loved, accepted, protected, guided, and held in the grace and loving embrace of the Limitless Light - God.

When we summit the crown, the climb is complete. On the seventh day God rests. We are in bliss, experiencing the ecstasy of the Cosmic Orgasm! Nowhere to go. Nothing to do. Divine Being! The noun and the verb in perfect balance. Here the sage dwells, high in mountains. We have entered the "upper room," where Jesus took his disciples to receive the higher truth. This is the "above" that completes the "below," the energy center at the base of the spine.

Now it becomes evident our foundation is really the crown, the place of cause. What we experience in the four dimensions (width, height, depth, and time) is created "above," in the realm of Spirit/Energy. Each chakra's energy is supported by the one below (lower in vibration). In order to fulfill some desire (sacral), we must move the body (root). A healthy self-esteem (solar plexus) grows out of our knowing we are worthy of having good in our lives (sacral). Our ability to love others unconditionally (heart) requires we accept ourselves completely (solar plexus). The power of our word, (throat) to manifest our intentions, is predicated on our open heart chakra. If we are to fully access our intuition (third eye), we must walk our talk with the integrity of our word. Finally, when we are relying completely on our inner knowing (third eye) we are in tune with and channeling divine Presence (crown).

The crown chakra is associated with The Magician card, in the Tarot. He is channeling divine energy from Source, the Sun pictured in The Fool card. He channels as much power as he knows he can. The Magician is a Master of the mind (Mercury), so he has mastery over the elements.

The crown chakra is therefore Master of the body, as it is the conduit for the energy that underlies our thoughts. The Source, the root of the tree, certainly dwells here at the crown. In the Kabbalah, creation is seen as an upside-down tree.

You Can Leave Your Hat On

There are many who have attempted to bring energy to the crown chakra, by placing objects on their heads. Some witches have worn pointy black hats. Some seekers place pyramids on their heads. These funnel shaped hats serve as a vortex, a means to channel power. Even the original use for the "dunce cap" was to stimulate a student's brain, à la the wizard's hat. One can only assume all these "pyramid heads" were seeking the same effect.

Kings and queens wear crowns, made of precious metal, usually adorned with jewels. When we awaken the crown chakra, we will also rule our kingdom and experience an abundance of riches.

The purpose of wearing spiritual head coverings is to bring one's attention to the crown center. In the Hebrew tradition, the men typically wear a *yarmulke* or skullcap in synagogue.

There is an association in the wearer's mind between the top of the head and being in God's presence.

The tradition of women wearing Easter bonnets is part of the 16th c. custom of donning new clothes to celebrate the resurrection of the Christ, Jesus. This holy day always occurs when the Sun is in Aries (ruler of the head).

Hari Krishna devotees shave their heads, except a patch at the crown. Catholic monks' hair style is just the opposite. Either way, the focus is brought to the top. Egyptian Pharaohs wore headdresses with the *Ureaus,* or rearing cobra, while First Nations peoples draw energy to the crown chakra, by means of feather adorned headdresses. Each serves the same purpose.

Why not offer the masses the teachings of the Kundalini outright, and dispense with hats and hairdos? The consciousness has risen to a point where such teachings now can be understood and assimilated by humanity. It was not always the case. Consider, for example, what happened to wise women deemed witches…. Fortunately, we have entered a new age, one where higher consciousness will again reign supreme. More and more of us are aware God dwells within and "up" means a "higher" vibration, not a direction. We are lifting the old-age veils, the occult is coming to Light, and up and down now take on a totally new meaning.

Know Fooling

At right, we see a pouch, which symbolizes the soul, tied at one end of the staff the Fool carries over the right shoulder. Contained in it is the essence of all previous experiences from this life and others. On the bag's front is an eagle, on the flap an eye. They represent the lock and the key to our own personal *Akashic Record*.

The Kundalini is typically associated with Scorpio, whose triune nature illustrates its three energetic modes of expression. Its least evolved aspect is the scorpion, whose sting and deadly poison are in its tail. The scorpion strikes its prey from behind, or attacks when it feels threatened. If the root chakra energy is unevolved, we live in survival mode. Self-preservation becomes key, and fear dominates our motives. When rooted in this low energy vibration, it is difficult to recognize we are the creators of our own experience, and we only ever reap what we sow. Our view of life becomes poisoned by blame and denial of responsibility.

As Scorpio raises its vibration, it becomes the snake. The Kundalini has awakened and is progressively moving upward to activate each chakra in the system. The snake must shed its skin, in order to grow. We must release outmoded habits of thought and behavior, if we wish to transcend our perceived limitations, and merge with the divine aspect of our being.

The next highest manifestation of Scorpio is the eagle, which appears on the Fool's soul-pouch. First Nations peoples of the Americas say the eagle is the only bird able to stare directly into the Sun. A soaring eagle's vision is so powerful it can spot a rabbit from about two miles away. The soaring eagle is symbolic of spiritual sight (the eye on the flap of the pouch), which is activated when the Kundalini raises to the third eye point. Though the third eye may be open, we still must be willing to look through it.

When we have been re-born in God's mind, following the death of the false mind (false ego), duality falls away. We no longer view life binocularly, but, rather through the singular, all seeing eye of Spirit. Then our inner vision or intuition becomes our only guide and we no longer rely on external input. Once the ego is transmuted and has been purified in the "funeral pyre" of the Heart Flame, we rise from the ashes as the resurrected phoenix, the highest vibration of Scorpio's energy.

The Fool card indicates we must raise the serpent to the brow, in order to remember other lives. To achieve this state, must we give up sex? Yes, but what is meant by giving up? It doesn't mean abstinence, it means raising the sexual energy up the spine, allowing it to be tempered by the Heart Light and channeled through the third eye chakra!

If at some point we allow the raised energy to descend again, we must refrain from binding it there with guilt. There is no good and bad. When we make a judgment regarding our own or other's behavior, we create an energy knot, which inhibits the free flow of the divine Life Force energy. We may think we are binding back a bad habit, but we are only imprisoning ourselves. If we live without judgment, with no good and bad, right and wrong, the knots dissolve.

At one time, there was even a misconstrued Catholic teaching, meant to deter masturbation, which stated it would eventually lead to blindness. Now we can ascertain they were really talking about the loss of spiritual sight. Remember, no judgment. The open and activated third eye chakra offers a real ability to see in a new way.

The fourteen *Stations of the Cross*, of Catholicism, are also connected to the Kundalini. Originally, there were seven stations, affiliated with the primary chakras. In time, the devotion expanded to fourteen. In this way, we might regard them as an expression of the seeming opposite polarities of these energy centers.

If you are interested in learning more about this correlation, read the *Mystery of the Christos*, by Corinne Heline, who was a student of Max Heindel, the founder of The Rosicrucian Fellowship.

The scourging (whipping) Jesus experienced reflects an accelerated raising of the Kundalini, which, when raised too fast, feels like being whipped across the back. His crown of thorns is symbolic of the energy center at the crown chakra opening up. The literal understanding of the Passion is a very superficial view of a powerful spiritual initiation. We believe the whipping and the crowning must have been painful, but it is only our ego-based perception.

The Christ, Jesus, was finally raised above the earthly plane, through the resurrection and ascension. His journey is symbolic and was offered by him as a path of salvation for the world to follow, so we too might experience this initiation. We do not need to experience the literal crucifixion, however. We get caught up in the details and miss the bigger picture.

The crucifixion is living symbolism. Many think they know what happened, but few ever look beyond the surface image. Jesus, it is said, was pierced through the hands (historically, one crucified was actually nailed between the radius and ulna bones at the wrists), feet and side, these represent, in some systems, the other five or lesser chakras.

Jesus was not the first to play out this role. Historically, there have been over a dozen messiahs, all born of virgins, who are attended by three wise men who are guided by a star to bring gifts to the child. The savior eventually dies and is resurrected. (Mithra, Osiris, Zoroaster, Adonis, Krishna, and others) Much more on this subject can be found in *The World's Sixteen Crucified Saviors,* by Kersey Graves, written in 1875.

The point is, it wasn't about Jesus. Jesus' death and resurrection were about the pattern of initiation. Jesus did take on the pattern and became the "Lord of Earth," but there were other Lords before him, and others will follow. Still, the Christ remains. Each "messiah" is a Christed Being. One day we will each claim this glorious position. It's just another step on the cosmic path. Jesus said,

"Come, follow me."

Luke 18:22, Matthew 19:21 KJV

THE CADUCEUS

The Caduceus, a healing symbol associated with the medical arts, perhaps seen at the local drugstore, is a diagram of the Kundalini. Two serpents intertwine around a central shaft. The heads of the snakes align with the third eye center. (snake = Scorpio = third eye) These represent the Kundalini's three distinct circuits.

The *sushumna nadi*, is the central and most direct path toward enlightenment, which runs along the spine. It is known as the "straight and narrow." The serpent on the right, *pingala*, is gold and represents the masculine, solar energy current, and *ida*, on the left, is silver and symbolizes the feminine, lunar energy flow, whose synergy gives us electro-magnetism.

Now, apply the Kundalini caduceus symbol to the image of the crucifixion handed down to us. The thieves either side of Jesus are symbolic of the two snakes. They are "thieves," because each, as one half of the equation, only gives a half-truth. When we believe the duality, which our mind creates is reality, our original state of Unity is "stolen" from us. As our Kundalini raises and activates the heart center, the awakened Christ Consciousness allows us to transcend all pairs of opposites. We move from our polarized consciousness back to our original Unity Consciousness. The death of the ego brings the resurrection of the Self.

On the cross, at the point of death, Jesus said,

"My God, my God, why hast though forsaken me?"

Matthew 27:46 KJV

At this point, it does feel as though God has forsaken us, as we must let go of our idea of what is God. We must let go of our current relationship with God, so we can have a completely new and more authentic one.

We can equate the seventh chakra with the seventh day, the Sabbath. For now, the work is over; it is time to be still. The crown chakra is the seat of Self-Mastery, the crown we wear when we are the ruler of our four lower bodies.

Attaining the summit of the crown is a goal of our work. Although, the Tarot teaches it is only once we reach this level we truly begin to walk the spiritual path. When the chakras are properly and gradually opened up, the change in consciousness greatly increases our energy.

Most people's consciousness dwells at the root chakra. They are stuck in "survival mode." With our focus on self-preservation, the world may seem a dangerous, inhospitable place. The unpredictable world of matter we perceive through our senses seems very real, because we know no other. In the Tarot, the crown chakra is represented by The Magician card.

The key is to have the occult knowledge (Air), while swimming in the mystical sea, the womb of creation (Water). The path of the mystic is one where we "feel" our way along, operating outside of the conventional mindset. The "knowledge" we acquire serves to neutralize the erroneous information we accepted as truth through our early life conditioning. Knowledge, however, is not the goal. Once we return to our original divine state of being, there is nothing we need to know, for we already have access to everything.

BUDDHA, KUNDALINI & DRAGONS, OH MY!

The crown chakra is symbolized by a thousand and one lotus petals. Years ago, David visited the ancient Sanjusangen-do Temple, in Kyoto, Japan. Inside was a huge statue of Kannon (Quan Yin, goddess of compassion and mercy) surrounded by 1000 unique life-sized Buddhas. As he sat in meditation at her feet, he realized each Buddha represented one of the petals. When our crown chakra is open and activated, we have access to 1,000 Buddhas, each with its own special quality. The One is surrounded by the thousand.

When the Kundalini, creative Life Force, prana, or qi reaches this summit and remains, we move above our worldly awareness and beyond thought, where the Buddha dwells. Buddha is always depicted as peaceful, because his mind is clear. There are no thoughts to disturb or distract. The word *Buddha* means "awakened." We wake from the dream (or nightmare) of thought. We transcended, because our trance has ended.

In India, the Kundalini is a feminine force, because it is perceived as the "Great Mother" birthing all of creation. As the high vibration at the crown lowers, the Kundalini descends, coils around the base of the spine three-and-a-half times, creating the physical universe. In the West, the realm of the dragon, we are taught the upward path, and therefore experience the serpent power in a more masculine, active way.

In the practice of Kundalini Yoga, one way to awaken is to practice spinal twists. (don't attempt without direction from a qualified instructor). When "The Twist" became a popular dance in the West, in the early 1960s, David thought the "fad" would actually begin the awakening of the Kundalini for his generation. (Then again, he thought the Beatles were the Four Horsemen of the Apocalypse…)

The Strength Card of the Tarot represents the dragon (Kundalini) awakening. This creature is prevalent in both Eastern and Western literature, lore, and legend. Both the Kundalini and dragons fly, and both breathe fire. The Tarot card pictures a red lion, as opposed to a dragon. The lion is Leo, the sign of fixed-fire.

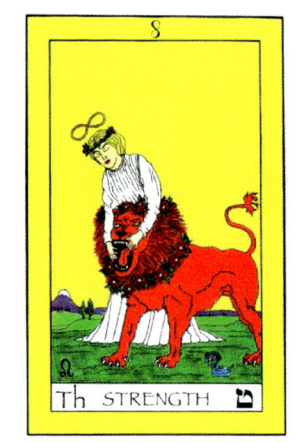

In the East, the dragon is a benevolent beast that signifies the Life Force energy. It is a Master of the elements, and the bringer of good luck.

In the West, the dragon is depicted as a malevolent creature that scorches villages, terrorizes villagers, guards a priceless treasure of gold and precious gems, and needs to be vanquished by noble heroes. Here, symbolically, the dragon represents the lure of power, which diverts our focus away from the inner treasure. We may also see the dragon as the lowered Kundalini that guards our inner riches.

In either case, the dragon symbolizes our own energy. How we choose to use it determines if we are moving closer to Source or farther away. As the Kundalini spirals, we can easily get caught up in the energetic vortex, which pulls us into and out of the world (whirled). The serpent continues to 'tempt.' We must remember, gold is the Heart, the Sun, the Light, and the glimmering jewels are the chakras.

Eventually, we will need to let go of all this information about the chakras. Ideally, we want to build our new foundation on information that has come from within the Self. Often, external information only leads to concepts that hinder us from actually experiencing truth.

If any of these lessons resonate with something inside you, that is entirely different. Then the truth is emerging from within you. You are simply remembering you are God. We cannot tell or teach you anything you do not already know at some level of your being. Remember, you are God, after all!

Explore the *Solar Meditation* below, to reawaken your awareness of the divine Presence within. We recommend you experience the meditation using the available audio recording, *Ten Gates into the Garden: Spiritual Exercises and Meditations.*

Solar Meditation

Come sitting at the front of your bolster, with legs crossed, supported by bolsters if you wish. If sitting is uncomfortable, you may also choose to experience the meditation lying down. Allow the lower body to descend, rooting through the sits bones at the base of your pelvis. From this solid foundation, let the spine grow long, as the crown of the head ascends skyward.

Close your eyes. Let them rest like gentle pools floating in the skull. Soften the inner ear. The brain is alert but remains passive. There is awareness without thought. Release the mind from its tasks. There is no need to analyze, qualify, comment, or judge. Simply be. Be present to the body and to the breath. The root of the tongue now descends in your mouth. Drop the jaw, slightly, so there is space between the upper and lower teeth. Allow your sensory organs to recede further, as you gradually release your attachment to the external environment.

Fall into the center of your Being. Fall into the Grace of who you are. Fall into the center of the Sun, the Pure, Radiant Light, the Christ or Buddha Consciousness, the bridge between the personality and the I AM Presence, our divine, essential essence. Become present to the Life Force that permeates and activates your subtle bodies, which in turn animate and vitalize your physical form. This is the essence of who you are.

Bring your awareness to the heart center, the swirling disc of the Anahata Chakra. The Sanskrit word Anahata, means un-struck. It refers to the Vedic concept of the un-struck sound, the sound of the celestial realm. The Eternal OM.

In your mind's eye, image the Anahata Chakra, it's color, a brilliant emerald green. It is depicted as a 12 petaled lotus, within which resides an upward facing triangle, representing Purusha (the Supreme Being), merged with a downward facing triangle, prakrti (Mother Nature, or all causal matter). This merger, creating a six-pointed star, represents the union of the masculine and feminine energy principles, the positive and negative poles that are essential to all creation.

Just as the physical Sun, the Heart of our solar system, is the child consummated in the union of Purusha and prakriti, so are we. We too are Sons of God. The essence of our being is the offspring of this same divine union. We share the same power to create as our solar system's radiant Sun. When positive and negative forces blend in harmony, energy is the result; its triune forms are Love, Light and Life.

As you breathe, visualize the heart chakra opening; visualize the brilliant green disc rapidly swirling in a clockwise fashion. The inhalation is receptive, representative of the feminine principle; the exhalation is active, representing the masculine force. The heart is the center, where these two energies intermingle in their cosmic dance of creation…

Solar Meditation, Cont'd

Sense the Life Force moving through you in the rhythmic inflow and out go of the breath. With each cycle of breath, move your awareness more deeply into the altar of the Heart. Fuel the divine Flame of the divine Consciousness. Let it radiate from the core of your being. Coeur, in French, is the heart. Here resides the Source of all that you are. Activate the Light body. Let it shine forth, illuminating you from within. As you open your heart fully, the Light emanates, showering all in your presence with the creative force of Love.

Now breathe in through the heart center and exhale out through the crown of the head. Feel the radiant warmth spill forth from the crown, like a fountain of Light, flowing down the sides of the head, over the shoulders, chest and back, down the arms and legs, enveloping you in a golden sheath. This is the golden embrace of divine Light, pure Consciousness. Let it cradle you. Let it carry you. Let it buoy you, as you move through your day. Float in the arms of Grace. Fully embrace the All that you are so you may fully embody All that you are.

Remain with the breath held within the Light for as long as you desire. When you do emerge, slowly allow your awareness to return from the depths of your inner exploration. Reenter the external environment invigorated and centered in the Light.

CHAPTER 8

The Divinity of Destruction

THE BEGINNING OF THE END?

The Apocalypse, Armageddon, End Times, the Third Wave, the New Age, the Aquarian Age, and the Second Coming of Christ are all concepts floating in the unconscious soup of what is known as the "mass-mind." What is going on?

We are moving into a period of great polarity, a split in realities. People are taking sides, though the sides aren't what we think. It's not good guys against bad guys. It's not a split between Islam and Christianity, or terrorists against law abiding citizens. The sides are much subtler. They are the sides or stances taken on the polarities of knowing, belief, and intent.

Do we believe it is the beginning of the end? Do we believe we are powerless? Are we simply being tossed around by forces beyond our control? Do others create our reality? Many accept such beliefs as their reality. We have a choice, however. If we function with the idea the Earth is our foundation, then we will be at the mercy of whatever happens in the world. The planet shakes and we shake with it. If Spirit is our foundation, we can never be shaken.

If we sit in a dark room, all is dark. If we introduce light, we will see light and shadow. The brighter the light, the darker the shadow appears. The great Light of divine Consciousness, is entering the Earth now, so it appears there are great shadows. The shadows are caused by an obstruction to the flow of this Light. If we let the Light or divine Consciousness shine through us, we cast no shadow. When we close our hearts and minds to others, we allow the darkness to manifest.

MULTIPLE REALITIES

We are presently experiencing what appears to be two worlds, two basic realities. We are the only ones to determine the one in which we want to live. If we choose the world of darkness and fear, we will live in a place where it appears that things are done to us, or to others, a helpless place of frustration and anger. We will live a life where we believe we are at the mercy of things beyond our control. We may choose, however, to live in a place of Light, Love and Peace. That place exists within us. That place is the Heart.

These worlds run parallel, so we may appear to be in one, when we are living in the other. It's our consciousness that makes the difference in our experience. We aren't imagining another reality. It isn't a creation of our mind. There is another reality.

This is not easy work. All around, people are feeling victimized. People are angry. There is a great call for justice, although many confuse it with revenge. We are surrounded by pain and confusion. It is not easy work.

Look at the specific acts of terror committed on September 11, 2001. How many different realities did the victims experience? People were stabbed to death on the planes. Some died in plane crashes, while others died as a result of explosions. Many were burned to death, as others suffocated from smoke inhalation. People fell to their deaths from the tower windows, while some were crushed. Many were hit by falling objects. Several consciously committed suicide through their acts of aggression.

Many realities were experienced. People were killed heroically, grappling with those on the plane that went down in Pennsylvania, or as first responders at the scene in Manhattan. Some died without a clue. No two people had the same experience. All of us will die to the Earth. We have all died thousands of times. The point is it's not really about death all.

ANCIENT TERRORISM

Let's consider another group of terrorists for a moment, the ancient Roman Army. At one point, the roads leading to Jerusalem were lined with the crucified. What could be more terrifying than being eaten alive by lions in the Forum, as tens of thousands watched and rooted for the animals?

Jesus dealt with the terrorists of his day, not by praying for revenge or justice, but that they be forgiven, as he knew they had no idea of what they were doing. We may think today's terrorists know exactly what they are doing. They have no idea.

Did the 9/11 terrorists know they were creating, at least for a short time, a greater sense of unity, not only among the people of the United States, but the entire world?

Jesus told us that his *'kingdom'* is not of this world. *(John 18:36 KJV)* The physical world is not the main concern. From the planet Earth's perspective, these and countless other attacks mean nothing. Many more around the world die of starvation, AIDS, and other diseases every single day.

All who go through transition in these ways, do not return to Spirit in tears, but in joy. The tears flow at our birth into the physical plane. For the survivors, there is grief and great pain. We grieve the loss, the separation. Our hearts open to those who have had their realities torn open.

The families' pain is very real to them. Our work is not to ignore the horrors that surround us, but rather to be compassionately non-attached. It is not easy to be of help, if we ourselves are in a state of imbalance. People are looking for stability. If our foundation is built on Spirit, we will manifest that stability and balance.

MODERN TERRORISTS

The violence seems to come from many different factions. A "spiritual" group, in Japan, releases poisonous gas, while right-wing militarists in the US bomb public offices, snipers out for revenge pick off passersby below, and cars are driven into crowds on busy sidewalks. Students are murdering their classmates, while others attack clinics where abortions are offered. Extreme religious fanatics blow up civilians in cities all around the world, hiding behind their own misunderstanding of their religion. All of these perpetrators are ignorant of the truth that souls are eternal and can never be killed.

The terror appears to be coming from all sides, or at least from the "outside." And it does seem terrible out there. What can we do? Jesus told us not to fear those who could only kill the body. *(Luke 12:4 KJV)* The body, or our connection to it, our miss-belief that we are a grouping of material cells, leads us to feelings of fear and the false need for self-defense.

We hear over and over from the gun advocates they have a God given right to defend themselves and their property. No, this is false. Jesus, the Christ, said:

"Whosoever shall seek to save his life shall lose it, and whosoever shall lose his life shall preserve it."

Luke 17:33 KJV

Many in this camp profess they are Christian but forget to follow Jesus. We do have the right to be our Self, which ultimately can lead to the transcending (trance-ending) of our bodies, and to the non-attachment to things.

When we have achieved this state, the terror cannot touch us anymore. We can be at peace in the midst of the storm, calm in the center of the confusion. That is not to say we have checked out and don't care.

When we watch the TV news, we feel the pain, as we see our brothers and sisters slain before our eyes. It is the soul of humanity being crucified again and again, in all places, at all times, until the Great Liberation, when we all wake up and remember God is One. For those who are still operating in the space-time continuum, the age is changing. The Christ, within each of us, is coming. The Apocalypse is at hand.

ARMAGEDDON

In the personal spiritual quest, there comes a time when we become conscious of the battle of the forces of Light and darkness, and we are finally aware it is occurring within us. It is our own personal war of Light and darkness, and the Light does always win, because we are consciously on the path and have the intent to persevere. When enough people are on the spiritual path, raising their consciousness and aligning with the Light, we achieve a critical mass that cannot be stopped.

We are undergoing this process now, and external events are out-picturing our own internal struggles. We are going through a spiritual initiation on a global, rather than merely a personal level. It may appear as though things are beyond our control and we are being swept-up by some great external dynamic forces. All the upheaval is ultimately working us toward a renewed state of balance.

THE OTHER SIDE OF 9/11

What will come of all of this terror? The terrorists' intent is chaos, but the intent of the people of America is the maintenance of the "United" States. Around the world, more and more individuals are uniting in defiance of these increasing acts of terror. David has spoken to a number of people who experienced an incredible rush of Spirit, as the Twin Towers, in Manhattan, collapsed, in 2001. In his meditation, immediately following the towers' destruction, he saw Archangel Michael surrounding the towers, and was given the words "transformation" and "temperance."

The feeling from the other side was one of calm and acceptance, there was no judgment at all. Divine action was in process. A doorway opened, through which many souls ascended, as Spirit descended. It seemed from Spirit's perspective very matter-of-fact. There was no extra concern. Those overseeing the souls' transition were not alarmed. The feeling from the other side was, "This happens, so we do this." David, however, still had to let go of judgments. Everything was going along fine "upstairs," concern would only get in the way.

The Tarot's Tower card depicts the tower being hit from above and burning, while the man and woman fall from the heights. The Tower represents personal isolation, a structure erected on a foundation of false premise. The lightening flash comes to destroy the illusion of separation. Now we move into a new reality. Now the premise transforms to: "Anything is possible in the limitless unity of the Divine." The old structure falls away to make space for our greater growth and expansion, the reclamation of our birthright.

We must fear not, nor bear anger in our hearts. We send Love and Light to all. The victims, the grieving, the perpetrators, without exclusion, we direct Love and Light to all. Even the beings, who appear the most "evil," are still God. They are doing evil deeds, because they have forgotten they are God. When we send them hate, their forgetfulness only amplifies, as we empower their actions with our words, focus, and fear. When we send them Love and Light, we can penetrate through their armor of human forgetfulness, and access the Divinity of their souls. They will eventually begin to remember.

PRIORITIES & THE BOTTOM LINE

Once we have begun our process of spiritual development, there comes a time when we need to re-examine our intentions, goals, and true beliefs. What is our bottom line? What result do we seek from our strivings?

In the Kabbalah, there is a major symbolic system, based on the *Tree of Life*, which we will focus on in greater depth in subsequent volumes. It is composed of ten spheres, called Sephiroth, placed on three columns, four spheres in the center column and three on each side. The spheres are connected to each other by paths. The use of these in spiritual development is known as path-working. Each sphere and path represent a specific state of consciousness.

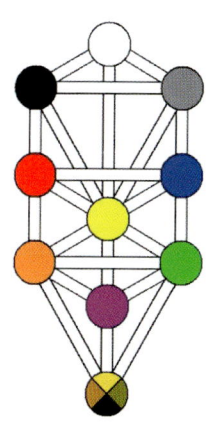

The Tree symbolizes God's connection with creation. The top sphere is called the Crown, and references, in part, the crown chakra, centered above the head. The bottom most sphere on the tree is the Earth, as we know it, mirrored in the root chakra.

This Tree has its roots in Spirit, not in the earth. The tree appears to be upside-down, which is the real key to spiritual awakening. Our roots are our foundation, our stability. Through roots we draw our sustenance, the true Source of Life. From divine perspective, the physical creation is the fruit that Spirit bears. Generally, most regard Spirit as the fruit of matter. For example, we may build a church or temple structure with the hope it will bring us closer to the Divine. This perspective is a reversal of reality.

The Suspended Man, in the Tarot, places us upside-down, hanging from a rope, which is fastened to the gallows. Our only support is the spiraling energy, represented by the twisted cord. The earth that once seemed so solid disappears from around our head. It wasn't so solid as we imagined. As study of this card reveals, we only find that out after we completely let go.

The tunic pockets are shaped like crescent moons, which indicates we have to let go of our memories and the past. This challenges our conscious mind, because we base our present-day identity on our past experiences. When we are asked to let go of the past, it feels like we must let go of our self. We must finally release our attachment to the false ego, which feels like a death of sorts, but the soul is eternal, and we can never be disconnected from who we truly are. We can never experience the "now," as long as we cling to the past.

There are many surprises awaiting us, when we let go of the false memories. We remember the true ones, what we were doing before this lifetime. We remember the essence of what and who we really are. We begin to have access to the Cosmic Memory or Akashic Record.

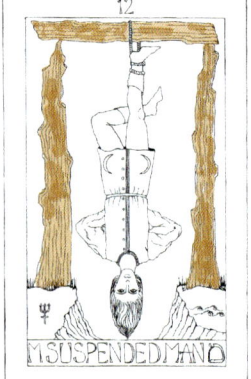

The Kabbalistic Tree of Life and the Suspended Man confront us with the notion that our thinking has been the cause of our shift away from Source. As the paths of the shaman and mystic are revealed to us, we recognized they walk contrary to the world. In the world, we are typically motivated by self-preservation, whether of our biological form or the fragile false-ego. The mystic and shaman know there is no death, and our sense of self is what actually keeps us from being our real Self. The sages do not practice self-defense. They understand it is as silly as the ocean defending itself, or the wind. Who we really are is in no danger of extinction.

The Suspended Man hangs from the Hebrew letter *Tav*, aligned with card 21, the Cosmos or The World card. The letter represents both the limited world, in which we find ourselves, and the limitless Cosmos we seek to inhabit. The two may appear the same, yet there are no two things further from each other. It is a paradox.

First there is a mountain. Then there is no mountain. Then there is.

This Zen saying would have us reflect on the reality we think we see, the mountain. As we consider the mountain, we begin to realize it is just our concept, our belief of what we think is the reality of "mountain."

As we do our spiritual work and cast out our false ideas, our distorted vision of the mountain disappears, and we become aware of the real underlying nature of its essence. Our vision is now based on the true foundation. We look again and the mountain has returned, though our vision of the mountain has changed. Now we see the mountain as it is.

The truth is the mountain has not changed a bit. All the transformation has occurred in our own consciousness. We can spend our whole lives working to change the mountain to no avail. The only work that results in lasting change is our work on our self. What is this work? Do we build new structures, and learn new facts? Do we learn how to control or how to manifest our will?

The true work is to let go of all the false ideas we have collected over the course of our many lifetimes. In reality, the work begins when we lose our mind. Really! We have each taken a limited allotment of divine Mind and called it our own. We have set up the rules and established our walled kingdom. Now, it is time for revolution. We must overthrow our own creations.

If we have revolution in mind, we can get complex and imagine overthrowing the government. The root of revolution is "revolve," which means to turn around. Can we turn the government around? Do we kick out the current government? Which government? The federal, state or local government? Do these people govern us? Are they that in touch with reality and truth that we so easily give away our power to them?

No one has any power over us, unless we give it. This may seem preposterous, when we think of our upbringing with parents, who may never have given us any option regarding our own autonomy. It is unlikely Mom and Dad sat us down as infants and discussed who was in control.

But who was really in control? Did they dictate when we were born? Were they in charge of our breathing? Did they command we digest our food in a particular way? And during our teen years, we may likely have more boldly exerted our will, to various consequence.

How are we looking at this concept of control? Is it from the point of view of Spirit or matter? Spirit reveals we have the power, no one else. Spirit shows us we have so much power we specifically choose our parents to incarnate through. We were absolutely in control of those early "helpless" years. We set up all the situations we experienced in our early life and beyond, before birth.

We may ask ourselves, why did we pick this specific experience? This question opens a door. When we have answered it, we will be able to walk through the opening the question has created. It may seem to take a long time, before we find the answers; however, there is no more important focus of our energy. All else is mere distraction.

Western society puts distraction on a pedestal to be worshiped. We reward those who distract us the most, heaping fame and fortune on professional athletes and movie stars, who play for us in stadiums, on stages and silver screens. Many politicians, and celebrities alike, focus attention on any number of meaningless things. We may choose to read gossip magazines and romance novels and will gladly give our attention to the ups and downs of the stock market.

We live in houses of distraction that require endless maintenance. We spend all our time and energy maintaining the illusion. We work really hard at it and do it very well. The dishes are clean. The laundry is done. The floors are swept. All done? Almost, just repeat for eternity.

What if we stop perpetuating the illusion? What happens to the dishes, the laundry, the floors? Do we care, if Aristotle wore dirty clothes? Would his teachings be any different? Are Jane Austin's writings any better or worse, if she didn't sweep the floor? If Marie Curie had consistently left dishes to stack in the sink, would her contribution to humanity have been any less?

Please recognize we are not saying stop washing the dishes or doing laundry. After all the outer is always a reflection of the inner. The problem arises when we allow these endless tasks to take precedence over deeper work. They become a means of avoidance. Some even use meditation as a way of avoidance. It's never about what we are doing, rather, it's about why we are doing it. Everything comes down to our intention.

Whatever appears to be going on without is always a reflection of what is going on within. This is the nature of the paradox. What ideas do we hold that actually hold us? All of them! When we possess, we are possessed. When we hold, we are held. Can we practice non-attachment with our thoughts? Are our thoughts really ours?

We think our beliefs are justified, because they are based on our previous experiences. Our previous experiences, however, are an outward manifestation of our belief systems. Life is a self-fulfilling prophesy. What we believe, we become. The cycle has to be broken, or it will keep us in eternal bondage.

Can we experience anything we do not believe exists? Our minds will quickly fill in the blanks, as we explain to ourselves what we think we are experiencing. The Amazing Randi, a famous magician, has made it his life's work to debunk all psychic abilities. He has offered a hefty reward to anyone who can prove that psychic abilities are real. He still has all his money. He stares at reality but cannot see beyond his own limited consciousness. No matter what the experience, his rational mind always comes up with an explanation.

Quantum physics shows us the observer observes what they expect to observe. God has such great love for us, we are given the ability to create. When we are awake to reality, this becomes a wonderful tool for liberation. When we are asleep in the dream of our own reality, it only gets us into trouble.

As we are created in God's image and reflection, so too are we creators. The difficulties arise, when we begin to create in our own image. When we create from our own limited state of consciousness, how can we then create anything but limitation? The enlightened allow God to create through them. When this happens, we experience limitless creation.

CUTTING THE TIES THAT BIND

The Master, Jesus, stated:

Think not that I am come to send peace on Earth: I came not to send peace, but a sword.
For I am come to set a man at variance against his father, and the daughter against her mother, and the daughter- in-law against her mother-in- law.
And a man's foes shall be they of his own household.

He that loveth father or mother more than me is not worthy of me: and he that loveth son or daughter more than me is not worthy of me.

And he that taketh not his cross, and followeth after me, is not worthy of me.

He that findeth his life shall lose it: and he that loseth his life for my sake shall find it.

Matthew 10:34 KJV

In the New Testament, these words are written in red, to signify their divine origin, which means the words come from the Christ that dwells within each of us. When Jesus said, "not worthy of me," he was not referring to his personal self, but to the Christ. The Son of Man is the Sun of God, just on a smaller scale. It is this divine Self within he teaches must be put first. Not our friends, family, or even our self (false-ego)! This is a hard lesson, because it cuts to the quick. This is only another way of saying:

"Seek ye first the kingdom of God, and his righteousness; and all these things shall be added unto you."

Matthew 6:33 KJV

How can we perceive true reality, if we don't put God first? We will only ever see reality through the lens of our own finite mind. From this vantage point, we invariably get a partial view. Must we place God before our parents or our children? Well, God is before them, as they are all God's creations. If we don't put God first, we continue experiencing the life we have now.

Jesus's mission, as the Christ, was also to break the patterns of the past, traditionally passed on from parent to child. We have conscious patterns of etiquette and behavior, as well as unconscious patterns of the same. As we get older, we find ourselves, at times, acting or speaking just like one of our parents. We might use a particular phrase, or move our hands in the same way as our mom or dad. We may perpetuate emotional states our parents regularly manifested. Maybe it's a bad temper, not being able to say no, or a tendency to tell the same bad jokes. We realize these traits are passed on from our grandparents and earlier ancestors. So, whose temper is it? Which of our traits are really ours?

Let's make it easy and just dump them all. These inherited limitations of false beliefs have not served our family well. Jesus came as a sword, because he needed to cut through the connections. This requires we relate to God as our Father/Mother, not the guy with the sperm and the gal with the egg. This cutting and re-connecting has been practiced for eons and is why we receive a new name each lifetime. Once we are reconnected with our true Source, Jesus no longer must come as a sword.

In order to put God first, we must be aware of God's Will. We must uncover God's word within us, which is the Self. The Self can be heard. We don't need to tell God to speak up! We need to learn how to listen.

Imagine a small number of people talking all at once. If we try to take in the totality of what is being said, we end up hearing nothing. If we focus, however, it is possible to pick up specific bits of conversation here and there. As we focus in on a particular sound, just one voice, we begin to discern and hear, at least what that person is saying. Through our meditation and inner listening, we eventually tune in to the one voice we are attempting to hear. We can then begin to filter out the distractions, that is, everything else.

"Be still, and know that I am God…"
Psalms 46:10 KJV

As Jiminy Cricket, from Disney's *Pinocchio*, would say, "Let your conscience be your guide." We need to become quiet inside enough, to hear the still small voice, which requires practice. It does get easier, truly. We do hear it, eventually. At first, is comes softly, then a bit stronger, until it comes through more forcefully than everything else. The challenge, then, is to follow our inner guidance.

When we heed it regularly, we change our foundation from matter to Spirit. Then we are no longer motivated by fear and pushed around by the requests of the world. As we follow the inner Light, the source of Love, our whole attitude changes. The junk falls away, all the justifications we offered in defense of our unproductive thoughts, feelings and actions.

As we begin to break down our inner limitations, we find they were always our own thought creations. We seek inner freedom and find it is always there. Now we reflect it outwardly, that we might manifest this inner reality in the world. Though we may pray God's kingdom will establish itself on Earth, each of us, individually, is the means to that end.

THE FINAL WALL

As we begin to bring this new reality forth, we typically come up against a wall. The walls we run into now are those erected by the unenlightened. It is not enough that we have rid ourselves of our self-created limitations; we must also move past the limitations others place on themselves, and those they would also place on us. To reiterate, "At least they aren't killing us anymore."

As we move past another's limitations, a variety of reactions may surface. Jesus showed this to the extreme, when he walked on water. The disciples were crossing the sea by boat, as a storm rolled in. Jesus was alone praying on a mountain. The disciples were afraid, and Jesus walked out to them on the water. What was the reaction, as he walked past their limitations? Initially they were very afraid. When Peter saw it was Jesus, he asked to join him, and he walked out on the water to Jesus.

> *"But when he saw the wind boisterous, he was afraid; and beginning to sink, he cried, saying, Lord, save me. And immediately Jesus stretched forth his hand, and caught him, and said unto him, O thou of little faith, wherefore didst thou doubt?"*
>
> *Matthew 14:30 KJV*

Peter also wished to walk past his limitations, and for a moment he did. Then he saw the 'boisterous' wind, which *Dictionary.com* defines as:

> *1: Rough and stormy; violent.*
> *2: Loud, noisy, and lacking in restraint or discipline.*

Remember, Air is the element of the mind. It is likely Peter's mind was loud, noisy and undisciplined, the source of most of our doubt. What is real; what is normal? In Jesus' reality, walking on water was not some great miracle. It was normal.

The Earth is obviously being shaken at the moment. As long as we look to the fruit of the tree for our sustenance, rather than to the root, we will shake with the Earth. The more we build our foundation in Spirit, the more normal miracles become. The following quote is often associated with Albert Einstein, though its attribution to him is disputed.

> *"There are only two ways to live your life. One is as though nothing is a miracle. The other is as though everything is."*

When things get heavy out there, be Light!

Explore another variation of the *Egg of Light Exercise*, when you are feeling the weight of the world triggering any sense of limitation.

We recommend you experience the spiritual exercise, using the available audio recording, *Ten Gates into the Garden: Spiritual Exercises and Meditations.*

Egg of Light Exercise

We'll explore another variation of this ancient spiritual exercise introduced in an earlier chapter.

Step 1: Sit in a relaxed position in a straight-backed chair, or on a meditation cushion. With eyes closed, release the muscles of the face and jaw. Visualize an egg of light surrounding your body The Egg is filled with the White Light of the Christ Consciousness. Its shell reaches above the head and below the feet. See it. Feel it. Be secure and fearless within it. Visualize the golden light of the Sun as the golden yoke, emitting from your solar-plexus. See it grow to fill the entire oval engulfing you. Allow it to become more intense, until there is only the light within the shell. Become the light.

Step 2: Become the Love and Peace that is Light. Be filled with the Life the Light carries. Cast all negation out of the egg, all negative thoughts and feelings. Release all the pain, fear, guilt, and separateness. Let there be Light! As you go through the day, know this shield of light is filtering out the thoughts and fears that are directed toward you from "out there" in the world. As this is your knowing, you become a true point of Light in the world.

CHAPTER 9

Religion

PERSONAL RELIGION

What is religion? When we contemplate religion, we typically think of the various world religions. Let's begin to expand beyond our own concepts. According to Wikipedia, there are around 4,200 world religions, the examination of each is beyond the scope of this volume. We will, however, look at religion through a different lens. Every person on this planet has their own personal religion. Many people may be in the same sect, but each will have a slightly different experience.

The top organized world religions and sects, by number of followers, are Christianity, Islam, Catholicism, Hinduism, Agnosticism, Buddhism, Atheism, Anglicanism, Seventh-Day Adventists, Mormonism, Sikhism, Judaism, Bahai, Confucianism, Jainism, and Shintoism. Like fingers on the hands of God, these beliefs are intended to be tools that build bridges between humans and God.

Even a pagan, agnostic, or atheist has a particular set of beliefs, perhaps even daily practices, and a code of conduct by which the individual makes their way in the world. Though one may not believe in God, per se, there may be a sense there is something greater, some Force or Energy, a larger Current of Creation within which we move through the universe.

As previously stated, the word religion comes from the Latin word *"religare,"* meaning "to bind." Religion is a tool used to reconnect us to the Divine. Religion is not the goal, it is a means. God is the goal. We can be religious for eternity, or we can be one with Source now. When we are One, time no longer exists, eternity dissolves into the now.

When we focus on the means rather than the goal, we have hitched ourselves to the never-ending wheel. We are called seekers, but we never find what we are looking for, until we go within. Though there are many paths that lead within, until we jump fully into the center of our being, we are still treading an external path.

The spiritual path has been offered as a way to enlightenment, which is all well and good, but we must eventually give up the path too. Buddha said his teachings are a bridge to carry one over the river of illusion. His teachings encourage us to stop standing on the bridge and move to the other side. We must make the leap from religion to God. We may become so attached to our religions that they keep us from ever attaining the goal. When we travel to a new place, we use a map or GPS. Once we have arrived at our destination, we no longer need the map.

Which is the right path to follow? If our goal is to reach the top of a hill, there are infinite paths to get there. We can begin anywhere. Our path may meander, or we may choose to make the ascent going straight up, which is typically more challenging, but gets us there quicker. When we reach the summit, the path we took to get to the top no longer matters. All the experiences we had along the path we chose were essential to our unique climb, necessary lessons to further us along our way.

SUPERSTITION AIN'T THE WAY

Most religions are based on a collection of beliefs, which are the main ingredients in their "truths." Some call themselves the believers and separate themselves from the nonbelievers. Belief, however, is a tool that is no longer needed. The key phrase for the sign Pisces, the dominant energy of the last age, is "I believe." Many of our beliefs greatly evolved, during that period. As the disciplines of science and medicine became more prominent, ignorance and superstition lessened. People rarely know the origin of their superstitions, which are long-held false beliefs perceived as true. Many still adhere to them, even though they know such beliefs are bogus. They exist, active in the collective subconscious, and are closely connected to feelings and emotions. We generally connect them to our luck, both good or bad.

For example, though we rationally know it's ridiculous, many of us avoid walking under ladders. "Just in case." What is the source of this idea? A ladder forms a triangle, whether set on its own or leaning against a wall. The triangle is a representation of the Holy Trinity, and one would "break" the sacred pattern, by walking through it. Is there any difference between this and a religious belief?

Our difficulty stems from belief itself, which, in itself, is not wrong. It is merely a step toward knowing. At points in our life, when we are stuck or we are mired in the darkness of our ignorance, belief can offer a way out, providing us hope. Hope is not our goal, as it implies a future that necessitates time, which is all an illusory construct conjured in our own minds.

Do we believe day follows night, or do we know day follows night? Do we believe we know something, or do we know that we only believe it? These concepts are not interchangeable.

Aquarius, the new age we are entering, uses the key phrase "I know." These major shifts in consciousness happen every 2,100 years. It is the inevitable movement of spiritual evolution. As we leave the Age of Pisces, rooted in belief, many religions will begin to fade and beliefs will dissolve. All the riddles will be solved and the mysteries explained. Many so-called "miracles" will be seen to have scientific explanations. We are moving beyond the fairytales, myths, and beliefs.

Knowing is the product of experience. Experience can also be the result of knowing. I know this will be a good day, and so it is. I know I will do poorly on this test, and so I do. Knowing is a creative power. It fixes energy into specific patterns. Aquarius is a fixed sign. Knowing is a fixed idea, and is the source of its own actualization, a seed carrying the pattern of its own fruit.

FAITH

"Now faith is the substance of things hoped for, the evidence of things not seen."
Hebrews 11:1 KJV

Faith and belief are not the same energy. Faith, by this definition, is an actual substance. Belief is not. It's an acceptance of an idea presented to us, which has no basis in reality. It is usually a concept that has been accepted for generations, as with religions. Faith is based on knowing. It is a thought-form that one knows will manifest. The word belief contains the word "lie." Beliefs change. Faith can be lost but does not change.

The living Master Teacher, Sai Maa Lakshmi Devi, has said we have more faith in our doubt than we have faith in our faith. Doubt can undo anything, it is not a creative force.

EARLY DAYS

As humankind evolved beyond its animal nature, it began to question, to look for the meaning in life. People looked to the stars, which were a mystery. The stars offered humanity a framework, a reflection, to out-picture itself, a means to see things from a different perspective. Stories were created to answer questions, to illustrate and explain various facets of life.

The Bible's creation story answers questions about where we came from, and how the creation came about. At the time it was written, it gave that particular group of people a framework they needed, just as the First Nations people of North America, or the Aboriginals of Australia formulated creation myths specific to those populations.

Such stories, in many cases, are being superseded by scientific discovery, which has begun to unveil the roots of matter, and the mechanisms of creation. Science, however, still doesn't really know our origin. They may, for example, have figured out where our bodies come from, but we are not this body.

Evolution moves in life-waves of growth. All life on Earth, mineral, vegetable, animal and human are seen as one, from divine perspective. Confusion arises when we believe we are our bodies. The human body, the result of our physical evolution on this planet, is a form that can house our soul.

As these forms became available, humanity began a cycle of incarnation. If we came from monkeys, as some erroneously believe evolution teaches, where did the monkeys come from? Our physical body evolved from the apes, but we are not this body. All life (consciousness) comes from the One. Divine Source expresses itself infinitely through all forms, so-called animate and inanimate.

Visualize two wheels, one above the other, making a figure eight. The upper is a wheel of evolving souls, the lower is a wheel of evolving matter. The wheel above conveys souls down into the physical then back up to Source. The wheel on the bottom evolves material substance (atoms) up from mineral through vegetable, then animal, and eventually to the more complex human form, then dissolves it back into its component parts, when we depart the body. Where the two wheels touch, the form has become sufficiently evolved to house a human soul.

The stars provided humankind a calendar, a way to divide the world into day and night, a way to see the cycles of the year. The first great teacher was repetition. Consider the axiom "repetition equals reality." The repeating cycle, out-picturing the polarity of day and night, of summer and winter, established the illusion of time. Though our present-day calendar uses the Sun, the first calendars used the cycle of the Moon to establish months.

ASTROLOGY & RELIGION

Early humans circled around the fire for warmth, which created a magical energy. A living symbol, with the fire at center, it linked them into the pattern of our solar system, the fiery Sun at its center. Though they likely had no conception of the pattern, it was still activated. As above, so below.

"Earth religions" are those that are based on the cycles of the Moon. They teach the lunar mysteries, incorporating rituals that are offered through the span of the human lifetime. They include rituals of purification, an early form of baptism, the rite of passage from childhood to adulthood, similar to the Jewish Bat Mitzvah and Bar Mitzvah, as well as the marriage rite, and the final rite of transition. These rituals, prominent in pagan religions, highlight particular moments of life on Earth, and are referred to as the lesser mysteries, in that they deal with our more mundane physical life.

The Greater or Solar Mysteries, deal with experience beyond the world, such as enlightenment, Self-realization and God-realization. When we direct our focus toward the solar orb we experience a huge shift in consciousness.

In astrology, religion is associated with the planet Jupiter, the largest planet in our solar system. It is also associated with philosophy and positive energy. It rules Sagittarius, the sign of expansion and travel. As we travel far, our awareness expands. It is also a sign of resurrection and rebirth. True religions offer pathways toward higher consciousness, mind expansion, and growth.

In the zodiacal system, Sagittarius follows Scorpio, which deals with the energy of death, among other things. The greatest mystery for the living, and a focus for most religions is what happens after death. Some religions share similar beliefs, others do not. What should we believe? Don't believe anything.

The vegetable kingdom and the animal kingdom experience death with no religion at all. Because they are in harmony with the greater cycle of Nature, they experience it as simply another aspect of the circle of life. There is no dread. More highly evolved animals can experience grief and loss, as human's do, but there is no philosophy underlying it.

Most religions also tap into the planetary and stellar cycles, the earliest forms arising out of astrological and astronomical events that were ritualized on Earth. In Christianity, the holiest day begins Easter morning, which always falls on the first Sunday after the first full Moon, after the Sun goes into Aries, at sunrise - *son rise*. This is the optimal time in the Greater Cycle for Jesus to transcend death, through his divine resurrection, and when nature yearly experiences its own resurrection in spring. How, then, is this aligned with the larger celestial movements?

This cycle, as just mentioned, begins with the Sun, the Christ's symbol, moving into the sign Aries, commencing the first day of spring (Northern Hemisphere). In astrology, the Sun finds its highest energetic expression, or exaltation, in Aries, ruler of the first house. Spring brings the rebirth of the vegetable kingdom. Animals come out of hibernation, the tree sap changes direction, moving back up the trunk.

At the next full Moon, as the solar energy intensifies, more light is reflected back to Earth. Additionally, Easter falls on Sunday, named for the Sun. Finally, the holy day begins at sunrise, when, due to the Earth's rotation, relative to the observer's position, the solar orb appears on the eastern horizon.

Connections between astrology and religion run deep. The Old Testament is filled with astrological symbolism. The twelve signs of the zodiac are represented in the twelve tribes of Israel, and Jesus' twelve apostles.

This astrological symbolism is found particularly in the Abrahamic religions, Judaism, Christianity, and Islam. Some Eastern religions have their own astrology, and all utilize symbolism to express their theologies. For example, Hinduism's pantheon of gods and goddesses are always depicted with various meaningful symbols, while Islamic symbolism is prevalent, for example, in the geometric patterns used as decoration in architecture and artworks.

Virtually no symbols are used in Zen Buddhism. The very work of Zen takes the practitioner beyond words and imagery, beyond the mundane mind. Taoism also dispenses with symbols, for the most part, though the yin yang or taiji symbol is well-recognized as associated with Taoism. At the foundation of Taoism is the Tao, "the way," which illuminates the way to be in balance and harmony with creation. Rather than a religion, it might be more aptly described as a way of life.

In ancient Egypt, the Pharaoh Akhenaten brought monotheism to the people, creating the city of the Sun, Heliopolis. There, the Sun was the emblem of Divinity. The "gods" became the one God. Later, the Hebrews reintroduced the concept of monotheism, with their faith in one God. As previously mentioned, the Divine is manifest for Hindus in a multitude of gods and goddesses, all of whom represent various aspects of the one God.

One way to approach reading the Bible is to identify with every person in it, as they also represent the different aspects of the one God. The Greek and Roman mythologies do the same. But are these aspects of God or of humanity? What is Divine and what is mundane?

The truth is hidden within the polarity of Spirit and matter, which are poles of the same energy. It is only our human mind that creates the divisions. Although one aim of religion is unification, bringing people together, typically we focus on the perceived differences, which create the illusion of separation, dividing humanity into hundreds of belief systems.

Any solution will only become another problem, if we hold fast to it. There are no universal remedies, as there are no universal problems. Answers that worked thousands of years ago do not work today. At the time, they were true, but now they are no longer. For most, taking "an eye for an eye," literally, is out of alignment with the prevailing consciousness of humanity. In truth, it is an expression that points to the nature of karma. What goes around comes around. It is not meant to suggest we inflict physical harm on another in retribution. Our attachment to old ways of being keeps us from moving forward. Religion helps until it hinders.

Today, many Christians do not follow Jesus, they are adherents of "churchianity," not practitioners of Christianity. How many Christians would actually turn the other cheek, or is revenge still active in their hearts? Look at all the wars we support. Few Buddhist's truly follow Buddha. Who today can live without any possessions? This is a major stumbling block for many, but one must be completely unattached to everything, even thought, to find the Source of all. Remember, non-attachment does not mean we must do away with all of our possessions, just our attachment to them.

Religion is one way to explain life; science offers us another. Very often their explanations appear to differ. We also have our own explanations, regarding where and who we are. Computer programs that manage lists have a set of filters to narrow the search, to limit the data. We also have filters. We call them our belief systems.

CHRISTIANITY & BUDDHISM

Christianity centers on the Christ, though for many it is centered on Jesus. These two are not the same, yet they are. In mystical studies, the Sun of God and the Son of God are the same, which brings us back to ancient Egypt, when the Sun was a representation of the Creator. Scientific research demonstrates that our solar system was created by our Sun. In fact, all life on Earth depends on the Sun. The vegetable kingdom, through photosynthesis, turns sunlight into food. The food chain begins with the Sun.

This Sun is also within us, it is the Son/Sun of Man, or the Christ Consciousness. Our life depends on the Christ within us. Life on Earth is nourished by solar radiation. As we let our inner light shine forth unimpeded, we nourish our own inner kingdom. True Christians have the "Christ-in." They are those who follow the pattern Jesus demonstrated with his life, for he said:

"Come, follow me."
Matthew 4:19; Mark 1:17 KJV

Buddha also had a following but worked in a much different manner. Jesus stood up, Buddha sat down. They represent the active and passive paths. Buddha lived around 500 years before Jesus. They are both team members in the cosmic relay race.

Buddha never spoke on the subject of God. "God" is just a word, a concept, an idea. Buddha's teachings are founded on direct experience and clearing the mind of thought, or rather, non-attachment to thought. Buddha taught all suffering comes from unfulfilled desires. The solution is simple, we must conquer our desire nature. We are instructed to stop wanting anything. For it is our desires that are the source of all our suffering. Yes, it's very simple but can take lifetimes to master. It can be very difficult to be simple.

Religion offers us codes by which we may live. It lays down rules, like the Ten Commandments, for example, and morals to uphold. After a time, these rules do not free the soul but bind it ever deeper, which may result in fear and guilt. We are afraid to break the rules and feel guilty when we do. This negative feedback loop will never offer us peace or lead us to Source.

Sometimes extreme practice is encouraged or advised, in order to reap the necessary spiritual fruits. There are religions that teach harmlessness toward all life, including insects, or those that involve regular fasting and other purification practices.

ANGELS, HEAVEN & HELL

What religion are the angels? They appear in the Old Testament, the New Testament and the Koran. Baha'i and Sikhism also reference angels.

Neither Hinduism nor Buddhism speak of angels, per se. There are non-physical spiritual beings but they are not referred to as angels. Angels have no religion but are seen as the "hands of God." They are and always have been connected to God and need no belief system.

Each human soul has a guardian angel, regardless of one's religious belief system, even if it doesn't recognize the presence of angels. If we don't believe we have a guardian angel, then we will have no interaction with it, and we will miss the benefit of its presence. If we do accept the reality of this partnership, we will not only find guidance and protection but angelic grace.

How do we work with our guardian angel? We call it, talk to it. We give our angel our love and thankfulness. The more we draw close to it, the more it will unite with us. If we doubt it, it disappears in our consciousness, but never fully disappears in our experience.

Zoroastrianism, which began about 1,000 years before Buddha walked the Earth, also accepted the existence of angels. The main extant contribution this religion offers to our present consciousness is the idea of duality. Zoroaster first proposed the concepts of heaven and hell.

Do heaven and hell exist, or are they simply a cosmic carrot and stick? Either way, they are both human creations based on our beliefs. On the "other side" there are many heavens. Each group or religion has its own idea of heaven. When we drop the body, at the end of this Earth journey, our belief system stands before us. Wherever we believe we are going, after death, is usually where we end up.

There are as many heavens as there are individuals, each will experience it based on their personal concept. A Catholic will experience the Catholic version of heaven, the Hindu, Jew, Muslim, etc., will experience heaven as it is conceived in that religion. Upon our physical death, after a while, that false perception begins to fade from our consciousness. There is no religion in heaven.

The Robin Williams film *What Dreams May Come* gives us an in-depth look at the after-life experience. As various beings make off-world journeys after death, each ends up in a different place, based on their earthly experience. We are all watching our own film, illumined by the Self and projected through our soul onto the infinite screen around us.

Some religions answer questions and create a structure of beliefs. Other religions free us of the structures, so the soul may move beyond the world of thought. Do we need religion? Initially, it may be of great benefit, but eventually we do not. God dwells within us. Religion can bring us closer to God or move us farther away. Believe nothing! Know the truth and be set free!

THE NEW AGE

Theosophists say, "There is no religion higher than truth!" Theosophy, derived from the roots "theo" and "sophy," means the "science or wisdom of God." This movement arose in the late 1800s, and drew from many sources, with a strong connection to Hinduism.

Many "New Age" religions practiced today have tried to synthesize the teachings of various older religions. These earlier religions are often called organized or established religions. As the age changes, we see fewer people identifying with the establishment. Until relatively recently, we typically took on our parent's religion without question. When we grow up within an organized religion, the roots are deep. We subconsciously carry the entirety of the belief structure embraced by that religion from the moment of its inception. This becomes the foundation we stand on, the platform from which we spring into this life. As we incarnate into the same religion life upon life, those roots are deeply anchored in our soul memory.

In order to expand our soul consciousness, we will necessarily incarnate into circumstances where we experience different sets of beliefs. As a result, we may find in this lifetime we have an affinity with other religions. Over countless lifetimes, we have experienced a multitude of religions. Which ones are right? The answer is all of them.

In each lifetime, we face different situations and learn soul-lessons that only apply to us. We each have a spiritual blueprint of reality that we have covered with our illusory beliefs. These belief patterns will not lead us to our inner Divinity. God is beyond belief. In order to know God, we all must, eventually, move beyond belief, as well.

God is Spirit and God is form. We are eternally surrounded by the loving, divine Light eternally expressing within, without, and as us!

"I have said, Ye are gods; and all of you are children of the most-high."
Psalm 82:6 KJV

MYSTIC ORIGINS & PRACTICAL SPIRITUALITY

Google's online dictionary defines a mystic as:

"A person who seeks by contemplation and self-surrender to obtain unity with or absorption into the deity or the absolute, or who believes in the spiritual apprehension of truths that are beyond the intellect."

All religions have mystical roots. The beings through which true religions originate were connected to God directly, in a real way. As many years pass, divine connection is lessened and rules and beliefs increase. Yet, there are, at the core of many such religions, a few who still, literally, "keep the faith," dedicating their lives to their spiritual work.

As we move further into the Aquarian Age, we will find these institutions gradually falling apart. This is necessary, as the path to Source has changed. More specifically, the goal has not changed, our starting point has. We are approaching this all from a more enlightened point of view. If our goal is to keep our front walk clean, it may require we must, variously, rake leaves, and shovel snow. The goal has not changed, but our actions have to align with the present conditions.

Originally, religion was developed to give people a framework, a code of ethics, a belief system. All this, however, was outer work. Far fewer were able to do the necessary inner work, the real foundation of religion. The outer work is a step toward the inner. Unfortunately, few of the early proponents walked or even saw the way to the Divine within. As a result, religion, in many respects, became a way to control people. Though the initial intensions were good, many religions eventually disempowered and bound the individual to a set of rigid dogma. We have seen how religion, fused with politics, furthers the descent, and the abuse that follows.

Today, in the West, and particularly in the United States, more people are moving away from organized religions toward a practical spirituality. This is the natural flow of evolution. We all come from Spirit, our true home, and to Spirit we all shall return. Enjoy life, experience life, grow into life. Be not distracted by the world. It is only a temporary passing.

As long as our religion serves us and draws us closer to God, we should surely allow it to guide us. Our path must be a practical one, that is one we can practice daily, not just once a week, or for a sacred month, or on special holy (holi) days. Ultimately, we will seek the jumping off place that will allow us to move beyond form toward infinite divine expression. Let God be that foundation. When we seek within, surely, we will find!

CHAPTER 10

The Self

THE NATURE OF THE SELF

A monk asked Zen Master Ummon, "What is the true self?" Ummon said, "It does not hold six things."

These six things are the five senses and the mind, the tools we use to function in the material world of physicality. If we released our hold on our sense of touch, the world would appear a lot less physical. The same could be said, if we no longer had access to the other four. Sense by sense, our experience of the world would diminish and eventually disappear. Though we may not feel, see, hear, smell, or taste it, we could still think about the world.

In a sensory deprivation tank, with virtually all sensory stimuli but touch removed (one floats in a dark, soundless tank filled with salt water), the mind continues to see images and hear sound, if only the movements of the water. Even if our senses are not engaged, still the mind is active. What happens when we let go of the mind? Though it may appear to be a death, it is when we truly awaken to the spiritual realm of heaven. So why are we here on Earth? Few consciously come to seek the Self; though, it is Self that incarnates to gain experience.

A master sculptor, speaking of their work, tells us all they need do is remove what is not necessary to reveal the essence of their carving. They are not doing, they are undoing. We can apply this same process in our own lives. God lives within us. All we need do is remove everything that is not God. This great undertaking is the path toward sainthood. It's so hard, because it is so simple. There is nothing that can remove our Divinity, it can only be covered up, hidden from the ego mind. The only things we can truly lose are those that we are not. Let go.

In the previous Age of Pisces, the focus of the Great Work was purification and renunciation. Once we have been stripped of the illusion, we are ready to enter the next age, Aquarius.

As the misconception of our separation from God is transformed to a state of Unity Consciousness, we can truly work as a group, a network of souls.

Within each individual soul lives the universal Self. The same Self is in an infinite variety of souls. In this way, we are all different, and yet all the same. This soul-Self connection extends throughout creation, a relationship between the Divine within us and the impressions received through our sensory apparatus as we interact with the creation.

Who are we? Our source is Source, the Creator, the Eternal Flame of Life, underlying all manifestation. Our very being is a divine spark, one with the whole of creation, yet distinct. We each have this same divine flame within us. In this way, we are really all the same being. As previously mentioned, this spark has many names: Atman, Blue Pearl, Philosopher's Stone, Rock of My Soul, Sun of Man, Self. In this work we use the term Self.

It all begins with movement. As the Self moves into the creation, it encounters experience. This experience is different for each divine spark. As each one moves farther away from Source and into the creation, the more each is differentiated. Each spark's experiences leave an impression, which initiates the birth of the soul. Though at the core each spark is the same, each one's experience is different. No two souls are alike.

The soul is an expression of one energy, the Self, manifesting in and as an ocean of energy fields that vibrate at different frequencies. These frequencies were originally harmonious. Though the soul is created to reflect the Self through these many fields, most people are only manifesting through the mental, emotional and physical bodies in ways that are greatly discordant and distorted. Our goal in each lifetime is to continually bring the frequencies of all these energy systems back into alignment.

We say, "It's never the thing." So, why do we become so concerned with the thing itself? We become attached to things, because of our distorted view of who we are. Let's look, for example, at the thing we call money. We may think our problems come from not having enough money, so we shift the blame onto a set of numbers. Everything, even the numbers reflected in our bank account, is a mirror. They do not reflect reality, but rather they reflect our emotional state and mental perspective regarding our experience.

KNOWLEDGE

In the biblical creation myth, Adam and Eve were told not to partake of only one tree in the Garden of Eden: *The Tree of the Knowledge of Good and Evil*. When we are able to see how the duality of good and evil are merely two expressions of the same energy, we can transcend them and detect a higher truth. We are going beyond good and evil, but should we avoid knowledge too?

On the Kabbalistic Tree of Life, there is an eleventh "invisible" sphere, called Knowledge. The Tree can function fully without knowledge, because it still retains Wisdom and Understanding.

Knowledge is static, old information, like that bound in books. When we make a decision, based on our knowledge, we stop listening to our inner voice and lose our connection with Source.

When Adam and Eve, representing the conscious and subconscious minds, partook of the knowledge of good and evil, they lost Unity Consciousness, they forgot the Self. Their Light bodies, activated at their creation, were covered with "coats of skin," as they descended in vibration into the physical plane. (*Genesis 3:21 KJV*) They moved from an inner reality to an outer false reality. This is where we find ourselves today. And yet, we are still in the garden, whether we are conscious of it or not. It's time to awaken our consciousness.

As we again move closer to the Divine, through our soul evolution, we realize we, as ego, know nothing, and can only rely on our inner guidance, the Self, based in Source. At this point, we truly become servants of the Most-High, or the ascended consciousness.

Though it may appear people are contradictory and say one thing at one time and the opposite, perhaps moments later, it is because we compare, which lands us in a state of judgement. Their polarized words appear to be opposing, because we are viewing everything in our experience from a dualistic perspective.

When the mind is no longer cleaved in two, and we are centered in the now, we begin to understand that each statement is true for that individual when it is said, even if the statement is actually a distortion of the truth. This will only frustrate the divided mind, though the Self, who we truly are, remains placid in Unity Consciousness. Our intention is to derail the train of thought that is caught in its endless cycle of illusion. The confusion ends, when the eye is single and the mind is clear; self becomes Self.

Who are we? We may think we know, but we rarely do. Fundamentally, most people believe we are the body. What is the body? Except for a few, all the cells that comprise the body have been replaced numerous times since our birth. Our physical bodies have died many times at the cellular level.

So, who are we? We are in the body, not of the body. Our body is a product of the earth, as an outgrowth of what we eat. Yet, we are not this body, and, therefore, not truly of the earth. We are actually consciousness, who we are between each lifetime, once we drop the body. We all existed infinitely before birth, and we will all exist eternally after death.

Though we have use of our emotions, we are not the energies we call our emotions. We identify with the mind and its thoughts, though we are neither. If we were the thoughts, how could we have them? In order to have something, there necessarily must be a separation, a division of some sort. If we have a mind, we cannot be the mind. When we think, who is the one thinking? Who is listening to the thoughts? Who is the observer? Self.

We all have a personal identity we refer to as ego. This is our small self, who we think we are. This false self is not the Self we are truly. The Buddhists speak of a smaller truth and a greater truth. The smaller truth is that we are humans living on the Earth. The greater truth is that we are one with all of creation; we are the Universe.

We may think we know who we are, but who is doing the thinking? As in *The Wonderful Wizard of Oz*, by L. Frank Baum, we are also the one behind the curtain running the show. In spiritual initiation, this curtain is referred to as the veil. It exists to separate our self from the Self. A literal veil was used in the ancient Hebrew temples to separate the Holy of Holies from the non-initiates. It is said our body is a temple containing a veil. Is this why so many people choose to honor the body?

The Temple is a symbolic representation of our body. We must look beyond the physical body and recognize that the flame within the Holy of Holies, in the center of the Temple, is our true Self. The Torah, within the Ark of the Covenant, represents the soul, which, symbolically, holds the history of our existence.

The ancient Temple of Jerusalem contained three areas. There was the outer court, where all people could enter, which represents our physical body, open to all things through the senses. Beyond it was the inner court where only the Jews were allowed to enter. This area is where we accept spiritual practice with the intent of drawing closer to God. Farther beyond that is the veil, the other side of which is the Holy of Holies, where only the priests could enter. This is where the Self resides within us. We become the priest of our salvation, when we move beyond the inner veil. When Jesus was crucified on the cross, the veil in the Temple was split, opening the Divine to all!

"And the veil of the Temple was rent in half, twain from the top to the bottom."
Mark 15:38 KJV

The Divine was no longer hidden, and the door was opened. In the Mystery Schools, both ancient and current, this veil is also removed within the initiate, to open the door to Self-realization. It may, however, take time for the initiate to enter and fully become who they are. Like the pattern Jesus showed us, one must "die" to the outer world, in order to enter the other side.

As we enter this new Age of Aquarius, the veil between Spirit and matter is thinning. More people are sensing energies of a higher vibration. More people are perceiving auras and working with Light. The transition is becoming easier. We are moving from our false self to our true Self, also known as the Higher Self. This Self is who we are throughout all our incarnations. Surrounding the Self is the soul. If we use the analogy of an egg, the yellow center represents our inner Sun, the Self. The albumin surrounding it represents our soul, and the hard, outer shell is our material body.

The Self witnesses our experiences and the soul records them. All our lives are recorded in our soul memory. How do we get there? How can we access this information? What would be the point of having the experience, if we couldn't retrieve it? For the average person, our connection to our soul is through the unconscious and subconscious minds. Our conscious mind can access our subconscious mind, and the subconscious can access the unconscious mind. Our unconscious mind runs all the bodily systems so we can continue to live even when we are in deep sleep.

In self-healing work, we consciously plant suggestions in our subconscious. These are then offered to our unconscious mind. This is how a placebo works. When healing others, our word, said with complete knowing and confidence, can easily enter the subconscious mind of the client or patient, and is why we should always speak in ways that support the greatest and highest good of the individual.

The Self dwells within the soul. When we observe the soul from outside, our own distortions and attachments to the world may reveal only limited information. Most psychics access information in this realm of awareness. In order to fully read the soul, we must go within it, to the Self. Then we can look at the soul from divine perspective.

The Self, Christ, or Sun of Man, dwells within us, as the expressed image of God. As we continue in our spiritual unfolding, the next realm we must access is that of the Supreme Self, or the unexpressed aspect of God, also referred to as the Great Central Sun. It dwells above us, both physically and vibrationally, even as we are one with it. It is the home of the Christ Consciousness.

Christ Consciousness is not Jesus consciousness, it is the consciousness that Jesus expressed. The Christ that Jesus embodied is the same Christ that dwells within all. Jesus revealed it within himself, while most of us are still searching for it in our outer experience.

In Esoteric Christianity, the first coming of the Christ was out in the world, through the man called Jesus. The second coming will manifest within each of us, right here, right now. It's the same but not the same. The pattern remains, but the scale is much different. The Christ within us is as one cell in the body of the Divine. The Christ that Jesus manifested expanded as he interacted with the world.

"Another parable spake he onto them; The kingdom of heaven is like unto leaven, which a woman took, and hid in three measures of meal, till the whole was leavened."

Matthew 13:33 KJV

We can interpret this lesson in a few ways. The leaven (yeast) represents the Christ Consciousness, while the three portions of meal are our physical, emotional and mental bodies. If we can receive even a small amount of Light, of Truth, of divine Consciousness, eventually it will grow until we are completely transformed. The work goes on. Hidden within our human consciousness our divinity grows. If we expand this idea further, Jesus, the Christ, is the leaven and the world is the meal.

There is no limit to the expansion of consciousness. So why do we limit it? Our ego, or false sense of self, imposes these limitations. We hold on to our identity, even though it stunts our growth. When we are "born again" our previous life is no more.

As we allow our higher nature to impact everything around us, it grows. We have stepped onto the path to the Divine. Jesus said,

"The gate is straight and narrow is the way."

Matthew 7:14 KJV

Indeed, it is. The spiritual path requires discipline and focus, so we are no longer distracted by all the things going on to our left and right (polarity).

self, Self, SELF

How many different 'selfs' are we? We know of three: who we think we are, who others think we are, and who we really are. Our soul is continually expanding. As we continue to incarnate in a human form from lifetime to lifetime, we evolve. We are an unchanging Self, within a continually evolving soul. All the planets have consciousness. The being that is Earth, or Gaia, is evolving beneath our feet. Still it is held in orbit, circling the Sun. More accurately, it spirals around our solar orb. As the Sun travels, it spirals on its own course through space-time.

Along the road of cosmic evolution, each of us will eventually become a planet, caring for the life-forms that inhabit our form. Does this sound a bit far-fetched? Our physical form already supports and feeds billions of cells, and even more bacteria that live on and within our body. Our physical and energetic bodies are already a reflection of the solar (soul-er) system, as we view it through the lenses of astrology and the chakra system.

Our Sun is a conscious being, which houses the Christ Consciousness of its own entire solar system. We too will become stars. When we view the stars at night, we are looking at our own cosmic family. The evolution continues, as we become a galaxy and then a universe. The pattern is the same, only the scale is different.

Our only task is to be our Self, giving our reality a truer perspective. We are already complete. There is nothing that we need. There is nowhere to go but within. Our true Self is God, deep within us. Explore the meditation at the end of the chapter, holding this awareness in your Heart.

As we investigate the Tarot, in the second level studies, we will explore the path of evolution through which the soul progresses from Spirit into matter and then on to God Realization. It all begins with Twenty-two keys. Two is the number representing duplication, as well as polarity, duality, and doubling. Twenty-two represents coming into duality and then emerging out of it.

The Tarot is the totality of the known and the unknown, the Fool and the other twenty-one Major Arcana cards. Which is which, or are they both the same? Energy and matter are two expressions of the same thing. Each is the other. The Fool knows nothing and everything.

Astrologically, Aquarius' key phrase is "I know." Uranus, ruler of Aquarius, is the planet aligned with the Fool, who doesn't know anything. What the Fool does know, actually, are the cycles of creation, the everything, the All. It has a unique perspective, because its planetary ruler, Uranus, has its axis running perpendicular to the other planets. The creation, or the twenty-one Arcana, contains all knowing and yet knows nothing.

Explore this final meditation, *Becoming a Conduit for the Divine*, with an open heart, mind, and soul. Enter the Self. We recommend you experience the meditation using the available audio recording, *Ten Gates into the Garden: Spiritual Exercises and Meditations.*

Join us for further exploration in the next volume: *The New Light Tarot: The Circular Path of the Soul*, as we step off the cliff with the Fool and continue on the evolutionary path of the soul toward Self…

Meditation: Becoming a Conduit for the Divine

Come sitting, toward the front of your chair, or on a firm cushion, with spine erect. If in a chair, plant your feet firmly under your knees. Rest your hands on the thighs palms up. Close your eyes and begin to draw your awareness inward. Center yourself in the rhythmic cycles of your breath.

As you breathe, begin to envision your body as a great tree, ancient and wise in the ways of Nature. Visualize roots descending into the earth from the soles of your feet. The legs and torso become the stable, yet supple, trunk of the tree. Your arms and head extend from the trunk, like branches, your hair and fingers are its leaves.

With each exhalation, sense the roots descending from the trunk, through the legs and feet, growing deeper, stabilizing you in the earth. At the same time the trunk grows taller, your branches and leaves extend skyward, reaching for the Sun.

When we observe a tree, we see only what is on the surface. Our physical eyes behold the elegant aspen's smooth white bark with its wise, black, knotty eyes that observe the world in silence. Its delicate branches dance in the breeze. Its verdant, pale, green leaves open, to receive the Suns light. Yet, there is so much more. The greater part of the tree is hidden from our view.

This limited view, this ignorance of the greater whole, lulls us into the mistaken belief that what we see is all there is. We fall into the illusion that we are lonely, isolated in our personal separateness. We forget that this individual tree has a deep and ancient root system that connects it to all the other aspen in the grove.

As we turn inward in meditation, the illusion of separateness begins to fall away, as we open to the unknown, to the unseen that lies deep under the surface, and tap into the underlying, unifying web of **SPIRIT** that supports and sustains us all. This practice helps us view, with spiritual sight, the wonders of the inner landscape.

As you breathe, begin to visualize your soul's intention for illumination, which resides in your Heart, as a tiny seed deep within the womb of the earth. In the stillness of the dark this seed of understanding begins to germinate. In your quest toward enlightenment, driven by this inner soul impulse, you can no longer remain encased in the constricting shell of illusion. The seed cracks open, and you send your roots deep. The shoot of your aspiration wends its way through the illusory obstacles of maya to surface into the brilliant Light of the Sun's Infinite Consciousness.

Meditation: Becoming a Conduit for the Divine, Cont'd

Continue to breathe fully and deeply, again sense the roots that descend from your feet toward the core of the Earth. Draw the energy of the divine Mother up through this intricate system, allowing it to vitalize your entire being. See this Life stream flowing through and cleansing each of the chakras, from the base of the spine, the energy center which connects us to the material plane, into the sacral region, the seat of the creative and procreative impulse, moving on to the solar plexus, the home of personal and spiritual power, then into the heart center, resplendent with compassion and unconditional Love. Here the seed of your intent is amplified by the energy of the divine feminine.

Inhaling again, allow the creative Life Force to climb higher to the region of the throat, the vehicle of creative expression and deliverer of truth, then onward to the 1ST eye of spiritual sight, culminating at the crown, radiant in its expression of the divine unity of the ALL. As you open to the limitless Light of the supreme Self, all sense of separation falls away.

Allow this divine flow of feminine energy to dissolve, through Love and compassion, the subconscious patterns of thought and habit that have bound you, that have held you encased in your self- made prison of limitation. Let this reawakened awareness remold you at the cellular level, then even more fundamentally in the structures of your DNA. As the body is the vehicle for our expression of self-mastery, we effect this transformation, by spiritualizing matter.

Now visualize the Great Central Sun, the source of the Life Force, luminescent in its radiant splendor, streaming down into the crown chakra. Continuing in your deep rhythmic cycles of breath, receive this pranic flow into the brain, with each inhalation. Feel it cleanse and purify your mind, burning away the false identification with personality that leads to a sense of separation, that you may release the reins of your own will, becoming a pure and open channel for the will of the Divine. With each exhalation release that which you cling to, that which still binds you to the material plane, by visualizing it flowing through the body and legs into the earth.

We will now begin to more fully amplify the Life Force to stoke the inner Flame of our Heart's intent. In a moment, we will demonstrate so you may gain a sense of the breathing pattern. Join in at any time and continue until you are directed to slow down and stop. Do NOT continue, if you feel overly dizzy or distressed. Be aware you are taking in a great deal of oxygen quickly and you may feel a bit LIGHT headed.

Place the thumb over the top of the nail of the pointer finger, with the other fingers extended in Gyan or Chin mudra. Now, inhaling, extend your arms straight up, like branches reaching skyward toward the LIGHT. Open fully to the cosmic flow of Love, Light and Life. As you exhale pull the arms down again, drawing the stream of Cosmic Consciousness through the Crown into the head and trunk. The arms move like pistons pumping. Inhale extend, exhale pull down, picking up the pace as you feel able. Let the breath become shallower, as you do so; and slow down or stop as you feel necessary.

Continue breathing and pumping. Feel this action harness the spiraling Life Force, purifying the brain, liberating the mind. You are creating a circuit through which the free flow of divine Consciousness imbues your entire being. This action, aligned with breath, raises your vibration. As you are liberated from your attachment to that which binds you, you open to the limitlessness of your vital essence, the supreme Self.

Begin to slow the arms and the breathing down, gradually coming back to stillness. Allow your right hand to rest in the left, tips of the thumbs touching, to retain the flow through the circuit. As you sit in silence, in this state of perfect union of the divine feminine and masculine energies, observe. Sense the One, Life, the Pivot and Source of the whole Cosmos, alive and active within you, knowing that through you this governing and directing power of the Universe flows into manifestation.

When guided by inner impulse to complete the meditation, remaining with your eyes closed, allow your breathing to gradually deepen. Begin to bring your awareness back to the external environment and your physical body, by gently moving your fingers and toes. Place your hands face down on your thighs to ground the energy, before you slowly open your eyes.

Sources

Book

Baum, L. Frank. *The Wonderful Wizard of Oz*, Chicago, George M. Hill Company, 1900

Dass, Ram. *Be Here Now*, San Cristobol, NM: Lama Foundation, 1971.

Graves, Kersey. *The World's Sixteen Crucified Saviors: Or Christianity Before Christ*, New York: Cosimo Classics, 2007.

Heline, Corinne. *Mystery of the Christos*, London: New Age Press, 1961.

Hesse, Herman. *Siddhartha*, USA, Bantam Books Publisher, 1982.

Jordan, Juno. *Numerology: The Romance in your Name*, Los Angeles: J. F. Rowny Press, 1968.

Lakshmi Devi, Sai Maa. *Petals of Grace: Essential Teachings for Self-Mastery, 2nd Edition*, USA: Sai Maa, LLC, 2013.

Piper, Watty, *The Little Engine That Could*, USA: Golden Press, 1975.

Film

Animal House, John Landis; Universal Pictures, 1978, Film.

Pinocchio, Hamilton Luske, Ben Sharpsteen; Walt Disney Productions, 1940, Film.

Internet

Dictionary.com. http://www.dictionary.com.

https://en.wikiquote.org/wiki/Albert_Einstein.

Google Dictionary. http://www.google.com/dictionary.

Gratitudes

I express my deepest gratitude to the many School of the New Light students, who were the first to receive these teachings and offer feedback in David's metaphysical classes, at Seven Rays Bookstore, in Syracuse NY.

I also thank our most recent students: Margaret Chao, Jane Dall, and Gail Fitterer, for serving as mirrors to reflect back to us the level of clarity of the teachings. They provided invaluable insights as to how we might improve the delivery of the material in both writing and verbal presentation. Anne Marie Higgins and Merlyn Fuller provided invaluable advice regarding the journey of self-publishing. You are both gems.

I offer great appreciation for Mark Nanni, our Recording Engineer, who dedicated countless hours to recording the text and accompanying spiritual exercises and meditations that support and augment the teachings. Learn more about his music and touring dates at www.facebook.com/MarkNanniMusic/. I am deeply grateful to David Young, multi-talented recording and visual artist, spiritual teacher and channel, for granting his permission to sample his inspirational music, which underlies the recorded spiritual exercises and meditations accompanying the book. Check out David Young's website for information on his work, music and touring schedule: www.davidyoungmusic.com.

Without the unceasing support, and unconditional love of Coe and Kate Hutchinson, Mark and Anjalee Hutchinson, Ronald and Kay Naumann, Melanie Stensrud, Paul Naumann, and Robin Costello, my beloved Cheddars, and countless other friends, this work would not have been possible.

Great gratitude to David Harry Davis, whose unending generosity, insightful guidance, and steadfast friendship have been instrumental in my soul's evolution in this lifetime.

To all my teachers, mentors and students across the ages, and the many seers and sages, who encouraged me to take on the work of bringing this book to fruition, I extend my heartfelt thanks.

Always, to my guru, Her Holiness Sai Maa Lakshmi Devi, I pranam. My heart overflows with your Grace, Shakti and Unconditional Love. Om Jai Jai Sai Maa   ~Katrin~

About the Authors

David Harry Davis

Born: June 3, 1948, New Rochelle, NY.

In 1969 David joined a Mystery School, the "Holy Order of MANS," where he studied the major religions and was brought through several spiritual initiations, giving him access to the Self, the source of his writing. After seven years of study and practice, he moved to Syracuse to start "Seven Rays Bookstore," a metaphysical, New Age bookstore, which he ran for 28 years.

It was a large store containing over 35,000 titles and items for spiritual support (tapes, incense, cards and so on. The store housed a large classroom where many authors and teachers came from all over the world. A publication was created, the "New Moon News," in which David contributed many articles.

He was serialized in a number of publications, including writing a monthly astrological column and a 22-part series on running a metaphysical bookstore, metaphysically.

During this period, he attended a spiritual retreat on the "Seven Rays," in Bali, Indonesia. There he was asked by John the Beloved, to create a Mystery School, which was accomplished by the turn of the century. The "School of the New Light" came into being.

Soon after meeting his Guru, Sai Maa Lakshmi Devi, David sold the store, entering into a more contemplative period of his life.

Retired from "business," he now resides on a hill, in upstate New York. He continues to write and teach. Contact David at: **brotherdavid@mac.com**

Katrin Louise Naumann

Born: October 1, 1964, Syracuse, NY.

As Director of Inner Balance Life Works: (R)evolutionary Self-Transformation, Katrin is a life-long student of inquiry and self-realization, through the focused study of World Wisdom Traditions and Practices, in the School of the New Light, with David Harry Davis, which include the Eastern and Western Mystery Teachings, Hermetics, Astrology and Tarot.

Katrin is a graduate of the Journeys of Profound Healing, Profound Awakening, Enlightened Awareness, Profound Abundance, and Divinization of Matter, with her beloved guru, Her Holiness, Sai Maa Lakshmi Devi. Additionally, she has completed various intensives in Transformational Healing, with Sai Maa.

She received Level III Qi Gong Therapy, and Traditional Chinese Medicine & Nutrition Certification from the Qi Gong Institute of Rochester, studying with Master Lisa B. O'Shea. Katrin studied Vibrational Healing, with Elizabeth Wright, of SpiritWorks.

A practitioner of Yoga for over 20 years, and a teacher for the past 14, Katrin holds Essential and Advanced Hatha Yoga Certification (E-RYT500) in the Iyengar tradition from Open Sky Yoga Studio, studying with Master Iyengar Teacher Francois Raoult. She currently teaches classes at Life Force Sanctuary, Syracuse Yoga, Synergy Center, the Syracuse VA, and to corporate and private clients in the area.

Katrin leads dynamic experiential workshops and meditations, which provide practical tools for realizing one's full life and soul potential. Katrin holds a BFA in Fine Art from St. Lawrence University, and an MFA in Design and Technical Theatre from Syracuse University. In this lifetime, she is blessed to be the mother of two amazing souls.

Contact Katrin through her website, and learn how her clairvoyant readings, holistic healing therapies, and spiritual and life guidance can support you, as you awaken your consciousness: **www.innerbalancelifeworks.com**